Reforming School Finance

Studies in Social Economics

TITLES PUBLISHED

STUDIES IN SOCIAL ECONOMICS

Reforming School Finance

*Robert D. Reischauer and Robert W. Hartman
with the assistance of Daniel J. Sullivan*

THE BROOKINGS INSTITUTION
Washington, D.C.

Copyright © 1973 by
THE BROOKINGS INSTITUTION
1775 Massachusetts Avenue, N.W., Washington, D.C. 20036

Library of Congress Cataloging in Publication Data:
Reischauer, Robert Danton, 1941–
 Reforming school finance.

 (Studies in social economics)
 Bibliography: p.
 1. Education—Finance.   I. Hartman, Robert W.,
joint author.   II. Title.   III. Series.
LB2824.R37   379   73-1080

ISBN 0-8157-7396-X
ISBN 0-8157-7395-1 (pbk.)

9 8 7 6 5 4 3 2 1

THE BROOKINGS INSTITUTION is an independent organization devoted to nonpartisan research, education, and publication in economics, government, foreign policy, and the social sciences generally. Its principal purposes are to aid in the development of sound public policies and to promote public understanding of issues of national importance.

The Institution was founded on December 8, 1927, to merge the activities of the Institute for Government Research, founded in 1916, the Institute of Economics, founded in 1922, and the Robert Brookings Graduate School of Economics and Government, founded in 1924.

The Board of Trustees is responsible for the general administration of the Institution, while the immediate direction of the policies, program, and staff is vested in the President, assisted by an advisory committee of the officers and staff. The by-laws of the Institution state, "It is the function of the Trustees to make possible the conduct of scientific research, and publication, under the most favorable conditions, and to safeguard the independence of the research staff in the pursuit of their studies and in the publication of the results of such studies. It is not a part of their function to determine, control, or influence the conduct of particular investigations or the conclusions reached."

The President bears final responsibility for the decision to publish a manuscript as a Brookings book or staff paper. In reaching his judgment on the competence, accuracy, and objectivity of each study, the President is advised by the director of the appropriate research program and weighs the views of a panel of expert outside readers who report to him in confidence on the quality of the work. Publication of a work signifies that it is deemed to be a competent treatment worthy of public consideration; such publication does not imply endorsement of conclusions or recommendations contained in the study.

The Institution maintains its position of neutrality on issues of public policy in order to safeguard the intellectual freedom of the staff. Hence interpretations or conclusions in Brookings publications should be understood to be solely those of the author or authors and should not be attributed to the Institution, to its trustees, officers, or other staff members, or to the organizations that support its research.

Foreword

As a taxpayer, parent, or student, every citizen is involved in the problems of the nation's elementary and secondary educational system. Increasingly, issues of finance have come to be seen as the common element in many of these problems. There is growing concern with the manner in which schools are financed, the influence of finance systems on the quality of educational services, the distribution of tax burdens and educational benefits, and the educational choices available to parents. Taxpayers have become alarmed by the rapid rise in school property tax rates; with growing frequency they have voted against school budget increases and school bond issues. In many parts of the nation teachers have begun to unionize, and some school districts have been faced with prolonged and bitter strikes. In over half the states, there have been legal challenges to existing systems of public school finance; many states are reconsidering their basic school aid laws. Among nonpublic schools, enrollment has declined and many institutions have been forced to close their doors.

The authors of this study examine the three major school finance issues facing the nation. First, they consider the aggregate fiscal position of the public schools and conclude that, although the existing revenue system was strained by the growth in school spending during the past decade, the financial pressure should ease markedly in the future. In their discussion of the second major school finance issue—the disparities in expenditures and tax burdens under current systems of school finance—they discuss the difficulties of devising a fiscal solution that would simultaneously meet the criteria of fairness, reasonable cost, and diversity of educational offerings. They point out that while there are many problems with the current systems of school finance—most stemming from the heavy reliance on local property taxes—any movement toward increased state or federal support may entail significant expenditure increases. Moreover, they emphasize that compromises will have to be made between the conflicting objectives of reducing disparities in expenditures among local school districts and of ensuring that the same districts remain free to determine the quality of public education they provide.

The fiscal and enrollment problems facing nonpublic schools, the third issue discussed in this study, are largely confined to Catholic and a few other denominational institutions. According to the authors, much of the decline in nonpublic school enrollment is not directly related to rising costs or fiscal pressures. Hence, they conclude that even a major program of government support for nonpublic schools probably would not halt or reverse the decline. In their discussion of alternative roles that the federal government might play in mitigating some of the problems of school finance, the authors stress the conflicting nature of the many possible objectives of federal policy. Especially when—as now—the federal budget is likely to become more stringent, fulfilling the objectives of existing federal education programs, particularly that of aid to students from low income families, will compete for federal resources with new efforts to provide relief from the property tax, to equalize expenditures per pupil, and to aid nonpublic schools.

Robert D. Reischauer, Robert W. Hartman, and Daniel J. Sullivan are, respectively, research associate, senior fellow, and research assistant in the Economic Studies program at the Brookings Institution. The authors wish to thank Henry J. Aaron, Stephen Barro, the Reverend Ernest Bartell, Walter McMahon, and Alice M. Rivlin for their valuable comments and criticisms of the manuscript. Secretarial assistance was provided by M. T. S. Schifter, whose patience and cryptographic skills were very much appreciated, and by Margaret Su and Virginia Crum. Evelyn Fisher checked the text for statistical accuracy and consistency.

This volume is the eleventh publication in the Brookings series of Studies in Social Economics. The series presents the results of research focused on selected problems in the fields of health, education, housing, social security, poverty, and welfare. This study was supported by a grant from the Edna McConnell Clark Foundation.

The views expressed in this study are those of the authors and should not be attributed to the trustees, officers, or other staff members of the Brookings Institution or to the Edna McConnell Clark Foundation.

January 1973   KERMIT GORDON
Washington, D.C.   *President*

Contents

ix

Tables

x

xi

Tables (*continued*)

Figures

chapter one Introduction

In the past half decade the problems of school finance have been transformed; the perennial headaches of local governments and nonpublic school administrators have become issues of national importance and public concern. As a result of this transformation, numerous commissions, advisory councils, and study groups have been established to help define the pertinent problems and to suggest possible solutions. A President's Commission on School Finance was created in 1970 to examine the "needs and resources of the Nation's public and non-public elementary and secondary schools."[1] Similar public and private bodies were established in more than half the states.

Three forces have been largely responsible for the great upsurge of interest in the methods by which schools are financed, and each has served to raise a fundamental question for the nation. The first of these forces was a taxpayers' revolt that raised the basic issue of whether traditional sources of school revenues were capable of supporting the future burden of public education. Faced with rapidly rising educational expenditures, voters began to balk at efforts to increase local and even state education taxes. Since 1966, school bond issues and budgets have been rejected with increasing frequency. The taxpayers' resistance was for the most part interpreted not as a popular rejection of the need for greater school spending, but as a repudiation of the prevailing methods of raising school revenue; it was a revolt against the heavy reliance on local school property taxes. Property tax relief thus became an integral part of the discussion of school finance reform, and the search began for methods of substituting state and federal revenues for local school property taxes. Echoing this development, President Nixon promised in his State of the Union Message on January 20, 1972, a "revolutionary" new program "for relieving the burden of property

1. Executive Order 11513.

1

taxes and providing both fair and adequate financing for our children's education."[2]

The second force that propelled school finance problems into the national limelight was a series of court decisions that dealt with the constitutionality of prevailing methods of financing public education. In California, Minnesota, Texas, New Jersey, Wyoming, Arizona, Kansas, and Michigan, judges held that existing systems of finance violated the equal protection clause of the Fourteenth Amendment to the Constitution, in that they made "the quality of a child's education a function of the wealth of his parents and neighbors."[3] These decisions were negative in nature; while they specified that the existing forms of financing public schools in these states were unacceptable, the courts did not spell out methods that would be tolerable. Thus, the second question facing the nation is to find ways to meet the challenge posed by the courts: how to ensure that a school district's wealth or poverty does not unduly influence the quality of the education it provides.

Finally, the decline in nonpublic school enrollments drew further public attention to the issues of school finance. Virtually all the enrollment decline took place in the Catholic schools, which educate four out of five of the nation's nonpublic school students. After peaking in 1964, the enrollment in Catholic schools fell steadily from 5.6 million in 1964 to 4.0 million in 1971. Although many factors contributed to this decline, the financial pressures on parochial schools have received the most attention. To counter these pressures, both church leaders and political leaders, from President Nixon on down, have sought to bolster the parochial school system through government financial assistance. However, many recent state efforts to provide public revenues for nonpublic schools have been overturned by the courts on the grounds that they violated the constitutional requirements of separation of church and state. Thus, the third set of questions before the nation was whether and how public revenue could be used to assist the nation's nonpublic schools.

This book discusses in detail each of the three major school finance issues facing the nation. It also analyzes the alternative solutions to these problems. As a background, the following chapter contains a brief description of the way in which public and nonpublic schools are currently financed. Chapter 3, which deals with the overall "fiscal crisis" facing the nation's public schools, delves into the roots of the problem and its likely

2. *Weekly Compilation of Presidential Documents,* Vol. 8 (January 24, 1972), p. 71.
3. *Serrano* v. *Priest,* California Supreme Court 938254, L.A. 29820 (1971), p. 1.

future, before discussing the costs and other problems associated with a major shift away from local financing of public schools. Chapter 4 analyzes the problems of defining equal educational opportunity, and the difficulties inherent in ensuring that financial inequities do not undermine equal educational opportunity. It then reviews the possible remedies, shows how they interact with the solutions to the fiscal problem, and considers their ramifications in the private school sector and their probable costs. The next chapter deals with the sources of the problems facing nonpublic schools and with possible remedies. The last chapter discusses the alternative roles the federal government might play in reforming school finance.

Public concern with school financing reflects two assumptions, which we accept: (1) the availability of money and resources is an important determinant of the quality of education, and (2) the quality of education significantly affects educational achievement. Although the extent to which money influences educational performance is the subject of lively debate, analyses of the available data have not been conclusive. However, a detailed study of the actual or potential impact of school finance on educational achievement lies beyond the scope of this book.

chapter two **Current Systems
of School Finance**

In the 1971–72 school year, elementary and secondary education ranked third only to national defense and income security as a consumer of government resources: $46.8 billion was spent on the education of the nation's 48.2 million public school students. Another $2.6 billion in private funds were devoted to educating the 5.4 million children attending nonpublic schools. In both the public and the private sectors a variety of methods was used to raise these revenues.

The Public Sector

The financial responsibility for the nation's public schools is shared by federal, state, and local governments. Historically, Washington's role has been limited, in large part because education was not one of the functions the Constitution delegated to the federal government. The basic division of labor—that between states and their school districts—is determined at the state level, where the ultimate constitutional responsibility for providing public education rests. States have usually delegated much of the administrative, and often most of the financial, responsibility for education to school districts or to municipalities, counties, and other local governments that operate schools.

Slightly more than half of all funds allocated to public schools are raised by school districts and these local governments; 40 percent is derived from state sources, and the remainder is contributed by the federal government. Although the state share increased markedly between 1930 and 1950, while the local share declined, little change has occurred during the past twenty

4

Table 2-1. Percentage of Funds Allocated to Public Schools by Level of Government, and Percentage of Total Allocations Derived from State Sources for Selected States, Various Years, 1929–30 to 1969–70 School Years

Level of government or state	*Years*					
	1929–30	*1939–40*	*1949–50*	*1959–60*	*1965–66*	*1969–70*
Percentage of funds allocated to public schools						
Local	82.7	67.9	57.3	56.5	53.0	52.7
State	17.0	30.3	39.8	39.1	39.1	40.7
Federal	0.3	1.8	2.9	4.4	7.9	6.6
All levels	100.0	100.0	100.0	100.0	100.0	100.0
Percentage of total allocations derived from state sources						
Idaho	7.7	10.7	23.5	27.6	39.1	43.2
Delaware	87.9	84.4	83.5	82.5	79.7	70.6
Iowa	4.3	1.1	19.1	12.0	12.5	30.1
New Mexico	21.8	45.3	86.0	74.4	63.5	62.7
Oklahoma	10.6	34.0	56.5	27.7	27.9	40.8
Wyoming	27.1	4.3	42.0	47.5	39.2	25.4

Sources: Data for all years except 1965–66 from Roe L. Johns, "The Development of State Support for the Public Schools," in Roe L. Johns and others (eds.), *Status and Impact of Educational Finance Programs* (Gainesville, Florida: National Educational Finance Project, 1971), pp. 20, 22. Data for 1965–66 from U.S. Office of Education, *Digest of Educational Statistics, 1969 Edition* (1969), Table 67, p. 50. Percentages are rounded and may not add to totals.

years (Table 2-1). The federal share expanded somewhat in the mid-1960s, with the passage of the Elementary and Secondary Education Act (ESEA) of 1965, but this expansion has not continued. Of course, tremendous shifts have occurred within some of the states, but as Table 2-1 shows, most of the changes reflected no consistent trend, either within one state or across the various states.

Local Support

In the 1971–72 school year, 55 percent of the total receipts[1] used by public schools was raised by the local school districts in which it was spent. The great bulk of this money—roughly 82 percent—came from property taxes, which are often the only form of taxation available to school districts (Table 2-2). Only in a handful of states do other taxes constitute a significant source of school moneys.[2] Even in these areas, how-

1. Total receipts includes revenue receipts derived from taxes, grants in aid, fees, and charges, as well as nonrevenue receipts from bond sales, loans, and sales of certain types of property.
2. Pennsylvania, Maryland, and Kentucky are among those states in which local nonproperty taxes are substantial. See Duane O. Moore, "Local Nonproperty Taxes for

Table 2-2. Estimated Public School Revenue and Nonrevenue Receipts, by Level of Government and Source, 1971–72 School Year

Thousands of dollars

Level of government and source	Amount	Percent from source	Percent of total
Local, total	28,033.0	100.0	54.7
Property taxes	23,000.0	82.0	44.9
Other taxes	469.4	1.7	0.9
Fees and charges	1,895.8	6.8	3.7
Borrowing	2,667.8	9.5	5.2
State, total	19,877.8	100.0	38.8
Sales taxes	9,477.7	47.7	18.5
Income taxes	4,940.5	24.9	9.6
Other taxes	2,720.3	13.7	5.3
Miscellaneous, fees, and other	2,739.3	13.8	5.4
Federal, total	3,305.7	100.0	6.5
Personal income tax	1,990.0	60.2	3.9
Corporate income tax	690.9	20.9	1.3
Other	624.8	18.9	1.2
All levels	51,216.5	...	100.0

Sources: Derived from National Education Association, Research Division, *Estimates of School Statistics, 1971–72* (NEA, 1971); Irene A. King, *Bond Sales for Public School Purposes, 1970–71*, U.S. Office of Education, National Center for Educational Statistics (1972), Table 6; U.S. Bureau of the Census, *Estimates of State Revenue and Expenditure for 1972*, State and Local Government Special Studies 58 (1971), Table 2; Bureau of the Census, *State Government Finances in 1970*, GF70-No. 3 (1971), Table 7; *The Budget of the United States Government, Fiscal Year 1973*, p. 65; and unpublished data provided by the Advisory Commission on Intergovernmental Relations. Figures are rounded and may not add to totals. The federal government's contribution was allocated among the sources of federal general revenues in proportion to the relative magnitudes of these sources. A similar method was used to derive an estimate of each state's contribution of revenue receipts to public schools. State nonrevenue contributions were treated separately.

ever, property taxes still provide most of the locally raised school receipts. Borrowing, the second largest local source of school finance, is for the most part reserved for school construction and other capital outlays. Fees and charges imposed for school lunches, tickets to athletic events, tuitions for nonresidents, book sales, and excursions are the third largest source of local receipts for school districts. On the whole these charges form only a minor and inflexible source of public school support; they often defray only a fraction of the cost of providing the services against which they are levied.

In general, school districts are free to raise as much as they want from local sources. Although many states set a maximum permissible tax rate that a school district may impose, the local voters in most areas of the

Schools," in Roe L. Johns and others (eds.), *Status and Impact of Educational Finance Programs* (Gainesville, Florida: National Educational Finance Project, 1971).

country can override such limitations through special referenda. In every state but Utah, local school districts are allowed to keep all the revenues they raise from their own sources, and in none is the amount of state aid reduced if the local district takes it upon itself to raise more money from local sources. In effect, the school districts themselves are the units of government that ultimately decide how much shall be spent on education in their areas.

State Support

State governments provided 39 percent of the money used to support public elementary and secondary schools in 1971–72. State educational support is usually derived from general revenue funds, almost half of which come from sales tax receipts. Most of the remainder is raised through personal and corporate income taxes.

Except in Hawaii, where the school system is administered by the state government, only a tiny fraction of state outlays for elementary and secondary education represents direct expenditures for such services as the operation of state departments of education or contributions to state-run teachers' pension systems. The great bulk of state educational outlays takes the form of intergovernmental grants to school districts to achieve three major objectives.

The first objective is the support of basic educational programs in every district in the state. Usually, a school district can apply such general educational aid in any way it sees fit. In its most rudimentary form, general state aid may be provided through a flat grant based solely on the number of students enrolled in, or the number of personnel employed by, the school system. In some states, grants are adjusted to reflect cost differences that arise from the nature of the district or the mix of pupils that it educates. For example, extra weight may be given to students enrolled in high school programs on the grounds that such programs are more specialized, and hence more expensive, than basic elementary schooling. In a few states additional money is provided for districts with hard-to-educate children— the handicapped, the disabled, and those from disadvantaged homes. Sparsely populated rural districts or congested central cities are given extra consideration under some state aid plans on the grounds that the cost of providing educational services in such areas is abnormally high.

The second objective, to which one-eighth of all state assistance to school districts is devoted, is the stimulation of special services or programs; the use of such funds is restricted to specific program areas. State categorical assistance for transportation, driver education, vocational education, textbook purchases, and school construction are examples of this type of state aid. One justification for such categorical assistance lies in the belief that, left to their own devices, local school districts would not allocate as much money to these programs and services as the state feels is desirable. Another is that since the need for such programs is often distributed unequally among the school districts of a state, it is inequitable to put the entire burden of support on the taxpayers of a few districts.

The third basic objective of state educational assistance has been to compensate local school districts for the differences in their abilities to raise educational revenues from local tax sources. In 1968–69, forty-seven states had programs designed to help equalize the revenue-raising abilities of their school districts. Minimum foundation state aid plans, percentage equalization schemes, guaranteed tax base systems, and the other programs devoted to this objective, absorbed about 58 percent of all state aid in that year.[3] All such programs are designed to vary the amount of state aid per student with the relative wealth of the district. Other things being equal, a district with a relatively small tax base (usually measured by the value of its taxable property per student) receives more state aid per pupil than one with a larger amount of taxable resources. Under a minimum foundation plan, the size of the state grant received by each district is equal to the difference between a foundation level and the revenue that would be raised by applying a stipulated tax rate (required "effort") to the local district's tax base. If the foundation level were $500 per pupil and the required tax effort 2 percent, a school district with a tax base of $25,000 per pupil would receive nothing ($500 − 0.02 × $25,000); a district whose tax base was $10,000 would receive $300 per student ($500 − 0.02 × $10,000). Under a percentage equalizing scheme, the state reimburses each district for a fraction of its expenditures. The fraction varies with the relative wealth of the district, richer districts receiving a smaller percentage of their expenditures than poorer ones. Guaranteed tax base plans act to ensure that each district receives at least as much from its current local tax effort as it would if its tax base were equivalent to the guaranteed level. In effect, the state makes up the difference between the amount the local tax rate

3. Roe L. Johns and Richard G. Salmon, "The Financial Equalization of Public School Support Programs in the United States for the School Year, 1968–69," in Johns and others (eds.), *Status and Impact of Educational Finance Programs*, Chap. 4, pp. 141–90.

would generate from the guaranteed tax base and the actual yield.[4] While in theory a high degree of fiscal equalization might result from such plans, the practice in most states does not achieve the potential. One reason is that most state equalization programs guarantee all districts a minimum level of state aid; not even extremely wealthy districts are required to pay part of their local revenues to the state. Other factors also limit the effectiveness of many equalization programs. For example, the minimum foundation is often set at an extremely low level, or the expenditure ranges through which percentage equalization or guaranteed tax base plans operate may be severely constricted.

Federal Support

The federal share, which represents less than 7 percent of the total, comes from personal and corporate income tax receipts, excise levies, and the other sources of federal general revenues. Most federal aid is intended for specific types of educational assistance rather than for general aid. Title I of ESEA, the largest of the federal aid programs, provides school districts with $1.6 billion for compensatory education programs for children from disadvantaged homes.

The program of aid to federally impacted areas, another major form of federal educational assistance, distributed an estimated $566 million in fiscal year 1972 among the school districts that educate significant numbers of children whose parents either work for the federal government or live on federal property. Other significant federal programs include aid for vocational education, supplementary services, education of the handicapped, school lunches, libraries, and state educational agencies.

4. Algebraically, the size of the state grant per pupil G under the simplest forms of these equalization programs can be expressed as follows:

Foundation plan	$G = F - t^*B$
Percentage equalization	$G = t[\overline{B}/k - B]$
Guaranteed tax base	$G = t[B^* - B]$

where F is the foundation level of expenditures per pupil, t^* is the required tax effort of the foundation program, B is the per pupil tax base of the district, t is the locally determined tax rate, $\overline{B}$ is the state average tax base per pupil, $(1 - k)$ is the state share of support in a district with an average tax base under a percentage equalizing scheme, and B^* is the guaranteed tax base per pupil. Although theoretically the grant under these programs could be negative—that is, the school district could be required to pay money to the state—states have precluded this possibility by establishing a minimum grant in their equalization programs.

Differences among and within States

This picture of the aggregate division of fiscal responsibility for public education in the United States hides the tremendous variations among states. At one extreme lies Hawaii, where the state government has assumed the entire financial burden for current educational expenditures, and local governments are required to pay only for the bonded debt incurred before the state assumed control in 1965. A number of states in which administrative control does not rest with the state government as it does in Hawaii, but rather is exercised by local school districts, also provide major portions of school revenues (Table 2-3). In Alaska, Delaware, and North Carolina, more than 65 percent of school revenues is raised by state taxes. At the other end of the spectrum lies New Hampshire, where 85 percent of the financial burden is borne by local governments, the state contributing only 10 percent. In Massachusetts, Nebraska, Oregon, South Dakota, and Connecticut, 70 percent or more of the financial responsibility for education is borne by local governments—that is, by local taxpayers. The variation in the fraction paid for by the federal government—from almost 30 percent in Mississippi to less than 3 percent in Connecticut—is a function of the level of state and local expenditures and the number of school children eligible for the various forms of federal categorical assistance. Since two-thirds of the federal aid is distributed according to the number of children eligible for the ESEA Title I and impacted area programs, there is little a state or a school district can do to increase significantly the amount it receives from the federal government.

Within states there are also great differences in the methods by which school districts raise money, and the amounts raised vary considerably among districts (Table 2-4). In most states, the total revenue available per student in high-spending districts exceeds that of low-spending districts by two to one, or more.[5] Although high-spending districts generally raise the greatest fraction of their revenue from local sources, even among districts that raise roughly equivalent amounts of money there are significant differences in sources of revenue. To take an extreme example, Fort Covington, a very poor rural school district in northern New York, obtained more than 90 percent of its revenue from the state in 1968–69; whereas New York City, whose total receipts per pupil from local, state, and federal

5. The disparities are examined in Chapter 4. See also *Review of Existing State School Finance Programs*, Vol. 2: *Documentation of Disparities in the Financing of Public Elementary and Secondary School Systems—By State*, A Commission Staff Report Submitted to the President's Commission on School Finance (The Commission, 1972), p. 13.

Table 2-3. Distribution of Federal, State, and Local Financing of Public Schools, by State, 1970–71 School Year

State	Percentage of revenue receipts		
	Federal	State	Local and other[a]
Alabama	18.9	60.5	20.6
Alaska	17.6	71.5	10.9
Arizona	8.7	43.4	47.9
Arkansas	18.5	44.2	37.3
California	5.1	35.2	59.8
Colorado	7.9	29.4	62.7
Connecticut	2.3	23.3	74.3
Delaware	7.2	70.8	22.0
District of Columbia	15.4	...	84.6
Florida	10.9	55.0	34.1
Georgia	10.9	54.7	34.4
Hawaii	7.7	89.4	2.9
Idaho	11.8	39.3	48.9
Illinois	4.9	34.8	60.3
Indiana	5.1	31.5	63.4
Iowa	3.3	27.9	68.8
Kansas	6.8	29.9	63.3
Kentucky	16.7	53.7	29.6
Louisiana	14.3	56.2	29.5
Maine	7.9	31.9	60.1
Maryland	5.8	35.3	58.9
Massachusetts	5.4	25.0	69.6
Michigan	3.8	41.3	54.8
Minnesota	4.4	46.0	49.6
Mississippi	28.1	47.6	24.2
Missouri	7.7	31.2	61.1
Montana	8.0	24.0	68.0
Nebraska	6.0	18.9	75.1
Nevada	6.7	37.5	55.8
New Hampshire	4.8	9.9	85.3
New Jersey	4.8	26.1	69.0
New Mexico	17.5	61.5	21.0
New York	4.3	47.9	47.7
North Carolina	15.0	66.2	18.8
North Dakota	10.0	28.2	61.8
Ohio	6.3	27.9	65.8
Oklahoma	10.6	41.1	48.2
Oregon	5.9	19.6	74.5
Pennsylvania	5.5	43.7	50.8
Rhode Island	7.2	34.4	58.4
South Carolina	17.7	56.3	26.0
South Dakota	10.6	14.3	75.1
Tennessee	14.6	44.5	40.9
Texas	9.1	47.9	43.0
Utah	8.3	52.5	39.2
Vermont	6.6	32.8	60.6
Virginia	10.5	33.8	55.8
Washington	7.4	50.7	41.9
West Virginia	12.9	49.4	37.7
Wisconsin	3.5	30.6	65.9
Wyoming	10.1	32.9	57.0
50 states and District of Columbia	7.2	40.0	52.8

Source: National Education Association, *Estimates of School Statistics, 1971–72*, Table 9, p. 34. Figures are rounded and may not add to 100.
a. Includes revenue receipts from local and intermediate sources, gifts, and tuition and fees from patrons.

Table 2-4. Local, State, and Federal Revenue Receipts per Pupil, Selected New York School Districts, 1968–69 School Year

Amounts in dollars

	Local		State		Federal	
School district	Percent	Amount	Percent	Amount	Percent	Amount
Hempstead	75.8	1,108	22.9	334	1.4	20
New York City	56.3	757	39.3	529	4.4	59
Buffalo	33.1	342	57.2	592	9.7	100
Trenton	22.9	251	73.4	807	3.7	40
Fort Covington	5.8	71	90.5	1,113	3.8	46
State average	49.1	628	46.9	600	4.0	51

Sources: *Review of Existing State School Finance Programs*, Vol. 2: *Documentation of Disparities in the Financing of Public Elementary and Secondary School Systems—By State*, A Commission Staff Report Submitted to the President's Commission on School Finance (The Commission, 1972), p. 145; State of New York, Department of Audit and Control, *School District Data for Year Ending June 30, 1969* (The Department, 1970), p. 16. Calculations were made from data before rounding.

sources were only slightly higher than Fort Covington's, received less than 40 percent of its revenue from the state in the same period (see Table 2-4). Most such differences can be traced to the method of distributing state aid and to the relative concentrations of pupils eligible for the federal categorical programs.

While it is often convenient to speak as if there were a single, uniform system that finances public education in the nation, this is not the case. Important differences exist among the fifty states, and even within a single state there is a great deal of variation in revenue sources from district to district.

The Nonpublic Sector

Nonpublic schools include a wide variety of parish, diocesan, and independent institutions administered by the Catholic church, exclusive day and boarding academies, neighborhood "free" schools, sectarian schools affiliated with Protestant and Jewish denominations, and ghetto street academies.[6] The diversity and the general lack of available information make it extremely difficult to generalize about the fiscal situation of the nonpublic sector.

It is clear, however, that the expenditures of nonpublic schools vary

6. For an excellent picture of the diverse types of nonpublic schools operating in one state, see Donald A. Erickson and others, "Crisis in Illinois Nonpublic Schools," Final Research Report to the Elementary and Secondary Nonpublic Schools Study Commission, State of Illinois (The Commission, 1971; processed), Chap. 4.

even more than those of the nation's public schools. In the 1970–71 school year, Catholic schools, which educate four of five nonpublic school students, spent an average of only $307 per pupil,[7] less than 40 percent of average public school costs (Table 2-5). While Lutheran schools, and

Table 2-5. Average Expenditures per Pupil in Selected Types of Nonpublic Schools, and in Public Schools, 1970–71 School Year

Dollars

Type of school	Average per pupil cost
Nonpublic	...
Roman Catholic	307
Elementary	240
Secondary	530
Lutheran	410
Episcopal	1,320
Jewish	990
National Association of Independent Schools	1,781
Other nonpublic	600
Public	812

Sources: Catholic data from National Catholic Educational Association, Research Department, *A Report on U.S. Catholic Schools, 1970–71* (Washington: NCEA, 1971), pp. 9, 10, 27; Lutheran data derived from Al H. Senske, "Lutheran Elementary School Statistics, 1971–1972," Board of Parish Education, Lutheran Church-Missouri Synod (St. Louis: The Board, 1972; processed), and Arthur J. Corazzini, "The Non-Catholic Private School," in Frank J. Fahey (director), *Economic Problems of Nonpublic Schools*, Submitted to the President's Commission on School Finance by the Office for Educational Research, University of Notre Dame (The Commission, 1972), pp. 292–94; NAIS data from National Association of Independent Schools, *NAIS Report*, No. 39 (January 1972), pp. 2, 10 (using day school data only); public data from National Education Association, *Estimates of School Statistics, 1971–72*, p. 36; other groups are authors' estimates based on data in Corazzini, "The Non-Catholic Private School."

certain other sectarian institutions, do not spend much more, both Episcopal schools and schools affiliated with the National Association of Independent Schools (NAIS), most of which do not have religious affiliations, spend as much as, if not more than, the public schools in the wealthiest suburbs of the nation.

A major explanation for the relatively low expenditure levels in the Catholic and Lutheran schools is that these institutions receive a great

7. Although it is convenient to talk of "Catholic" schools there are very significant differences within this group of institutions. Expenditures per pupil in Catholic secondary schools far exceed those of elementary schools. Private Catholic institutions generally spend more than those administered by the dioceses, which in turn have greater expenditure levels than those under parish control. Private Catholic schools also depend heavily on tuition for their revenue, while parish schools rely primarily on church subsidies. For a good description of the differences between the various types of Catholic schools, see Henry M. Brickell and others, *Nonpublic Education in Rhode Island: Alternatives for the Future*, A Study for the Rhode Island Special Commission to Study the Entire Field of Education (The Commission, 1969), pp. 61–95.

deal in the way of "contributed services." For example, members of religious orders, who comprise about half the staff of Catholic schools, are paid wages well below those of the lay teachers, who themselves receive less than teachers in the public sector.[8] Furthermore, in schools that are adjacent to churches, maintenance and operation services are often provided by the church's custodial staff. Another reason for the low spending levels reported by parochial schools is that the in-kind services provided by governments—transportation, free textbooks, and health services—are not generally included in the school budgets either as revenues or as expenditures. Like the contributed services, this practice makes expenditures understate service levels. Finally, some low-spending non-public schools are operated with fewer inputs than their public or high-spending private counterparts. In Catholic schools, for example, classes tend to be large. In New York state in 1969–70 there were thirty-three pupils per teacher in the Catholic elementary schools, while the other nonpublic elementary institutions employed one teacher for every thirteen students. The public elementary schools in the fall of 1970 averaged one for every twenty-one.[9]

The reliance that different types of nonpublic schools place on various revenue sources provides as marked a contrast as do their expenditure levels. Only 46 percent of Catholic school income, and somewhat less than half that of the Lutheran institutions, is derived from tuition and fees. By way of contrast, the private schools associated with the NAIS rely on this source for more than 80 percent of their revenues (Table 2-6). Tuition charges per pupil are roughly one-tenth as high in the Catholic schools as they are at NAIS institutions.

The second major source of revenues for Catholic as well as for some of the other religiously affiliated institutions is church subsidies. Large Catholic school systems justify their reliance on church subsidies in part

8. Religious-order teachers in Catholic schools received an average salary of $1,995 in 1970–71, while the average lay teacher earned $6,328. If all teachers had been paid on the lay teachers' salary schedules, average expenditures per pupil in the Catholic schools would have been 31 percent higher in 1970–71. (Estimated from National Catholic Educational Association, Research Department, *A Report on U.S. Catholic Schools, 1970–71* [Washington: NCEA, 1971], pp. 24, 32.)

9. Louis R. Gary and associates, "The Collapse of Nonpublic Education: Rumor or Reality?" The Report on Nonpublic Education in the State of New York for the New York State Commission on the Quality, Cost and Financing of Elementary and Secondary Education (The Commission, 1971; processed), Vol. 2, Tables A-1 and A-3; National Education Association, Research Division, *Rankings of the States, 1972* (NEA, 1972), Table 34.

Table 2-6. Revenue per Pupil of Selected Types of Nonpublic Elementary and Secondary Schools, by Source, 1970–71 School Year
Amounts in dollars

	Catholic schools		National Association of Independent Schools	
Source	Average per pupil	Percent	Average per pupil	Percent
Tuition and fees	142	46.2	1,532	83.1
Gifts and endowments	6	2.0	208	11.3
Church subsidies	127	41.2	0	0
Government assistance	19	6.2	17	0.9
Other	14	4.4	87	4.7
Total	308	100.0	1,844	100.0

Sources: As for Catholic and NAIS data in Table 2-5. NAIS data are for day schools only. Calculations were made from data before rounding.

on the grounds that parochial schools should be quasi-public in nature, and that no Catholic child should be excluded because of his family's inability to afford the tuition. Much of the burden of supporting the schools is thus placed on the public—the parish or the Catholic community at large. Another reason for the use of church subsidies is the tax treatment of tuition and gifts. Because tuition payments are not tax-deductible, while contributions to churches are, religiously affiliated schools and parents of children attending these institutions have preferred to raise church subsidies rather than tuition. In recent years, some Catholic parishes have added special collections for the parish schools and have exerted pressure on the parents of school children to contribute to this fund.

Church subsidies for certain schools associated with non-Catholic denominations are for the most part small. On the other hand, gifts and endowments, which are the second largest source of NAIS school revenues, are an insignificant source of income for the Catholic schools.

In general, public revenues are not a resource upon which private institutions depend heavily. However, because these schools do not include in-kind government services in their budgets, the figures in Table 2-6 understate the importance of such aid. Most government aid is provided by states and localities. In many states, child support services are available to children attending nonpublic schools. For example, in New Jersey, children attending such institutions receive school transportation services from local public school districts. Textbooks, health care, and remedial instruction are provided from public school funds in a number of states.

Until the practice was struck down by the courts, New York compensated nonpublic schools for providing such state-mandated services as testing and keeping attendance records. In total, in 1970–71 revenues from state and local governments accounted for 4.2 percent of the income of Catholic elementary schools, and 3.2 percent for the Catholic secondary schools. Recent efforts to increase state aid to nonpublic schools have encountered constitutional problems. In Rhode Island, Connecticut, New York, and Pennsylvania, state laws that channeled public money into these institutions have been overturned by the courts in the past two years.

Nonpublic schools have also shared in a number of federal educational programs. In total, federal funds account for about 3 percent of the income of Catholic schools, and a lesser fraction of that of other nonpublic institutions. Almost half this money comes from the program of aid to the disadvantaged (Title I of ESEA), and another third from federal school lunch programs. Aid for supplementary services and library resources makes up the remainder. Most of the recent growth in federal assistance has resulted not from new programs, but from the discovery by the schools that they were already eligible for funds.

The nonpublic school sector represents such a diversity of financial situations, sources of revenue, clienteles, and affiliations with religious organizations that it is extremely difficult to design public programs to deal efficiently with the problems confronting these institutions.

chapter three **The General Fiscal Dilemma**

During the past decade concern has mounted over the pervasive fiscal plight of public education, that is, over the problem of financing public schools adequately from existing local and state sources of revenue. Two factors have combined to create this problem. First, school expenditures have risen at the extremely rapid rate of 10 percent a year since 1960. This growth reflects expanded enrollment, increased desires for education, and rising prices. Second, it has become more and more difficult to squeeze additional money out of the traditional sources. Voters have resisted increasing the local contribution because this would entail raising school property taxes, which many feel are both inequitable and already excessively high. Increasing state educational aid, on the other hand, would require either a reduction of state outlays for welfare, health, higher education, and other worthwhile programs, or an increase in state taxes, which are themselves none too popular.

This chapter attempts to assess the seriousness of the fiscal problems facing public education.[1] It seeks to resolve whether a genuine crisis is developing or whether the problem is of a different sort: while we all want better schools, we are not certain that more money will improve the schools, nor do we like the taxes we now pay to support education. The first section of this chapter reviews the recent growth in school expenditures and analyzes the factors responsible for this growth. It is followed by a discussion of the revenue sources that financed the extraordinary increase in public school spending. This discussion dwells primarily on the weaknesses of the local property tax, which have led many observers to conclude that further

1. Some of the material in this chapter appeared in Charles L. Schultze and others, *Setting National Priorities: The 1973 Budget* (Brookings Institution, 1972), Chap. 6, "Financing Elementary and Secondary Education," written in collaboration with Robert W. Hartman and Robert D. Reischauer.

expenditure increases cannot be financed from this source. Next there is a brief description of the fiscal situation that will probably face public education during the next decade. The final section analyzes the implications of alternative methods of strengthening the fiscal position of education, and the difficulties inherent in them.

Rising Expenditures

In the past decade and a half, total outlays for public elementary and secondary education have more than tripled, rising from $13.6 billion in 1957–58 to $46.8 billion in the 1971–72 school year. Many factors are responsible. Roughly one-quarter of the total can be attributed to the increase in school enrollments from 33.5 million in the 1957–59 period to 48.2 million in the 1971–72 school year. This enrollment increase reflected both the high number of children born during the 1950s and early 1960s and the increase in the fraction of children who remained in school.

Growth in Total Expenditure per Pupil

About three-quarters of the total increase in school expenditures is attributable to a rise in the amount spent per pupil, which increased from $335 per child in the earlier period to $929 in 1971–72. While every category of school spending has grown rapidly during this period, the fastest growing school budget items have been expenditures for administration and for such miscellaneous instructional materials as textbooks and teaching supplies (see Table 3-1). However, such expenditures still constitute

Table 3-1. Public School Expenditures per Pupil, by Purpose, 1970–71 School Year, and Increase over 1957–59 Average

	1970–71 school year		*Percentage increase over 1957–59*	*Percentage contribution to increase*
Purpose	*Amount, dollars*	*Percentage*		
Administrative and miscellaneous services	63	7	236	8
Salaries and fringe benefits of instructional personnel	554	64	162	64
Other instructional services	38	4	209	5
Plant operation and maintenance	90	10	129	10
Transportation	32	4	157	4
Capital outlays and debt service	90	10	124	9
All purposes	867	100	159	100

Source: Computed from Orlando F. Furno and Paul K. Cunco, "Cost of Education Index, 1970–71," *School Management,* Vol. 15 (January 1971), p. 14. Figures are rounded and may not add to totals.

rather small portions of the total budget. Capital outlays and debt services, together with plant operation and maintenance, neither of which bulks large in most school budgets, grew the slowest. The salaries and benefits paid to teachers, which absorb by far the largest share of school resources, grew fairly rapidly and contributed the largest increase in total expenditures.

Growth in Instructional Costs

Almost two-thirds of the increase in expenditures per pupil was related to increases in the amount spent for teachers and other "instructional personnel," such as librarians and guidance counselors. One of the reasons for the rise in teaching costs per pupil was the significant decrease in the ratio of pupils to persons engaged in instruction during this period. The number of pupils per classroom teacher dropped from about 26 to 22, and the number of pupils per "other instructional" employee from 325 to 160. Not all the reductions in pupil-teacher ratios resulted in smaller class sizes, since teaching loads for instructional staffs were also reduced.

More than 80 percent of the rise in outlays per pupil for instructional personnel resulted from rising salaries and benefits. During the past twelve years, the average annual salaries of teachers increased by some 90 percent, those for other instructional personnel by more than 100 percent. Pensions, medical insurance plans, and other fringe benefits of school district employees also improved considerably during this period.

As a group, teachers, like other public employees, fared somewhat better than the average American worker in the private sector, whose earnings increased by some 74 percent during this period. From 1965 to 1970, teachers' salaries rose one-third faster than private sector wages. A number of explanations have been suggested. Some contend that teachers' salaries rose rapidly to "catch up" to a level commensurate with the amount of education required for the job. But while many citizens and school district employees may have viewed teachers as being in some sense "underpaid," their salaries are more likely to have been influenced by the forces of supply and demand than by some notion of the "just" wage.

Others like to interpret the rise as a reflection of the more highly trained persons entering the teaching profession (Table 3-2). While it is true that most school districts automatically increase teachers' salaries when they obtain more education, a higher degree or more teaching experience, it is not true that teachers' educational attainment has risen faster than that of the rest of the labor force. Thus, greater educational attainment "explains"

Table 3-2. Distribution of Public School Teachers by Highest Degree Held, 1956, 1965, and 1970

Percent

Degree	1956	1965	1970
No degree or two-year diploma	22.2	8.6	3.6
Bachelor's	53.2	67.3	65.8
Master's or education specialist	24.3	24.0	30.3
Doctor's	0.3	0.1	0.3
Total	100.0	100.0	100.0

Sources: National Education Association, Research Division, *NEA Research Bulletin*, Vol. 49 (May 1971), p. 56; NEA, Committee on Educational Finance, *Financial Status of the Public Schools, 1971* (NEA, 1971), Table 8, p. 13.

the relative rise in teachers' salaries only in the sense that pay is more closely tied to degrees in the teaching profession than in other lines of work.

The "teacher shortage" that prevailed through 1968 provides a more plausible explanation for the increase in the relative wages of these workers. Although the supply of potential teachers expanded rapidly during this period, estimates by the National Education Association suggest that the demand for instructional personnel grew even more rapidly.[2] The demand increase was spurred both by the rapid rise in enrollments and by rising incomes, which led the public to support increased government budgets for education.

The increased militancy and unionization of teachers is another possible cause of the rapid increase in the salaries of school district employees. Unions and professional associations that often differ little from unions have come to represent an increasing fraction of the nation's teachers. Collective bargaining and negotiated wage agreements have become the rule rather than the exception in many parts of the nation, and teachers have frequently been willing to strike to achieve their demands, even where strikes are illegal (Table 3-3). Although the effect is not clear, several recent studies of the impact of unionization and collective bargaining on salary levels have reached the conclusion that collective negotiation may have boosted teacher compensation by as much as 5 percent over what it otherwise would have been.[3] These estimates suggest that while increased unionization and the shift to collective bargaining may have been major causes

2. See "Teacher Job Shortage Ahead," in National Education Association, Research Division, *NEA Research Bulletin*, Vol. 49 (October 1971), p. 71.

3. See Hirschel Kasper, "The Effects of Collective Bargaining on Public School Teachers' Salaries," and the comment by Robert N. Baird and John H. Landon, in *Industrial and Labor Relations Review*, Vol. 24 (October 1970), pp. 57–72, and Vol. 25 (April 1972), pp. 410–17, respectively.

Table 3-3. Negotiated Agreements and Work Stoppages Involving Public School Teachers, 1959–71

	Negotiated agreements[a]		Work stoppages		
Year	Percent of measurable districts	Percent of teachers	Number of stoppages	Number of workers involved (thousands)	Man-days idle (thousands)
1959	n.a.	n.a.	2	0.2	0.7
1960	n.a.	n.a.	3	5.5	5.5
1961	n.a.	n.a.	1	*	*
1962	n.a.	n.a.	1	20.0	20.0
1963	n.a.	n.a.	2	2.2	2.6
1964	n.a.	n.a.	9	14.4	30.6
1965	n.a.	n.a.	5	1.7	7.9
1966	25.0	41.5	30	37.3	58.5
1967	34.8	52.2	76	92.4	969.3
1968	43.4	58.7	88	145.0	2,180.0
1969	53.2	66.2	183	105.0	412.0
1970	57.3	63.6	152	94.8	935.6
1971	64.1	74.2	135	76.6	551.4

Sources: Negotiated agreements, National Education Association, *Negotiation Research Digest*, Vol. 5 (June 1972), Table B, and June issues for 1968–71; work stoppages, U.S. Bureau of Labor Statistics, *Government Work Stoppages, 1960, 1969, and 1970* (November 1971), Table 9, p. 6, and *Work Stoppages in Government, 1958–68*, Report 348 (1970), Table 9, p. 13, supplemented with work stoppage data for 1971 from BLS.
* Less than 50.
n.a. Not available.
a. The percentages are based on the number of respondents for the given year.

of rising teachers' salaries in certain school districts, only a small portion of the nationwide increase can be attributed to them.

Whatever the reasons, the relative rise in wages of teachers has contributed significantly to the growth in expenditures for education. Had the rate of increase of instructional salaries not exceeded the national average for other occupations over the past twelve years, school expenditures in 1971–72 would have been some $2.8 billion, or 6 percent, less than they actually were.

The Effects of Inflation

Wages of school personnel are not the only item in school budgets that have risen rapidly in recent years. The general inflation experienced by the economy has pushed up the costs of textbooks, teaching aids, and other supplies needed to operate and maintain educational institutions by about one-third in the past decade and a half. Construction costs for new schools have increased by more than 65 percent during this period—considerably

Table 3-4. Number of Public Elementary and Secondary School Bond Elections Held, Par Value of Proposed Bond Issues, Percentage Approved, and Bond Interest Cost, Fiscal Years 1962–71

Fiscal year	Number of elections	Par value of proposed bond issues (millions of dollars)	Percent approved		Net interest costs (percent)
			Number	Par value	
1962	1,432	1,849	72.4	68.9	3.33
1963	2,048	2,659	72.4	69.6	3.11
1964	2,071	2,672	72.5	71.1	3.25
1965	2,041	3,129	74.7	79.4	3.25
1966	1,745	3,560	72.5	74.5	3.67
1967	1,625	3,063	66.6	69.2	4.01
1968	1,750	3,740	67.6	62.5	4.57
1969	1,341	3,913	56.8	43.6	4.88
1970	1,216	3,285	53.2	49.5	6.39
1971	1,086	3,337	46.7	41.4	5.48

Source: Irene A. King, *Bond Sales for Public School Purposes, 1970–71*, U.S. Office of Education, National Center for Educational Statistics (1972), pp. 2, 3, 11.

faster than the rate of increase for private structures.[4] Finally, interest costs on the new bonds issued by elementary and secondary school districts have been far higher in the past five years than they were previously (see last column of Table 3-4).

In summary, increases in the numbers of teachers, books, and other inputs devoted to educating each student and increases in the prices of these factors have pushed up school expenditures in recent years. In part, the rise in expenditures was caused by an increase in the demand for educational services which in turn was related to the rapid growth of family incomes during the past decade. The increase in expenditures would have been less had there been gains in educational productivity similar to those that occurred in most other sectors of the economy. Unfortunately, however, education, like most public and private personal service industries, does not lend itself to innovations that increase productivity. So much of the learning process depends on personal contact between the teachers and students that no machine or other labor-saving device is likely to reduce the need for instructional personnel in the near future.

4. U.S. Department of Commerce, *Survey of Current Business*, Vol. 51 (July 1971), Table 8.7, p. 45.

Raising the Money

While expanded federal and state aid have helped, school districts have had to rely heavily on local revenues to finance the recent rise in educational expenditures. Nationally, 52 percent of the increase in school revenues over the past decade and a half came from local sources, while 40 percent was contributed by the states. In many of the most populous states—California, Ohio, New Jersey, and Massachusetts, for example—more than 60 percent of the increase in school spending was paid for out of increased local tax collections.

Recently, resistance to further increases in the local contribution to education has mounted. This "taxpayers' revolt," as it has been labeled by the media, is reflected in the refusal of local voters to approve school construction bond issues and property tax hikes for increases in current school expenditures (see Table 3-4). More than half of all school bond issues were turned down in 1971, whereas more than 70 percent were approved during the 1958–66 period. Similarly, about half of the requests for school tax increases were rejected in 1970. Although this revolt has not markedly slowed the national rise in school budgets, in some places it has resulted in shortened school years, reduced offerings of academic programs, teacher layoffs, and the abolition of sports and other special activities. Some large school districts, such as Chicago and Philadelphia, have sustained substantial budget deficits.

The Sources of Discontent

A great many explanations have been put forward for the taxpayers' revolt. Some educators hope that it is a temporary response to the uncertainty generated by the 1969–70 economic recession. Others fear, however, that it reflects a more permanent negative shift in the electorate's attitudes toward education. There seems to be widespread feeling among taxpayers that school expenditures have been rising "too fast" and that the increases have not produced a commensurate improvement in the quality of education, but have been eaten up by increases in the salaries and benefits of school district employees. There is also considerable dissatisfaction with the schools, ranging from concern over the relevance of educational programs to a fear and dislike of the lifestyles of the students. In some areas, racial conflicts and opposition to busing for purposes of racial integration may be adding to citizen reluctance to spend for schools.

Another explanation for the possible shift in public attitudes is the changing structure of the population. In many communities, the fraction of voters with school age children is dropping, while single, childless, and aged voters form an increasingly large segment of the electorate. In some places private school enrollments are quite large. When bond issues or tax increases must be approved by more than a simple majority, a small decline in the fraction of persons having a direct stake in the school system may be an important determinant of the election's outcome.

The Problems with the Property Tax

While these forces are no doubt partially responsible for the taxpayers' revolt, the cause that has most often been cited is the method used to raise the local educational share; the property tax is widely disliked. A number of polls and surveys have revealed that it is the most unpopular of all levies. A survey by the Advisory Commission on Intergovernmental Relations (ACIR) found that almost half of those interviewed regarded the property tax as the worst or least fair of the major federal, state, and local taxes.[5] The many alleged faults of this levy have led to a rising chorus of opinion that it should be abandoned as a major source of school financing. Because many policymakers and citizens are seriously entertaining this possibility, it is worth analyzing in some detail its alleged weaknesses. But before that we shall summarize some of its strengths, so that the criticisms will be placed in perspective: In the first place, the property tax has proved to be a tremendous revenue raiser. Among all the nation's taxes only the federal personal income and payroll taxes generate more money. Second, the receipts are extremely stable, allowing governments that depend on such revenues to plan their expenditures well in advance. Third, the major part of the tax base—real property—is both difficult to conceal and immobile, so that the tax is not easily avoided. These characteristics make property a good base for a tax levied by relatively unskilled taxing authorities. Finally, since local public services enhance the desirability of a community and thereby raise property values, the property tax to some extent tends to charge those who benefit from the services it finances.

5. See Advisory Commission on Intergovernmental Relations, "Public Opinion and Taxes" (ACIR, May 1972; processed). The same basic unpopularity was reported in "City Taxes and Services: Citizens Speak Out," *Nation's Cities*, Vol. 9 (August 1971), pp. 9–10. It is important to keep in mind that the property tax is often the only major tax on which the electorate can vote directly; some general antitax or antigovernment feelings may thus be vented in school budget elections.

LEVEL AND GROWTH OF THE PROPERTY TAX. Foremost among the complaints about the property tax is the belief that it is too high and has risen at an uncontrolled pace. From the scanty evidence that is available, it appears that effective property tax rates—the tax liability relative to the market value of property—have risen considerably in recent years. For the nation as a whole, annual property tax receipts in 1955 were equivalent to 1.41 percent of the market value of real property; fourteen years later they had risen to 1.80 percent. National figures are not available for more recent years, but evidence from several states suggests that the rise has continued (see Table 3-5).

While total property tax receipts have risen rapidly, their growth has been quite moderate in comparison with the increases in other state and local taxes. As Table 3-6 shows, in the postwar period property tax receipts have risen slightly faster than national income, but much more slowly than other state and local taxes. Whether this growth is excessive or the rates are now too high is, of course, a matter of opinion.

Irrespective of how high property taxes are or how fast they have grown,

Table 3-5. Effective Property Tax Rates, United States, New York, New Jersey, and California, Selected Fiscal Years, 1955–71

Percent

Fiscal year	United States	New York		New Jersey		California	
		Total	School	Total	School	Total	School
1955	1.41	n.a.	n.a.	n.a.	n.a.	n.a.	n.a.
1960	1.57	3.21	1.39	2.91	1.43	1.80	0.64
1965	1.79	3.19	1.52	3.12	1.61	2.00	0.72
1967	1.78	3.43	1.59	3.20	1.65	2.19	0.84
1968	1.79	3.37	1.71	3.25	1.76	2.17	0.86
1969	1.80	3.58	1.73	3.34	1.87	2.37	0.93
1970	n.a.	3.82	1.92	3.57	2.02	2.34	0.94
1971	n.a.	3.81	2.05	3.66	2.12	2.46	0.90

Sources: United States: Estimated from unpublished data on net stocks of structures from the U.S. Department of Commerce; unpublished data on property values from Edward F. Denison; one-family, multifamily, and land values from Allen D. Manvel, "Trends in the Value of Real Estate and Land, 1956 to 1966," in *Three Land Research Studies,* Prepared for the Consideration of the National Commission on Urban Problems, Research Report 12 (Government Printing Office, 1968), pp. 2, 9; and property tax receipts from Department of Commerce, *Survey of Current Business,* various July issues, Table 3.3.
   New York: *Report of the New York State Commission on the Quality, Cost and Financing of Elementary and Secondary Education* (The Commission, 1972), Vol. 1, Table 2.2, p. 2.30; New York State Division of the Budget, *New York State Statistical Yearbook, 1970* (Albany: NYSDB, April 1970), p. 180; U.S. Bureau of the Census, *Governmental Finances in 1970–71* (1972), p. 32, and three preceding issues.
   New Jersey: *Part III of the Report of the New Jersey Tax Policy Committee,* Submitted to the Governor (Trenton: The Committee), Table 3-13, p. 32.
   California: Unpublished data, California State Board of Equalization; *Annual Report of Financial Transactions Covering the School Districts of California, Fiscal Year 1960* (Sacramento: State Controller Office, State of California, 1960), and relevant succeeding issues; Bureau of the Census, *Governmental Finances,* various years.
   n.a. Not available.

Table 3-6. Property and Other State and Local Tax Receipts, and Property Taxes as Percentage of Total Taxes and of Potential Gross National Product, Selected Fiscal Years, 1927–71

Taxes in millions of dollars

Fiscal year	Property taxes	Other state and local taxes	Property taxes as percentage of total state and local taxes	Property taxes as percentage of potential GNP
1927	4,730	1,357	77.7	4.9[a]
1956	11,749	14,619	44.6	2.6
1962	19,054	22,500	45.9	3.2
1967	26,047	34,953	42.7	3.3
1971	38,260	56,019	40.6	3.4

Sources: Tax receipts, 1927–67, and GNP, 1927, U.S. Bureau of the Census, *Census of Governments, 1967*, Vol. 6, No. 5, *Historical Statistics on Governmental Finances and Employment* (1969), Table 4 and p. 1, respectively; and 1971, Bureau of the Census, "Quarterly Summary of State and Local Tax Revenue, April–June 1971," GT71 No. 2 (September 1971), p. 1. Potential GNP is estimated by authors.
a. Percentage of actual GNP.

taxpayers seem to find it extremely irritating to pay them. While sales taxes are paid a few pennies at a time and income taxes are generally deducted from paychecks before the money is actually in hand, the property tax is paid in large sums directly from the taxpayers' pockets. Most communities bill taxpayers annually or semiannually, and even when the property tax is included with the monthly mortgage payment the taxpayer may be more conscious of its bite than he is of other state and local taxes.

The large discontinuous jumps that occur in property tax liabilities also lead to taxpayer resentment. While property values generally rise gradually as income increases, the rise does not generate more revenue for a community unless property is reassessed or the millage rate is raised—both actions that are resented by the taxpayer. Since reassessments of property values are made infrequently, they may involve large increases in tax liability. For those whose incomes are not rising as rapidly, the increases may be difficult to pay. Although their homes may have appreciated considerably, they do not feel any wealthier. Nor can they easily convert the increased value of their asset into money to pay the property tax. Such situations often face older persons, who, for sentimental reasons and because of community ties, tend to remain in housing that is large and valuable in relation to their current incomes, which may be derived from relatively fixed pension and social security benefits. As is shown in Table 3-7, the value of housing per household member is usually greatest for those over 65.

ADMINISTRATION OF THE PROPERTY TAX. Discontent with the property tax also stems from the erratic manner in which it is administered. Assess-

Table 3-7. Average Value of Owner-Occupied Housing Units and Their Value per
Household Member, by Age Group and Income Class, 1972
All amounts in dollars

| | Average value by income class | | | |
Age group and value item	Under 5,000	5,000– 10,000	10,000– 15,000	Over 15,000
30–55 age group				
Value per household	10,765	14,776	19,135	22,963
Value per household member	3,209	3,531	4,405	5,144
55–65 age group				
Value per household	11,584	13,710	18,485	24,514
Value per household member	5,818	5,259	5,965	6,316
Over-65 age group				
Value per household	11,693	15,933	17,996	22,873
Value per household member	6,142	5,980	5,855	7,389

Source: Based on the Brookings SEO File of 30,000 family units for the year 1966, with values projected
to 1972 levels.

ment of property values is a judgmental process. Unless the property has
recently been sold, its market value can only be estimated. The possibility of favoritism, corruption, and carelessness is always present. The result
is that the ratios of assessed valuations to objectively determined market
values often vary greatly. For example, a study of Boston showed that in
1962 the ratio of assessed to market value of single family homes ranged
from 0.28 in East Boston to 0.54 in predominantly black Roxbury, while
assessment ratios on commercial property ranged from 0.59 in Hyde Park
to 1.11 in South Boston.[6] This suggests that some Boston homeowners
were paying double the tax rate that others paid, while owners of some
commercial property were paying at a rate four times that of the most
fortunate homeowners.

INCIDENCE OF THE PROPERTY TAX AMONG INCOME CLASSES. Another
major source of dissatisfaction with the property tax stems from the feeling
that it is highly regressive—that it absorbs a higher fraction of the incomes
of the poor than of the rich. This view rests on the belief that the property

6. Oliver Oldman and Henry [J.] Aaron, "Assessment-Sales Ratios Under the Boston
Property Tax," *Assessors Journal*, Vol. 4 (April 1969), pp. 18–19. For additional informa-
tion on differential effective tax rates within the same taxing jurisdiction, see David E.
Black, "The Nature and Extent of Effective Property Tax Rate Variation Within the City
of Boston," *National Tax Journal*, Vol. 25 (June 1972), pp. 203–10; "Statement of Ralph
Nader and Jonathan Rowe before the Senate Subcommittee on Intergovernmental Re-
lations, May 9, 1972" (processed); and William J. Beeman, *The Property Tax and the
Spatial Pattern of Growth within Urban Areas*, Research Monograph 16 (Washington:
Urban Land Institute, 1969).

tax on buildings and other improvements, if not the tax on land, is largely passed on or shifted to the final consumer of the services of the property, that renters bear the tax on residential buildings through higher rents, that consumers ultimately pay the tax on commercial and industrial property in the form of higher prices for the goods they buy, and that homeowners bear the tax on their residences.[7] If the tax is shifted in this manner, its incidence is similar to that of a consumption tax with an extremely high rate on housing services and a lower rate on other forms of expenditures. Because housing expenditures and outlays for consumer goods all tend to absorb a larger fraction of current family income among the poor than among the rich, many have concluded that such a consumption tax must be highly regressive.

Some economists, however, have pointed out that the observed tendency for housing and consumer expenditures to take up a smaller fraction of income of those in the higher income brackets is due largely to transitory factors and to the different age mix of the population at various income levels. Many families who in any one year find themselves at the lower end of the income distribution are aged or are there only temporarily either because of unemployment or because they are young and just starting a new career. The purchase of either a house or an expensive consumer durable good is a decision not usually made on the basis of a family's current economic status alone, but also on expectations about long-term income prospects and needs. Most studies have found that families with higher long-term incomes tend to own homes that are more valuable in relation to such income than lower income families.[8] This indicates that the property tax, for homeowners, is progressive when judged against longer-term indexes of ability to pay.

For renters the situation is more complex. Rental payments may absorb a larger fraction of the long-term incomes of poor renters than they do of wealthy renters, but property taxes are levied against the value of the property, not rents. Rental properties that house the poor tend to be older

7. The value of land constitutes approximately 40 percent of the value of all taxable real property (Allen D. Manvel, "Trends in the Value of Real Estate and Land, 1956 to 1966," in *Three Land Research Studies*, Prepared for the Consideration of the National Commission on Urban Problems, Research Report 12 [U.S. Government Printing Office, 1968], p. 1). It is generally agreed that the portion of the property tax that represents a levy on the value of land cannot be shifted and is borne by the owner of the land.

8. For a summary of these studies, see Frank de Leeuw, "The Demand for Housing: A Review of Cross-Section Evidence," *Review of Economics and Statistics*, Vol. 53 (February 1971), pp. 1–10. For a contrasting view, see Geoffrey Carliner, "Income Elasticity of Housing Demand," Institute for Research on Poverty, Discussion Paper 144-72 (University of Wisconsin, November 1972; processed).

and more costly to operate, to be in neighborhoods which offer little prospect for capital appreciation, and to involve higher risk than those that house wealthier tenants. Hence the ratio of value to rent for structures occupied by the poor is probably far lower than it is for buildings occupied by higher income groups. If so, the property tax, even if fully shifted to the tenant in the form of higher rental payments, may be mildly progressive for tenants as well as homeowners.[9]

In recent years a growing number of economists have come to challenge the view that the property tax is similar to an excise tax or to a sales tax that can be shifted to consumers. They argue instead that a complete analysis of the incidence of a property tax requires that one trace through the market forces set off by its imposition. The argument runs as follows: Initially, a property tax is paid by the owners of the houses, buildings, and factories upon which it is levied. Since this added cost reduces the profitability of real estate and other taxable property as a form of investment, it is likely to divert capital into untaxed or more lightly taxed sectors of the economy. Such a movement of capital will lower the profitability of capital in the untaxed sectors until a point is reached at which owners of all kinds of capital receive an equivalent rate of return after deductions and taxes. At this point, the question becomes how new investment responds to the lower rate of return on capital.

One possibility is that there will be a reduction in the aggregate flow of new investment. If this happens, the property tax will become a burden on consumers as well as on owners of capital, because as new construction and investment in capital goods are cut back, competition for the reduced supply of housing and other capital goods will drive up rents and prices[10]—and

9. If the incidence of a fully shifted property tax is defined as T/Y, where T is the tax and Y is the tenant's income, then $T/Y = tM/Y = t(R/Y)(M/R)$, where t is the effective tax rate on the market value, M, of the unit, and R is the rent. The tax would be progressive (that is, the derivative of T/Y with respect to Y would be positive), if the tendency for R/Y to be lower among richer persons were more than offset by a rise in the ratio of value to rent, M/R, caused by the factors mentioned in the text. These points are based on the work of George E. Peterson as reported in "The Regressivity of the Residential Property Tax," Working Paper 1207-10 (Urban Institute, November 8, 1972; processed).

10. Of course, even if new investment fell there are a number of obstacles that would impede the complete or immediate shifting of property taxes. Since new investment represents only a tiny fraction of the housing stock in any year, it may take many years for the supply to adjust to a new or increased property tax. Furthermore, the property tax is a local tax that varies among thousands of jurisdictions. To the extent that industry and landlords compete with others in neighboring taxing jurisdictions, they would be able to pass along only the tax that was common to all of them. The remainder would tend to be reflected in land values or in the price of other immobile factors of production. The large stocks of vacant commercial space in some central cities and the stock of single

the argument that the incidence of the property tax is similar to that of an excise tax would be valid.

The other possibility is that total investment may not change appreciably when the rate of return on capital drops. The basis for this view is that the flow of investment is limited by aggregate saving in the economy. Most studies have shown that aggregate saving is not sensitive to changes in interest rates or the profitability of capital, but rather depends on income and life-cycle factors. Thus, the imposition of a property tax would not affect the aggregate supply of homes, apartments, or commercial and industrial buildings, and the tax could not be shifted to tenants and consumers. Instead, according to this analysis, the burden of the property tax ultimately falls on all owners of capital, whose after-tax profits are reduced by the tax.

If the property tax is a tax on capital, it will be borne by individuals roughly in proportion to the value of their capital assets; the burden will be greatest for those whose holdings of capital are disproportionately large in relation to their incomes. One group with this characteristic is the elderly, but high income groups also tend to have large asset holdings in relation to their incomes.

In summary, it can be said that although politicians and the public may have been persuaded that the property tax is a regressive tax on housing expenditures, it is probably a tax borne by owners of capital and its incidence is therefore at least mildly progressive. Even if the property tax could be shifted to consumers and tenants, the incidence of the tax—when measured against long-run income—may be proportional to income or it might even be progressive.

The general proposition that the property tax may be inherently progressive does not preclude the possibility that other factors may work so as to make the nation's lower income families pay a larger fraction of their long-run incomes on property taxes than do the rich. For example, the tendency of some taxing jurisdictions to assess properties housing low

---

family homes temporarily rented for other than investment purposes could also act to impede property tax shifting.

For an elaboration of these points, see Peter Mieszkowski, "The Property Tax: An Excise Tax or a Profits Tax?" *Journal of Public Economics*, Vol. 1 (April 1972), pp. 73–96; M. Mason Gaffney, "The Property Tax Is a Progressive Tax," in National Tax Association, *1971 Proceedings of the Sixty-fourth Annual Conference on Taxation* (1972), pp. 408–26; C. Lowell Harriss, "Property Tax: Who Pays?" *Tax Review*, Vol. 33 (April 1972), pp. 13–16. A careful summary of the more traditional view is contained in Dick Netzer, *Economics of the Property Tax* (Brookings Institution, 1966), Chap. 3.

income families at a higher fraction of market value than those housing the wealthy is an administrative practice that would bias the tax in a regressive direction. The state and federal income tax provisions that permit families to deduct property taxes from their taxable incomes have the same effect. Homeowners who itemize their deductions benefit from these provisions in that they are able to shift part of their property tax bill onto the state and federal governments through a reduction in their income tax liabilities. Since, on the whole, such taxpayers have higher-than-average incomes the impact is regressive; but this effect should be viewed as a regressive element of the income tax, not of the property tax. The distribution of families with differing incomes among the thousands of local jurisdictions each with a different property tax rate may also influence the actual amounts paid by the various income classes. A progressive influence should be exerted by the fact that a disproportionate fraction of the nation's low income population lives in the South and in rural areas where property tax rates are relatively low. On the other hand, within metropolitan areas the poor are concentrated in the central cities and low income communities, where local tax rates are considerably higher than they are in the wealthier suburbs, resulting in a tendency toward regressivity.

With existing data it is not possible to estimate how these opposing tendencies influence the incidence of the property tax in the nation as a whole. Even if the pattern of incidence were found to be regressive, the cause of it could be the distribution of families among different taxing jurisdictions or discriminatory administration of the property tax, rather than any inherent characteristic of the levy itself.

DISTRIBUTION OF THE PROPERTY TAX BASE AMONG JURISDICTIONS. Another source of discontent is the way the tax base is distributed among jurisdictions. The fact that the distribution of the base is clearly unrelated to educational need creates, according to many analysts, inequities among taxpayers, because a higher tax rate is needed in a poor community than in a wealthy community to generate an equal amount of school revenue per pupil.

There is little doubt about the great disparities in the property tax base within every state. For example, the range of per-student property values among the school districts of New Jersey in 1971 was from $3,921 to $62,-598,621, or about 1 to 16,000.[11] Districts at such extremes are usually either rural areas with little in the way of taxable property or small manufacturing

---

11. *Robinson* v. *Cahill*, Docket L-18704-69, Superior Court of New Jersey, Hudson County (1972), App. A.

Table 3-8. Highest and Lowest Property Tax Bases per Pupil for School Districts in Selected Metropolitan Areas, Various Years, 1967–71

Dollars

Metropolitan area, school district, and year	Per-pupil property tax base
San Antonio, Texas, fiscal year 1967–68	
Alamo Heights	49,478
Edgewood	5,960
Essex County, New Jersey, 1971	
Millburn	99,653
Newark	19,815
Los Angeles County, fiscal year 1968–69	
Beverly Hills	50,885
Baldwin Park	3,706
Boston area, 1970	
Brookline	68,048
Norfolk	14,040
New York City area,[a] fiscal year 1968–69	
Harrison, District 2	229,866
Hempstead, District 3 (East Meadows)	20,055

Sources: In order of the table: *Rodriguez* v. *San Antonio Independent School District*, Civil Action 68-175-SA, U.S. District Court, Western District of Texas, San Antonio Division (1971), p. 26; *Robinson* v *Cahill*, Docket L-18704-69, Superior Court of New Jersey, Hudson County (1972), Appendix A, p. 2; *Serrano* v. *Priest*, California Supreme Court 938254, L.A. 29820 (1971), p. 24; Massachusetts State Tax Commission, "1970 Final Equalized Valuations" (tabulation, 1970), and U.S. Bureau of the Census, *Census of Population, 1970, General Social and Economic Characteristics*, Final Report PC (1)-C23, *Massachusetts* (1972); State of New York, Department of Audit and Control, *School District Data for Year Ending June 30, 1969* (The Department, 1970), Table 3.

a. The New York City area is considered to be New York City and Nassau and Westchester Counties.

enclaves and tax havens with only a handful of students. Yet, even within a single county or metropolitan area without such anomalies, the discrepancies are considerable, as Table 3-8 shows. In Los Angeles County, for example, the tax base of Beverly Hills is $50,885 per pupil, while nearby Baldwin Park's is a meager $3,706. Discrepancies such as these mean that school districts may have to impose very different local tax rates to raise equivalent amounts of money per student; Baldwin Park would have to levy a 13.7 percent property tax to generate the same amount that Beverly Hills could raise from a 1 percent tax. These discrepancies have led to a number of legal challenges to the existing methods of financing public schools (see Chapter 4).

While it is obvious that there are large differences in the size of various school districts' tax bases, a simple comparison of property values per pupil may overstate the inequities. Property value differences among districts reflect not only differences in ability to pay but also tax advantages and disadvantages that the housing market has translated into real estate values.

An example will demonstrate how this might happen: Suppose a large factory that imposed no costs on the local government suddenly moved into one of two neighboring communities that had identical housing, population, tax bases, and school tax rates. The tax base in the district with the factory would increase by the assessed value of the plant, so that the tax rate needed to generate the amount of revenue per pupil that was raised previously would fall. Families living in the other community, or those considering moving to either area, would see the tax advantage and want to move to the community with the factory, as long as it did not pollute its surroundings or reduce the attractiveness of the community as a place to live. The price of houses in that area would thus increase, even though the houses were identical with those in the neighboring community. The appreciation would continue until a price level was reached at which people felt there was no advantage either to living in the community with the lower tax rate and the higher cost of housing or to the one with the higher tax rate and the lower cost of housing. The appreciation of the value of homes would increase still further the tax base of the community with the plant, but it is not clear that the community would have a greater inherent ability to raise taxes. Of course, those who owned the houses when the factory moved into the community would have received capital gains, but subsequent owners would have paid higher house prices. If the incomes of families in both districts were about equal, despite the discrepancy in taxable property per pupil, the two areas would be on roughly the same fiscal footing. Those in the district with the factory would make higher monthly mortgage payments for equivalent housing, in return for the privilege of paying lower annual property taxes for a given level of per-pupil spending. Their counterparts in the other community would pay higher taxes, but their other housing costs would be lower. It is important to note, however, that from the standpoint of the resident in the community with the plant, the "price" of education and other public goods has fallen because part of each tax dollar is now raised from the plant. The price reduction should cause that community to increase its per-pupil spending above the level previously maintained by either community.

Within any labor market area it is probably safe to assume that communities housing families of roughly equal economic status have about the same fiscal capacities, whatever their per-pupil property tax base. The mobility of families would ensure that if a certain district enjoyed a real tax advantage, those living elsewhere would attempt to move into the area, and thus bid up housing prices. For racial and ethnic minorities that face housing discrimination this would not be true, since they are not free to choose their place of residence. It would also be wrong to infer that family mobility lessens the importance of differences in the tax bases of school districts housing families of very different economic levels. Discriminatory zoning, building codes, and public pressure have kept low income families from most exclusive suburban subdivisions. Nevertheless, if tax liabilities are reflected in property values, the actual variation in the fiscal capacity of school districts may be smaller than differences in the per-pupil values of taxable property would suggest.

INELASTICITY OF PROPERTY TAXES. The local property tax is also criticized for its slow growth. In the jargon of economists, the tax is inelastic with respect to national income. If effective tax rates are kept the same, the aggregate yield of the property tax increases with the expansion in the value of taxable property, which has historically been a little slower than the growth in the economy as a whole. In contrast, income tax yields tend to grow at a far faster pace than the gross national product (GNP) because of the progressive rate structure. Since local educational spending seems to increase more rapidly than national income, effective property tax rates will have to rise continuously unless state and federal aid are increased disproportionately. Furthermore, growth in the property tax base is not distributed equally among school districts. While new building activity and appreciation of existing properties send the tax rolls of one community soaring, its neighbor may experience little or no growth in its property tax base. In a number of decaying cities, such as Newark and East St. Louis, the aggregate market value of property has actually declined in recent years.

These and other complaints have led many to conclude that the nation should reduce its reliance on local property taxes to finance education and should look to other taxes and other levels of government.

Few of the criticisms of the property tax apply to the sources from which state and federal governments raise their funds for schools. On the whole, the federal and, to a lesser extent, the state tax structures are well administered and elastic, and do not suffer from as much interjurisdictional variability. Federal taxes, on balance, are also mildly progressive. Despite the advantages, however, there has been no marked increase in the reliance on federal and state funds for elementary and secondary education in the past two decades. While the total amount of federal aid has mushroomed, it remains a minor revenue source. What is more, the federal government has shown a great reluctance to provide any general educational assistance; virtually all its money is channeled into special categorical programs.

The Future

The past two decades have been difficult ones for those responsible for school financing. Are the problems likely to continue in the future? Is the existing revenue structure incapable of providing for the needs of the next decade? Although the answers to such questions hinge upon many factors, there are several reasons to expect the severity of the aggregate fiscal problem facing school districts to abate. In the first place, the growth in school enrollment that choked the system during the 1950s and continued into the 1960s has all but ended. As a result of the fall in the birth rate during the past decade, the number of school-aged children (from five to seventeen years old) has already begun to decline. The U.S. Office of Education's projections of public school enrollment indicate that in 1972–73 the number of students in public schools should level off, and that it should then begin to decrease slightly. Even the independent estimates made for the President's Commission on School Finance, which assume a continuation of the rapid shift of students from nonpublic to public schools, project that public school enrollment will be less than 2 percent greater in 1980–81 than it was a decade earlier, a far cry from the 29 percent increase of the preceding decade (see Table 3-9). This slowdown in the growth of enrollment

Table 3-9. School-Age Population and Public School Enrollment, by Five-Year Intervals, 1950–80
Thousands

School year	School-age population[a]	Public school enrollment	Percentage increase in enrollment in 5-year period
1950–51	30,861	25,111	8.1
1955–56	37,160	30,045	19.6
1960–61	44,189	36,087	20.1
1965–66	49,926	42,280	17.2
1970–71	52,517	46,531	10.1
1975–76	49,969	44,500	−4.4
		(47,325)[b]	(1.7)[b]
1980–81	49,174	44,800	0.7
		(47,211)[b]	(−0.2)[b]

Sources: Population from U.S. Bureau of the Census, *Current Population Reports*, Series P-25, No. 310, "Estimates of the Population of the United States and Components of Change, by Age, Color, and Sex, 1950 to 1960" (1965), and No. 476, "Demographic Projections for the United States" (1972), pp. 11 and 16 (Series D), respectively; past enrollment from Bureau of the Census, *Statistical Abstract of the United States*, 1948 and 1971 editions, pp. 128 and 114, respectively; projected enrollment from U.S. Office of Education, *Projections of Educational Statistics to 1980–81*, forthcoming. The projections in parentheses are from Joseph Froomkin and others, *Population, Enrollment, and Costs of Public Elementary and Secondary Education, 1975–76 and 1980–81*, A Report to the President's Commission on School Finance (The Commission, 1972), Sec. 2, Table 5.
a. Ages five to seventeen.
b. Alternative projections; see sources.

should reduce the need for more classrooms, books, instructional personnel, and other educational resources.

A second factor that should ease the fiscal plight of school districts is the drastic change that has occurred in the market for teachers. The shortage of the 1960s has become the glut of the 1970s. Growing numbers of newly trained teachers swell the ranks of those seeking positions. Estimates for the President's Commission on School Finance, the National Education Association, and the Bureau of Labor Statistics agree that the situation will continue during the next decade.[12] The supply of college graduates capable of teaching will significantly exceed the demand. The excess supply should reduce if not eliminate the relative wage gains instructional personnel have made in the last decade. Such a change might of course fail to materialize if there were a major increase in the demand for teachers, stemming, for instance, from an effort to provide universal early childhood education, or if the supply were artificially constricted by increased unionization or demands for statewide bargaining over teacher salaries.

Any reduction in the general rate of inflation should also act to slow down the growth in educational outlays. The rates of increase in the price of the materials, supplies, and capital construction items purchased by school districts are already slackening from the pace of the previous five years, and interest costs have fallen from their 1969–70 peak. While this will not reduce the cost of past debt service, it will reduce the cost of new bond issues.

The future growth of school expenditures may also be slowed considerably if the cost-saving innovations with which some areas are currently experimenting are adopted by a significant number of districts. Considerable savings could be realized from the rationalization of methods of purchasing school supplies and equipment. For example, the efficiencies and lower prices realized only by the larger districts that purchase in volume could be realized by small districts that joined together to form purchasing and storage cooperatives. School districts could also make a greater effort to solicit competitive bids on their purchases and to take advantage of the substantial discounts available to buyers who pay their invoices promptly. The need for and cost of new school construction could also be radically

12. Joseph Froomkin and others, *Population, Enrollment, and Costs of Public Elementary and Secondary Education, 1975–76 and 1980–81*, A Report to the President's Commission on School Finance (The Commission, 1972), Sec. 3; "Teacher Job Shortage Ahead," pp. 69–74; "Teachers, Teachers Everywhere!" U.S. Department of Labor, *Occupational Outlook Quarterly*, Vol. 14 (Fall 1970), pp. 6–10.

reduced. Improved scheduling of classes and adoption of extended or year-round school year plans such as those operating in more than 100 districts could increase the capacity of existing school structures by as much as one-third. New school construction costs could be reduced by using "systems building" techniques and by combining several schools in one larger one; noneducational parts of the larger building might be rented or used for community centers. A study made for the President's Commission on School Finance estimated that in 1970–71 the potential saving from such cost-reducing innovations was $5.2 billion, or 11.7 percent of total expenditures.[13]

Another factor that could lead to a slowdown in future expenditure growth is the recent outpouring of studies that purport to show that marginal changes in outlays per pupil produce very little in the way of improved academic performance.[14] While most of these studies contain emphatic warnings about the inadvisability of large-scale cutbacks, and although critics have questioned the validity of their conclusions,[15] it is conceivable that some communities will try to test the proposition that money makes no difference. The most likely approach is to allow class sizes to rise by failing to replace teachers who retire or quit. Within a few years such a policy could result in substantially lower expenditures even if the remaining teachers receive moderate wage increases.[16]

While it is impossible to project future expenditures with accuracy, the demographic, market, and efficiency factors discussed previously point to a

13. Cresap, McCormick and Paget, Inc., *Economies in Education*, A Report for the President's Commission on School Finance (The Commission, 1972), pp. 28–29.

14. See, for example, Harvey A. Averch and others, *How Effective Is Schooling? A Critical Review and Synthesis of Research Findings*, Prepared for the President's Commission on School Finance (Santa Monica: RAND Corporation, 1972); Frederick Mosteller and Daniel P. Moynihan (eds.), *On Equality of Educational Opportunity* (Random House, 1972); and Christopher Jencks and others, *Inequality: A Reassessment of the Effect of Family and Schooling in America* (Basic Books, 1972).

15. See Charles S. Benson (director), *Final Report to the Senate Select Committee on School District Finance*, Submitted by the Consultant Staff (Sacramento: The Committee, 1972; processed), Vol. 1. See also "Educational Equality and Intergovernmental Relations," Preliminary Draft Report of the ACIR Staff (Advisory Commission on Intergovernmental Relations, August 15, 1972; processed), App. (The data and views contained in this draft report are subject to revision. The final report will be entitled *Financing Schools and Property Tax Relief—A State Responsibility* [forthcoming].)

16. The National Education Association estimates that between 1971 and 1979 annual teacher turnover will be 8.1 percent in elementary schools and 8.6 percent in secondary schools ("Teacher Job Shortage Ahead," p. 72).

significant slowdown in the growth of educational spending. An estimate made for the President's Commission indicates that, without taking into account price increases, the growth of aggregate school spending should be about 55 percent between 1970–71 and 1980–81, or less than half as much as that of the preceding decade.[17] The projected slowdown does not include the potential savings from adoption of the innovations just discussed. Furthermore, it assumes a continued reduction in pupil-teacher ratios, upgrading of teachers' training, and a shift of half the current nonpublic elementary and secondary school enrollment to public schools.

In the aggregate, a growth in school spending of 50 to 60 percent over the next decade should not strain the existing revenue system. If the federal, state, and local governments increase their contributions to educational financing in proportion to the normal growth in their revenues, the total aggregate resources available to school districts should expand by roughly 55 percent over the next decade.[18] While this estimate assumes a return to full employment by 1974, it does not assume any increase in effective tax rates.

The prospect of a future aggregate balance between the needs and resources of school districts of course masks the more fundamental question of distribution. Will the growth in available resources take place in the school districts with the greatest growth in education needs? The answer to this question is clearly no. In states that rely heavily upon local revenue sources to finance education, much of the growth in the school tax base will occur in suburban jurisdictions, while the unmet needs for improved education will continue to be concentrated in the decaying cities and rural backwaters. As a result, while the fiscal system may seem healthy in the aggregate or in states in which local financing plays a minor role, increasing problems will plague many districts in states whose local taxpayers bear a significant share of the burden of school finance.

17. Froomkin and others, *Population, Enrollment, and Costs of Public Elementary and Secondary Education, 1975–76 and 1980–81.*

18. This assumes that the economy reaches full employment in fiscal 1974 and that thereafter real GNP grows at 4.25 percent per year. Like the estimates of expenditure growth, it abstracts from price increases. Revenues raised by school districts are assumed to have a GNP elasticity of 0.87; those of the states, 0.97; and those of the federal government, 1.19. These estimates represent a weighted average of the elasticities of the major taxes levied by each level of government. See Advisory Commission on Intergovernmental Relations, *Federal-State Coordination of Personal Income Taxes* (ACIR, 1965), Table 4, p. 42. It is important to note that under these assumptions federal aid will become an increasingly important source of school revenues, while local taxes will play an ever-diminishing relative role.

Alternative Solutions to the Fiscal Problems

The current and future fiscal problems of elementary and secondary education, while not as severe as they are often portrayed, stem largely from the nation's heavy reliance on the *local* property tax as a source of school financing. This revenue source has numerous administrative defects, many of which could be eliminated through fundamental reform; yet even a drastically reformed local property tax would be difficult to administer, inelastic, and inequitably distributed among jurisdictions. The only way to circumvent these problems is to shift to another revenue source.

Reforming the Local Property Tax

Over the course of the past decades, numerous reforms of the property tax have been suggested.[19] Although states and, for the most part, localities have been free to act on these suggestions, few have done so.

One suggested series of reforms of the property tax is motivated by the fact that many small units of local government do not have the capacity to administer the tax efficiently. The situation would probably improve considerably if the administrative responsibility for assessments and collections were transferred from the school district or municipal level, where it now rests in many states, to the county or even to the state level. Assessment practices could be upgraded and assessments made more equitable by improvements in the training and certification of assessors; neither electing assessors nor hiring private firms to make assessments is efficient. Standardized assessment practices and modern estimating techniques would also help to reduce the possibility of corrupt practice. Unequal assessment ratios within a taxing jurisdiction would be discouraged by the requirement of public disclosure of all assessments and by creation of a system that would make it easy for property owners to appeal any assessment. Assessment at full market value rather than at some small fraction thereof would also help to improve the equitability of the tax, leaving less room for favoritism and sloppy assessment, and would make it possible for the layman to judge the fairness of assessments.

A number of steps could be taken to make the property tax easier to pay and more equitable. Monthly or bimonthly billings would allow families to budget their tax payments better over the entire year. A system of with-

19. See Advisory Commission on Intergovernmental Relations, *The Role of the States in Strengthening the Property Tax* (Government Printing Office, 1963), Vols. 1 and 2; and Netzer, *Economics of the Property Tax*.

holding tied to state income taxes would have the same effect. The annual reappraisal of all property—even if only by estimate—would eliminate the large discrete jumps in tax liability that now accompany reassessment.

Changes could also be made to ensure that property taxes do not place an undue burden on low income families. One approach is the "circuit breaker" program, under which the state reimburses the taxpayer for any "excessive" burden. Twelve states currently have programs that shield the elderly poor from such a possibility, but only Oregon and New Mexico provide a comprehensive program for all their low income homeowners.[20] Most circuit breaker programs give a cash rebate or a state income tax credit equal to a specified fraction of the tax liability that is deemed to be "excessive." For example, Wisconsin reimburses elderly taxpayers with incomes below $1,000 for three-quarters of their total property tax liability; those with incomes in the range from $2,000 to $5,000 are repaid 60 percent of any property taxes that exceed 14 percent of the household's income. The extension of such "circuit breaker" plans to all states and their expansion to include all low income persons rather than just the elderly would go a long way toward reducing the complaints concerning the regressivity of the property tax. The cost of such a program, while not inconsequential, would certainly fall within the fiscal capacity of most states.[21]

Deferred payment plans offer an alternative means of ameliorating the impact of the property tax on the elderly or on those whose incomes are not rising as rapidly as their assessments. If a fraction of the tax liability were deferred until the property was sold or disposed of as part of an estate, the problems posed by a household's inability to convert the appreciation of its real estate into cash would be largely overcome. In effect, the taxing jurisdiction could be given a claim on the property, against which it could borrow the amount owed in taxes. A deferred payment plan, unlike a circuit breaker scheme, would not be a subsidy that either encouraged the overconsumption of housing or maintained the estates of the elderly for their heirs.

20. For a description of these programs, see "Property Tax Relief and Reform: The Intergovernmental Dimension," Preliminary Draft Report of the ACIR Staff (ACIR, August 31, 1972; processed), Pt. 2, pp. III–10 to III–37, and "State Programs for Relieving Property Tax Overloads: The Circuit Breaker Approach," preliminary draft prepared as Appendix E to accompany the above draft (ACIR, July 1972; processed). (The data and views in this draft report are preliminary and subject to revision. The final report will be entitled *Financing Schools and Property Tax Relief—A State Responsibility* [forthcoming].)

21. The comprehensive "circuit breaker" plan proposed in Benson, *Final Report*, pp. 14–17, would cost California $565 million, or roughly 10 percent of the amount currently collected from property taxes.

Differential treatment of various classes of property offers another more profound reform of the existing system of local school property taxes. One suggestion that has been put forward is to remove commercial and industrial property from the local educational tax base and to make it subject to a uniform state property levy. This would effectively reduce—but by no means eliminate—the interdistrict variation in tax bases, much of which is caused by a concentration of nonresidential property in certain communities. It would also eliminate the "tax price" differences that now exist between districts with differing relative amounts of commercial and industrial property. For communities that today have equivalent amounts of property behind each pupil, the cost to residents of raising a local dollar for education in a district half of whose property is nonresidential is half the cost to residents of a community whose tax base consists entirely of owner-occupied houses. The residents of the industrialized area, since they bear only half of the cost of schooling, may spend more than those in the community whose residents, because there is no commercial property, must pay the whole bill.

Another beneficial effect of removing nonresidential property from the local school tax base would be the end of the competition between taxing jurisdictions for clean industries, shopping centers, and other types of development that add to the local tax base but do not demand extensive local services. But removing commercial and industrial property from the local tax base would mean that those school districts that depend heavily on such property would have to find alternative sources of revenue.

A similar suggestion is to require by statute that different types of property be taxed at different rates. If the residential property tax is thought to be particularly onerous, the burden on such properties can be reduced by the requirement that houses be taxed at some fraction of the rate imposed on commercial and industrial property. Six states already require such treatment through laws that stipulate different ratios of assessment to market value for various classes of real estate. In many communities, even in areas where such practices are proscribed by law, differential rates of taxation are applied. Such discrimination, which is the product of the assessment mechanism, more often than not benefits owners of residential real estate, who are taxed at lower effective rates than holders of commercial and industrial property.[22]

Taken together these changes in the structure and administration of the property tax would represent significant improvement over the existing

22. "Property Tax Relief and Reform," Report of the ACIR Staff, Pt. 2, pp. VI-2 to VI-10. (The data and views in this draft report are subject to revision; see note 20.)

situation. However, the complaints that the overall tax burdens are too high, that they are inequitably distributed among school districts, or that the tax is an inelastic source of revenue may be reduced little by such changes. Only a shift to another source of revenue could effectively quiet such complaints.

Alternative Local Revenue Sources

There does not seem to be a realistic alternative source of local revenue that would be capable of raising even a small fraction of the amount raised by the property tax that does not have many of the same defects. Although local sales or income taxes might produce as much revenue, and could easily be administered by state governments if they were imposed as a surcharge on state income or sales taxes, neither is free from other drawbacks. State governments, which rely heavily on sales taxes for their own revenues, would be reluctant to share the revenue source with school districts. Furthermore, sales tax rates are already high in many parts of the nation; in seven states they are 5 percent or more, and there is no evidence that taxpayers would want to trade "excessive" property tax rates for "excessive" sales taxes.

More important, local sales are probably even more unequally distributed than property (Table 3-10). Cities and districts with large shopping centers would have very large sales tax bases in relation to their educa-

Table 3-10. Disparities in Various Tax Bases of School Districts, Boston Metropolitan Area, 1970

Tax base	High district (dollars)	Low district (dollars)	Coefficient of variation
Property value per pupil[a]	68,048 (Brookline)	14,040 (Norfolk)	0.321
Income per pupil[a]	53,970 (Brookline)	8,348 (Norfolk)	0.374
Discretionary income per pupil[a]	47,382 (Brookline)	6,128 (Norfolk)	0.417
Retail sales per pupil[b]	52,706 (Nahant)	1,104 (Millis)	0.869

Sources: Property value from Massachusetts State Tax Commission, "1970 Final Equalized Valuations"; income, population, and pupils from Bureau of the Census, Census of Population, 1970, General Social and Economic Characteristics, Massachusetts; discretionary income per pupil computed by multiplying the population per pupil by the difference between per-capita income and $750; retail sales from Bureau of the Census, Census of Business, 1967, Vol. 2, Retail Trade—Area Statistics, Pt. 2, Iowa to North Carolina (1970), pp. 23-8 to 23-13.
a. Based on all seventy-eight school districts within the Boston standard metropolitan statistical area.
b. Based on sixty-two school districts within the Boston standard metropolitan statistical area for which data were available.

tional needs, while rural areas and suburbs with few stores would find themselves with little to tax. This means that for all districts to raise equivalent amounts of local revenue per pupil, sales tax rates would have to be even more disparate than property tax rates. In areas that are broken up into many small taxing jurisdictions, shopping patterns could be dramatically altered if local sales tax rates differed greatly among communities. Another problem is that sales taxes are at best only slightly more elastic than property taxes. Without changes in rates, sales tax receipts tend to increase at about the same rate as national income. Finally, although the incidence of the property tax is still being debated, few would argue that existing state sales taxes are anything but regressive.

Like sales taxes, income taxes have not generally been considered the province of local governments, although in Maryland and Pennsylvania they provide a small fraction of locally raised school revenues. While this revenue source is both progressive and elastic, it also tends to be distributed rather unequally among jurisdictions. Table 3-10, which lists measures of the variability of several potential local tax bases for the school districts in the Boston metropolitan area, shows that on this score there is little reason to prefer a local income tax to a local property tax. Because of the variation in bases, local income tax rates would have to vary considerably among school districts if they were to raise equivalent amounts of revenue per pupil. If local income tax rates did differ greatly among localities, wealthy persons would have an even greater incentive than exists today to cluster in communities with other rich families so as to minimize their local tax liability. Whatever else may be wrong with the local property tax, it is levied against one of the least mobile sources of local revenue.

Revenue instability is another problem that would arise with heavy reliance on a local income tax for school finance. Since taxable incomes fluctuate considerably with cyclical swings in the economy, it is difficult to predict with any great accuracy income tax receipts for the coming school year. School districts that depended on this source of revenue would experience annual surpluses or deficits, whereas the receipts from the property tax are known in advance with certainty, since both the tax rate and the tax base are administratively determined.

State or Federal Financing for Schools

If a system of reformed local property taxes remains unacceptable to the majority of Americans and alternative local revenue sources cannot be used, the only remaining possibility is to shift more of the financial responsibility for education to the state or federal governments. Although a number of commissions[23] and committees, including the President's Commission, have recommended such a change, the move involves far more than a simple substitution of tax instruments. In the first place, it will probably entail a substantial increase in outlays; second, it raises questions concerning the distribution among jurisdictions; third, it may involve major shifts in tax burdens among individuals, communities, and states; and, finally, it implies some changes in the powers and authorities of local school districts.

OUTLAY IMPLICATIONS OF A SHIFT TO STATE OR FEDERAL FINANCE. A complete shift from local school property taxes to state or federal revenue sources in 1970 would have involved a minimum transfer of some $17.4 billion in fiscal responsibility from local to state or federal governments. There would be a tremendous variation among the states because of the great diversity they now exhibit in their reliance on local property taxes to support education. In Hawaii, a shift to the state level has already taken place, but in New Jersey, New Hampshire, and South Dakota, for example, a considerable amount of state or federal money would have to be raised to replace the educational revenue now generated by the local property tax.

The amount now raised by local property taxes, however, is only a part of the costs that would be incurred in a program that attempted to shift revenue sources. Recent court cases make it clear that shifting to state or federal financing of education would entail reducing the disparities in expenditures that now exist among school districts. It is not politically realistic to suppose that such equalization could be accomplished by "leveling down"—that is, by cutting school expenditures in districts that now spend large amounts per pupil. The only feasible approach to reducing the differences would be to "level up," or in other words to raise the level in all communities in a state closer to the highest levels. Depending upon the percentile norm toward which districts were brought, this would have cost from $1.7 to $7.0 billion more in 1969–70 (Table 3-11). Federal assumption of educational costs would also require elimination of at least some of the disparities among states, which would add another $2.3–$5.6 billion to the

23. Advisory Commission on Intergovernmental Relations, *State Aid to Local Government* (Government Printing Office, 1969); Committee for Economic Development, *Education for the Urban Disadvantaged: from Preschool to Employment* (CED, 1971), pp. 71–74; *Report of the New York State Commission on the Quality, Cost and Financing of Elementary and Secondary Education* (The Commission, 1972), Vol. 1, Chaps. 2 and 3; *Report of the New Jersey Tax Policy Committee,* Submitted to Governor William T. Cahill (Trenton: The Committee, 1972), especially *Part III* and *Summary.*

Table 3-11. Transfer and Equalization Costs of Complete State or Federal Assumption of School Financing, 1969–70 School Year
Billions of dollars

Type of cost	Amount
Transfer	
Replacement of all local revenue	19.8
Replacement of property tax revenue only	17.4
Equalization, intrastate[a]	
50th percentile	1.7
70th percentile	3.1
90th percentile	7.0
Equalization, interstate[b]	
Median state	2.3
80th percentile state	5.6

Sources: Local revenues and enrollments from National Education Association, Research Division, *Estimates of School Statistics, 1970–71* (NEA, 1970), p. 34. Property tax revenues estimated by authors. Equalization costs from *Review of Existing State School Finance Programs,* Vol. 2: *Documentation of Disparities in the Financing of Public Elementary and Secondary School Systems—By State,* A Commission Staff Report Submitted to the President's Commission on School Finance (The Commission, 1972), with adjustments.

a. Cost of bringing low expenditure districts up to the existing expenditures at the percentiles listed. Intrastate equalization levels refer to *student* percentile levels. An example: 10 percent of the students in a state have more spent on them than the ninetieth percentile level. An equalization program would raise the outlays for all students receiving less than this level until they were equal to that of the ninetieth percentile student.

b. Additional cost of bringing low spending states up to the level indicated after intrastate equalization at the seventieth percentile level.

cost, depending upon the level to which the low expenditure states were raised.

Even these crude estimates indicate that in many states substantial new revenue sources or vast increases in existing taxes would be needed if the local role in school financing were to be eliminated. Simple replacement of local school property taxes would require increases in existing state tax collections of 40 percent or more in nineteen states. Of course, in the aggregate, local property taxes would be reduced by an equivalent amount, but "leveling up" for equalization would require a net increase in expenditures and taxes.

STATE PROPERTY TAXES AND THE VALUE ADDED TAX. One new source of revenue to meet these needs is a statewide property tax. The Fleischmann Commission in New York recommended that such a tax capable of generating the amount of revenue now produced by local school property taxes be established to help finance the state takeover of all educational costs.[24] Several of the proposals before the California legislature also call for statewide property taxes to finance a state assumption of educational cost. Since a statewide property tax would be levied at a uniform rate in all

24. *Report of the New York State Commission on the Quality, Cost and Financing of Elementary and Secondary Education,* Vol. 1, p. 2.12.

jurisdictions and would be administered by the state government, it represents an improvement upon the existing system of local property taxes. But unless the state tax were levied at a low rate, it would not represent a significant decrease in property tax burdens for most persons.

The value added tax (VAT) is another potential source of new revenue for education. While few states have seriously considered establishing such a tax, it has been considered at the federal level as a means of financing a new national program of residential property tax relief.[25] In effect, a VAT would be similar to a national sales tax.[26] While it would have tremendous revenue raising ability—$5.6 billion would be generated by each percentage point of tax—it would be regressive. To overcome this defect a system of income tax credits and rebates could be designed for low income persons, but any such system would add administrative complexities.

PROBLEMS OF ALLOCATING FUNDS. Any increase in the financial role of either the federal or the state governments will raise thorny problems concerning the distribution of revenues. This issue is discussed in greater detail in the next chapter, but the basic nature of the problem is illustrated by the plan President Nixon asked the ACIR to study, which required that the portion of the local residential property tax used for education be replaced by the proceeds of a national VAT. In the aggregate, such property taxes raise about $12 billion, the amount that would be generated by a 3.25 percent VAT with a system of rebates for low income persons. It is inconceivable that the federal government would distribute this amount among the states in a way that would simply replace the revenue currently raised by local residential property taxes. Such a distribution would give New Jersey $445 per pupil, Alabama $32, and Hawaii nothing (Table 3-12). In effect,

25. See "State of the Union Address of President Richard Nixon," Jan. 20, 1972. In a letter to the Advisory Commission on Intergovernmental Relations, the President requested the commission to undertake a study of a plan prepared by the administration for a federal VAT to replace residential school property taxes. Letter from Richard Nixon to Chairman of ACIR, Jan. 20, 1972; ACIR Memorandum, "Revised Issues Paper on a Federal Aid Proposal for Replacing Residential School Property Taxes With a National Value Added Tax" (Feb. 9, 1972).

26. The VAT is applied to the increased value of goods and services at each stage of the production process. Thus a miller is taxed on the difference between the sales price of his flour and the cost of the grain he purchases, and the baker's tax is based on the increase in the value of the bread he sells over the cost of the flour and other ingredients. In the end, the price of bread incorporates not only the cost of its ingredients, the labor used in making it and the firms' profits but also the VAT. If all consumer goods but no investment goods are taxed, a VAT is equivalent in its incidence to a retail sales tax levied at the same rate. For a description of the intricacies of a VAT, see Clara K. Sullivan, *The Tax on Value Added* (Columbia University Press, 1965).

it would reward states for having made heavy use of the property tax in the past, and would tend to give most to the richest states in the nation and least to those that have the lowest spending levels. What is more, if it were a permanent program its constitutionality would be dubious.[27]

President Nixon, of course, did not advocate such a formula for distribution of the VAT proceeds. One administration plan, contained in a communication to the Advisory Commission on Intergovernmental Relations, suggested, by way of example, that federal VAT funds be distributed among the states that agreed to eliminate their residential school property taxes on a matching basis—$1 of federal aid for each $2 of state expenditure—up to a maximum grant of $400 per pupil.[28] Per-student grants resulting from this matching formula would vary considerably among states, although not as much as grants based strictly on present residential property taxes (see Table 3-12).

Two features of such a matching formula should be noted, however. First, distributing funds in this way would accentuate existing disparities in spending levels among states. New York would get more than twice as much per child as Tennessee. Second, although the total amount distributed would be as much as was collected for schools from the residential property tax, not all states would get enough to provide total relief from the property tax without raising state taxes. States such as North Carolina, Alabama, South Carolina, and Hawaii would receive more than enough from the VAT fund to replace their low school property taxes, while high property tax states such as New Hampshire, New Jersey, and California would receive insufficient VAT funds to replace their present yield. Thus, the matching formula would force some states not only to replace residential property tax losses but also to raise new revenues at the state level to replace the excess of residential property taxes over the VAT receipts. Indeed, distribution of the VAT funds on any basis other than strict replacement of current property tax yields would require either that some states take on a substantial new financial burden or that the VAT be adjusted to yield substantially more revenue than the property tax it is replacing. Thus a matching formula of the type suggested would raise both an equity problem (because disparities among the states would be accentuated) and a

27. Several of the alternative methods for federal grants suggested by the President's Commission on School Finance as incentives to push states toward full state funding would be distributed in such a manner, but these grants are explicitly designed to be temporary in nature. See President's Commission on School Finance, *Schools, People, & Money: The Need for Educational Reform,* Final Report (1972), App. H.

28. "Basic Ingredients of a Plan to Substitute a Federal Value-Added Tax for Residential School Property Taxes" (Feb. 9, 1972).

Table 3-12. Yield on Residential Property Taxes for Education Compared to Federal Matching Grants, by State, 1970

State	Residential property tax for education Total (millions of dollars)	Residential property tax for education Per pupil (dollars)	Federal matching grants of $1 for each $2 of state expenditure Total (millions of dollars)	Federal matching grants of $1 for each $2 of state expenditure Per pupil (dollars)	Difference between residential property tax and federal matching grant, per pupil (dollars)
Alabama	25	32	105	135	−103
Alaska	3	54	17	300	−246
Arizona	98	246	104	260	−14
Arkansas	35	87	65	159	−72
California	1,513	323	1,304	278	45
Colorado	130	259	113	226	33
Connecticut	238	359	170	257	102
Delaware	15	128	40	340	−212
District of Columbia	24	159	61	409	−250
Florida	205	156	320	243	−87
Georgia	161	158	215	210	−52
Hawaii	...	...	55	309	−309
Idaho	13	79	29	171	−92
Illinois	663	319	671	323	−4
Indiana	341	307	314	283	24
Iowa	120	184	155	237	−53
Kansas	102	205	129	260	−55
Kentucky	79	122	134	207	−85
Louisiana	50	64	137	177	−113
Maine	41	170	40	165	5
Maryland	259	300	222	257	43
Massachusetts	386	339	252	221	118
Michigan	587	273	576	268	5
Minnesota	203	206	280	283	−77
Mississippi	24	45	72	138	−93
Missouri	229	255	217	242	13
Montana	29	181	36	219	−38
Nebraska	64	196	70	213	−17
Nevada	20	173	25	219	−46
New Hampshire	58	386	31	206	180
New Jersey	655	445	448	305	140
New Mexico	17	62	52	189	−127
New York	1,130	337	1,352	403	−66
North Carolina	52	47	205	186	−139
North Dakota	12	81	25	171	−90
Ohio	774	323	569	237	86
Oklahoma	88	157	100	178	−21
Oregon	143	309	121	263	46
Pennsylvania	522	228	612	267	−39
Rhode Island	51	290	42	237	53
South Carolina	43	71	116	194	−123
South Dakota	24	146	35	209	−63
Tennessee	82	97	130	156	−59
Texas	247	102	474	196	−94
Utah	41	141	59	206	−65
Vermont	15	130	21	184	−54
Virginia	146	147	175	176	−29
Washington	151	191	229	288	−97
West Virginia	42	112	69	186	−74
Wisconsin	272	293	243	261	32
Wyoming	22	262	20	232	30
U.S. total	10,244	235	11,056	254	−19

financing problem (because some states would have to increase taxes to replace lost revenue).

An equally serious problem arises in the methods by which states would distribute increased federal or state revenues within their borders, because reliance on local property taxes to finance schools varies greatly within as well as among states. Table 3-13 shows an estimate of the residential property taxes per capita used to support schools in several major cities and their surrounding suburban counties in 1966–67. Even a state like New York, which under the administration proposal would receive enough VAT funds to replace in the aggregate the residential property taxes used for schools, would have to decide what to do about the enormous loss of property tax revenue in wealthy suburban Nassau County ($112 per capita in 1966–67) and the smaller loss in New York city ($29 per capita). Although the state could in principle simply replace Nassau's tax loss and give much less to New York city, it is hard to imagine a state's allocating funds to preserve current spending disparities associated with wealth—for that is what replacement of school tax losses means—when recent court decisions call for the reduction of wealth-related expenditure differences. Alternatively, New York state might allocate receipts from a federal VAT or increased state taxes on an equal per-pupil basis to all counties. As a comparison of the two columns of Table 3-13 will indicate, such a distribution would prove inadequate to replace the residential property tax for schools in the high-tax suburban counties. With equal per-pupil allocations, suburban school districts in Nassau County in New York, Bucks County in Pennsylvania, and San Mateo County in California would have to cut back school spending, even if their states as a whole received or raised enough to replace the statewide total of residential property taxes used to support the schools. Since such cutbacks are not likely to be politically feasible, state governments would have to face the problems not only of replacing residential property taxes but of raising additional money to increase expenditures in low spending districts toward the level of the higher ones. In the end, a much larger total of federal or state revenues would be required to replace the present aggregate amount of local resi-

---

Footnote to Table 3-12:
Sources: Residential property tax for education was calculated by multiplying property tax for schools (Advisory Commission on Intergovernmental Relations, *State-Local Revenue Systems and Educational Finance*, A Report to the President's Commission on School Finance [ACIR, 1971], Table 23) by the percent of property that is residential nonfarm (Bureau of the Census, *Census of Governments, 1967*, Vol. 2: *Taxable Property Values* [1968], Table 5); school enrollment data are from *Review of Existing State School Finance Programs*, Report Submitted to the President's Commission on School Finance, Vol. 2; federal matching grant = ⅓ × (total property tax for education from ACIR. *State-Local Revenue Systems. . . .* Table 23, + school revenue from state sources, from National Education Association, *Estimates of School Statistics, 1970–71*, p. 34); col. 5 = col. 2 − col. 4.

Table 3-13. Revenue Available for Public Education from the Residential Property Tax and from a 2.5 Percent Value Added Tax, Selected Areas, 1966–67 School Year
Dollars per capita

City and surrounding area	Estimated residential property tax revenue used for education	Equal distribution per pupil of 2.5 percent value added tax revenue[a]
New York City	29[b]	31
Nassau County	112	52
Suffolk County	86	57
Westchester County	83	42
Philadelphia	29	31
Bucks County	65	43
Chester County	47	52
Delaware County	52	35
Detroit	29	42
Wayne County (except Detroit)	42	56
Macomb County	43	57
Oakland County	60	60
Chicago	37	36
Cook County (except Chicago)	61	50
Du Page County	103	59
Lake County	79	54
St. Louis	36	39
St. Louis County	79	39
Denver	58	43
Adams County	36	73
Arapahoe County	78	73
Boulder County	63	61
San Francisco	40	35
Contra Costa County	81	69
San Mateo County	116	59
New Orleans	15	38
Jefferson Parish	5	41
St. Bernard Parish	16[c]	59

Sources: Residential property tax was calculated by multiplying property tax revenue of school districts (Bureau of the Census, *Census of Governments, 1967*, Vol. 5. *Local Government in Metropolitan Areas* [1969], Table 13, and [for Chicago and Detroit] Vol. 4, No. 1. *Finances of School Districts* [1969], Table 8) by percent of property that is residential nonfarm (*Census of Governments, 1967*, Vol. 2, *Taxable Property Values*, Table 19). Population and public school enrollment are from the U.S. Office of Education, Office of Program Planning and Evaluation, unpublished tabulations.
a. Estimated as $232 per public school enrollee.
b. Total residential property tax per capita × (education expenditures/total expenditures).
c. State average was used for percent of property that is residential.

dential property taxes for schools. The excess would depend on the degree to which states attempted to equalize intrastate differences. Property tax relief itself would do nothing to reduce expenditure disparities either within or among states, although if enough additional funds could be found it might provide an opportunity for enactment of new and more equal means of financing education.

SHIFTS IN TAX BURDENS. Substitution of increased state taxes, a VAT, or a statewide property tax for existing local school property taxes could result in substantial shifts in tax burdens among individuals, communities, and states. The exact nature of the changes would of course depend upon which taxes were substituted for the local school property tax and the incidence of the taxes involved. Low income homeowners living in high property tax districts stand to gain under any shift in tax sources, while high income homeowners living in tax havens would pay more under a shift to state or federal revenue sources. But beyond these groups, the effects of a shift in tax sources are difficult to predict, in part because we do not know who now bears the burden of property taxes. If the burden falls on owners of capital, renters stand to lose from any shift to nonproperty sources. If the property tax is a mildly progressive revenue source, as was suggested earlier in this chapter, lower income families would be hurt by a shift to a regressive VAT or state sales tax.

Certain changes would entirely relieve some groups of the responsibility of supporting public education. Replacement of the local educational property tax by increased state sales or personal income taxes, for example, would provide a windfall to the owners of commercial and industrial property, whose property taxes would fall without a commensurate increase in the other taxes they pay.[29]

In some states a shift from local property taxes to increased or new state-level taxes could produce dramatic changes in the tax burdens of various communities. For example, in New York, the uniform statewide property tax proposed by the Fleischmann Commission would increase property tax burdens in the state's six largest cities, because effective school tax rates in large cities tend to be lower than the statewide average. A statewide property tax could also be expected to raise the burden in many rural areas, because farmland in America tends to be underassessed[30] and tax rates in rural areas are generally extremely low. On the other hand, in New York

---

29. To compensate for such a possibility, Governor Cahill in New Jersey proposed an "excess gains tax" as part of his school finance reform package. This tax would capture the gains resulting from the net reduction in the property tax liability of business and industry.

30. Manvel, "Trends in the Value of Real Estate and Land," p. 6.

Table 3-14. Per-Capita Burden of Local School Property Taxes in Selected New York Jurisdictions, Various Alternative State Taxes Capable of Raising the Same Revenue, and Distribution on the Basis of Enrollment, Various Years, 1968–70

Dollars

Jurisdiction	Local school property tax, fiscal year 1969	State property tax, 1968	State income tax, 1969	State sales tax, 1970	Distribution on the basis of enrollment, 1968–69[a]
New York State	103	103	103	103	103
New York City	90	105	97	97	78
Westchester County	170	143	207	130	104
Nassau County	189	139	169	136	128
Suffolk County	142	104	76	105	140
Madison County	72	68	52	78	149
Sullivan County	146	142	54	193	118
St. Lawrence County	66	72	40	87	132

Sources: Population data for all columns are from Bureau of the Census, *U.S. Census of Population, 1970, Number of Inhabitants,* Final Report PC (1)-A34, *New York,* Tables 1, 6, 9. Columns 1 and 5 are computed from State of New York, *School District Data for Year Ending June 30, 1969,* Tables 1 and 3, and Table 2, respectively. Columns 2 and 3 are computed from New York State Division of the Budget, Office of Statistical Coordination, *New York State Statistical Yearbook, 1970* and . . . *Yearbook, 1971,* Tables H-25 and H-9, respectively. Column 4 is based on the distribution of state sales taxes collected in fiscal year 1971 (unpublished estimates from the New York State Department of Taxation and Finance), and sales tax data in *New York State Statistical Yearbook, 1971,* p. 164.

a. Computed as the ratio of enrollment to population.

at least, a statewide property tax would reduce the burden in some of the state's wealthiest school districts, such as Scarsdale and Hempstead. Table 3-14 illustrates the burden alternative tax sources would place on a number of counties in New York if statewide taxes were levied in such a way as to raise the same aggregate amount now produced by local school property taxes. By comparing the burdens of various taxes to the last column, one can get a rough idea of how each area would fare if the state were to distribute its receipts on the basis of enrollment. New York City and Westchester and Nassau counties would be better off under the existing system under which they keep all the money raised through the local system of property taxes. On the other hand, in rural Madison and St. Lawrence Counties, a shift to statewide taxation would generate about $2 of receipts for every $1 extracted from the community in state taxes. Two cautions must be observed in the interpretation of these estimates. First, other distributions of state funds are possible. If extra weight were given for children from disadvantaged homes or for low achievers, the large cities and rural areas would receive considerably more than they do under a flat per-pupil grant, while the suburban counties would receive less. Second, patterns of residence may be affected by significant changes in the way public schools are financed. For example, the number of families that left the large cities for the suburbs when their children reached school age might be reduced; if this happened, state aid would increase along with school enrollment in the cities.

Similar shifts in tax burdens would occur among states if local education property taxes were eliminated and a federal revenue source substituted. Table 3-15 provides a picture of these changes. Once again, if the money were distributed on the basis of enrollment, the poorer states such as Alabama and Mississippi would tend to gain, while the richer states would receive less from Washington than they contributed in increased federal taxes. This is not to say that there would be a reduction in the expenditure disparities among states; the opposite would occur if poorer states exhibited a greater tendency to substitute federal aid for state taxes.

If the property tax were reduced or eliminated altogether, and if property values reflect existing tax liabilities, a major redistribution of wealth would accompany the shift in tax burdens. The value of property would tend to appreciate because the ownership of a factory, house, or land would no longer entail as large an annual tax payment to local government. Unless owners of rental and commercial property were forced to pass on their savings to tenants and consumers, their apartments and factories would appreciate because the after-tax flow of income generated by the properties would increase. Removal of a 2-percent educational property tax might increase market values of real estate by roughly 20 percent if taxes were fully reflected in current real estate values. Since ownership of property tends to be concentrated among upper income groups, the inequality in the distribution of wealth would be exacerbated by such capital appreciation. The possibility of such a repercussion is one reason why many reform programs involving large reductions in local property taxes include a statewide property tax as part of a new revenue package.

A statewide property tax—even one levied at the average rate—would not preclude the possibility of dramatic changes in property values among various school districts. If the tax advantages of wealthy districts are reflected in current values of houses, one might expect the values of such real estate to fall with the imposition of a state property tax, while values in poor school districts would rise because the state property tax would represent a drop in tax liabilities in those areas.

SHIFTS IN CONTROL OF SCHOOLS. The final significant change that might result from a shift of revenue sources from the local to the state or federal

Table 3-15. Per-Capita Burden of Federal Income and Value Added Taxes, and Tax Distributed on the Basis of Public School Enrollment in 1969, by State

Dollars

State	Federal income tax	Value added tax	Tax distributed on basis of school enrollment
Alabama	36	45	63
Alaska	69	72	68
Arizona	49	55	62
Arkansas	33	44	63
California	65	66	61
Colorado	52	58	64
Connecticut	94	71	56
Delaware	75	64	63
District of Columbia	66	84	52
Florida	54	56	55
Georgia	46	52	64
Hawaii	63	66	61
Idaho	38	50	67
Illinois	76	67	55
Indiana	58	58	62
Iowa	48	56	62
Kansas	49	59	61
Kentucky	40	47	57
Louisiana	40	46	62
Maine	44	49	63
Maryland	73	62	60
Massachusetts	69	65	53
Michigan	68	60	64
Minnesota	52	58	63
Mississippi	25	40	68
Missouri	55	57	60
Montana	44	52	66
Nebraska	49	58	59
Nevada	86	67	67
New Hampshire	53	56	54
New Jersey	75	69	53
New Mexico	38	48	72
New York	75	69	51
North Carolina	41	50	61
North Dakota	35	45	63
Ohio	65	61	60
Oklahoma	44	52	63
Oregon	54	56	60
Pennsylvania	61	59	52
Rhode Island	57	59	50
South Carolina	35	46	66
South Dakota	34	48	65
Tennessee	43	48	60
Texas	51	55	65
Utah	39	49	75
Vermont	46	51	59
Virginia	54	55	61
Washington	63	60	63
West Virginia	42	46	60
Wisconsin	53	54	58
Wyoming	49	53	69
U.S. average	59	59	59

level would affect the relative power of local school boards. Although much has been said about the necessity for preserving "local control" in education, it is clear that complete state funding would remove from local school districts their most important power, the ability to decide upon the spending level within the districts. Most observers feel that there would be tremendous opposition to such a shift. For this reason, many of the reform plans currently under serious consideration permit local school districts to "add on" or supplement the amount provided by the state. The President's Commission on School Finance and the ACIR have urged that such local supplements be restricted to not more than 10 percent of the amount provided by the state. Others, such as the program suggested by New Jersey's Governor Cahill, place no limits on the amounts raised locally; such plans would result in systems similar to the present ones, with vastly increased levels of state support.

"Local control" of course implies more than determining the level of expenditure. Decisions affecting curriculum, staff patterns, textbook selection, salary levels, and school construction are made in many states by the school districts. The impact diminished local tax support would have on these powers is a matter of dispute. On one side it is argued that if the basic funding decision is made at the state level, local interest in determining how the money is spent will flag, or that local school administrators and school boards will seek to please the state department of education rather than local parents and voters. Local control would thus become an empty phrase. In addition, it is contended that state control of funding will lead special interest groups to press their educational positions at the state level, with a further erosion of local control. Teachers would pressure legislatures for statewide bargaining agreements, salary schedules, and tenure laws, and minority groups would lobby for special state provisions to guarantee that local units do not discriminate. All such developments would whittle away the prerogatives of local districts.

None of these eventualities is inevitable. The Urban Institute, after re-

---

Footnote to Table 3-15:

Sources: Federal income tax from U.S. Internal Revenue Service, *Statistics of Income—1969, Individual Income Tax Returns* (1971), Table 8.9, pp. 373–74; state and local taxes from Bureau of the Census, *Governmental Finances in 1969–70* (1971), Table 17, pp. 31–33; personal income from Department of Commerce, *Survey of Current Business*, Vol. 51 (August 1971), Table 1, p. 31; population from Bureau of the Census, *Statistical Abstract of the United States, 1971* (1971), Table 11, p. 12; public school enrollment from Office of Education, *Digest of Educational Statistics, 1970 Edition* (1970), Table 27, p. 24.

The total tax for all states is assumed to be $12 billion, which when divided by population gives the per-capita amount in the first column. Per-capita income tax for each state was reduced proportionately to yield the national total. Value added tax was computed as a constant fraction of per-capita personal income, less personal income tax and state and local taxes. The last column was computed by converting an equal per-student payment ($12 billion divided by total public school enrollment) to a per-capita value.

viewing the evidence from ten states, concluded that "increased state funding (1) does not lead to substantial state restrictions on local school district decision making, and (2) does not stifle the initiative of local school boards to adopt innovative educational practices."[31] Others have expressed the opinion that greater local control could result from a centralized system of school financing. For example, the ACIR concluded that "once liberated from the necessity of 'selling' local bond issues and tax rate increases, school superintendents and local board members can concentrate their efforts on the true interest of local control—namely the nature and quality of education that is provided for the children of their locality."[32] Moreover, new structures could be created under state-financed systems. Existing school districts, which have often been organized as efficient money raising units rather than as optimum districts for administrative purposes, could be broken up. New units consisting of either single schools or a high school and its feeder elementary schools could be created as the decision-making units. "Local control" might thus be brought closer to the individual parents and schools in many large cities. Any such change, however, would threaten the entrenched interests and powers of the administrative personnel in most districts. On balance, it is impossible to predict whether "local control" will flourish or wither away under new methods of school finance.

Conclusion

Reducing the role of the local property tax in school finance is not an easy task. Although administrative reforms or changes such as circuit breakers would have few universal effects, a major shift toward replacing property taxes would probably create major fiscal and political changes. There would be an increase in the level of educational spending; while property taxes might be reduced, aggregate taxes would rise. Important changes also would be likely to occur in the distribution of school tax burdens, the wealth of individuals, the variation in spending levels among districts, and the locus of educational decision-making power.

In view of the complexities and expenses involved in increasing the role

31. Betsy Levin and others, *Public School Finance: Present Disparities and Fiscal Alternatives*, A Report Prepared by the Urban Institute for the President's Commission on School Finance (The Commission, 1972), Vol. 1, p. 268.
32. *State Aid to Local Government*, p. 15.

of the states or federal government in school finance, it is not surprising that there has been so little movement in this direction despite the admitted faults of the existing system. However, court suits challenging the constitutionality of the present methods of financing education may well change the situation. It is with this issue that the next chapter deals.

chapter four Fiscal Paths
to Educational Equality

Citizens, politicians, legal scholars, and economists have long agreed that the quality and distribution of elementary and secondary education are a matter of social, political, and even constitutional importance. Until recently, it was assumed that these concerns were met by making schooling compulsory and by providing it as a free, nonsegregated public service. These criteria, however, have not guaranteed that children living in different jurisdictions receive roughly equivalent educations, or that taxpayers residing in different school districts pay approximately the same charges for education of basically the same quality. In many areas the system has even failed to provide children with an acceptable minimum level of schooling.

The inequities that riddle the existing system have been the target of both legal challenges and legislative attempts at reform. In the late 1960s the constitutionality of the school financing systems of Illinois and Virginia[1] was challenged on the grounds that these systems permitted "wide variations in the expenditures per student from district to district, thereby providing some students with a good education and depriving others, who have equal or greater educational need."[2] United States district courts rejected both these suits, and the decisions were affirmed without opinion by the United States Supreme Court. Then, in August of 1971, the California Supreme Court ruled that that state's method of financing elementary and secondary schools, because it discriminated on the basis of wealth, violated the equal protection clause of the Fourteenth Amendment to the Constitution.[3] In fairly rapid succession state or federal courts in Minne-

1. *McInnis* v. *Shapiro*, 293 F. Supp. 327 (N.D. Ill. 1968); and *Burruss* v. *Wilkerson*, 310 F. Supp. 572 (W.D. Va. 1969), respectively.
2. *McInnis* v. *Shapiro*, p. 329.
3. *Serrano* v. *Priest*, California Supreme Court 938254, L.A. 29820 (1971).

sota, Texas, New Jersey, Arizona, Wyoming, Kansas, and Michigan[4] hand-
ed down similar decisions, and legal challenges were pursued in more than
twenty other states. Since all states except Hawaii finance their public
schools in basically the same manner, these challenges, if upheld by the
Supreme Court, will have nationwide repercussions.

However, there is likely to be a fundamental change in the way some
states finance education, irrespective of the high court's ruling when it
reviews the Texas decision in its 1972–73 term, because many educators,
state legislators, and politicians have been pushing for such reforms for
years. In a number of states, efforts to increase the equitability of the school
finance system were underway long before public attention and pressure
were galvanized by the ruling of the courts. New York, New Jersey, and
Massachusetts, to name but a few, had established commissions to draw
up recommendations for change and the governors of Michigan and Minnesota had actively sought legislative action to reform school financing.

This chapter examines both the inequities that have stimulated the legal
and political attacks on the existing system of school financing and alternative methods that would reduce or eliminate the inequities. In the next
section the tremendous interdistrict disparities that have played such an
important role in the legal arguments are analyzed. This is followed by a
review of the logic of the courts' decisions and a discussion of the nature
of the states' responsibility for providing education. The final section of
this chapter discusses various methods of reducing the current inequities
and the problems associated with each.

School District Disparities

There are significant disparities among the 17,000 school districts in the
nation: in the quality of the education they provide, in the cost of providing
equivalent educational services, in the need for different types of educational programs, and in the tax burdens placed upon residents. These
disparities and their interrelations have prompted the efforts at reform.

4. *Van Dusartz* v. *Hatfield*, Civ. 243, U.S. District Court, District of Minnesota,
Third Division, Memorandum and Order 3-71 (1971); *Rodriguez* v. *San Antonio Independent School District*, Civil Action 68-175-SA, U.S. District Court, Western District
of Texas, San Antonio Division (1971); *Robinson* v. *Cahill*, Docket L-18704-69, Superior
Court of New Jersey, Hudson County (1972); *Hollins* v. *Shofstall*, Civil No. C-253652,
Sup. Ct. Maricopa County (1972); *Sweetwater Planning Committee* v. *Hinkle*, 491 P. 2D
1234, Wyoming (1971); *Caldwell* v. *Kansas*, No. 50616, D. C. Johnson County (1972);
and *Milliken* v. *Green*, No. 53809, Mich. Sup. Ct. (1972).

Educational Quality and Its Measurement

Although most public concern has correctly focused on the disparities in the quality of education children receive, it has proven difficult if not impossible to measure and compare the quality of schooling provided by different districts. Education produces many results that cannot be registered by even the most sophisticated "achievement" tests. The problem is compounded by the difficulty of separating the effect of the schools from the influence of native ability, home environment, peer group pressures, and other factors that seem to affect achievement but over which the formal school system has little control. Considering these problems, analysts have been forced to rely on proxy measures—such as the amount of resources or expenditures devoted to educating each pupil—to represent educational quality. Before looking at the expenditure disparities that exist between districts, it is worthwhile to review some of the shortcomings of using such a measure as a substitute for the measurement of quality.

Expenditure differences may fail to reflect the true variation in educational quality or even in amounts of real resources devoted to education because of the differences in the efficiency with which school districts operate, the differences in the prices they must pay for equivalent goods and services, and the differences in the educational tasks confronting them. Some jurisdictions are simply more efficient than others; with equivalent resources they can provide a better education. While poor management may be at fault in some cases, some districts have little choice but to operate inefficiently. For example, in rural areas many school jurisdictions have too few pupils to operate efficiently. For them, a physics or calculus class that requires a specially trained teacher becomes terribly expensive because the cost of providing the class can be spread over only a handful of students.

Expenditure differences are also a deficient measure of the quality or level of real resources devoted to education because a dollar may buy different amounts of educational inputs in different places. Although it is accepted that the price of the goods and services purchased by schools differs substantially among school districts, little is known about either the directions or the magnitudes of the variations. For some items, such as books and supplies, prices seem not to differ greatly; the variation that exists probably reflects the skill of each district's purchasing agent. For other items, such as land or school construction, price differences can be tremendous. For example, one survey of the twenty-five largest metropolitan areas revealed that while central cities paid on the average $68,000 per acre for school sites, suburban jurisdictions paid only \$3,500.[5] Land costs are presumably even lower in rural areas.

Although teachers' salaries are the biggest component of educational costs, virtually nothing is known about the variation across school districts of the salary needed to attract teachers of equal quality. While it is tempting to use existing data on beginning or average teacher compensation for a crude indication of the variation, such measures often reflect not true cost differences but rather differences in the training, experience, or quality of the teachers employed by each district.[6] Thus, while Table 4-1 shows that central cities generally pay higher teachers' salaries, it is not necessarily correct to infer that the cost of hiring teachers of equal quality is greater in cities than in suburbs or rural areas, because cities often employ teachers who are more experienced and have more advanced degrees. Differences in the cost of living, the level of wages in alternative occupations, the strength of unions, and general working conditions presumably contribute to determining the salary needed to attract equivalent personnel to various school districts. In pleasant suburban districts with attentive middle class students, the wage would probably be lowest. Because small towns and rural areas have traditionally held little attraction for college-trained labor, it is possible that extremely high salaries—or "boredom bonuses"—would have to be paid to lure highly qualified educators to isolated school districts. In similar fashion, some inner city poverty areas may be forced to offer "combat pay" to induce skilled teachers to forsake the safety and pleasant surroundings of the suburbs. Thus, variations in teachers' salaries, which account for much of the difference in expenditures among school districts, do not measure pure cost differences; to a large degree they reflect differences in teacher qualifications. But neither do they measure "teacher quality." A number of studies have shown that although teachers' experience and degree attainment are usually rewarded in salary schedules, they are not the major indicators of a teacher's ability to educate.[7]

5. S. P. Marland, Jr., "Education's Rigged Lottery" (speech delivered to the National Association of State Boards of Education, Atlanta, Georgia, October 12, 1971; processed), pp. 5–6.

6. James W. Guthrie and others, "Geographic Distribution of Teaching Talent," in State Committee on Public Education, *Citizens for the Twenty-First Century* (Sacramento: State Board of Education, 1969), cited in Charles S. Benson (director), *Final Report to the Senate Select Committee on School District Finance*, Submitted by the Consultant Staff (Sacramento: The Committee, 1972), pp. 35–36.

7. See U.S. Office of Education, *Do Teachers Make a Difference? A Report on Recent Research on Pupil Achievement* (1970).

Table 4-1. Teacher Characteristics in Five States, by Type of District,
1968–69 School Year

Salaries in dollars

State and type of school district	Starting salary with bachelor's degree	Average salary	Years of experience	Percentage with advanced degree
Delaware				
Central city	6,400	10,616	11.1	24.9
Suburbs	6,448	9,179	8.6	28.0
Rural	6,108	7,828	9.5	16.0
Washington				
Central city	6,175	9,144	8.5	19.8
Suburbs	5,995	8,538	6.6	15.2
Rural	5,914	8,133	7.2	13.1
California				
Central city	6,916	10,166	7.6	22.6
Suburbs	6,419	9,608	6.9	23.8
Rural	6,146	8,904	6.8	15.7
Michigan				
Central city	7,500	10,702	11.0	36.0
Suburbs	6,930	10,544	8.5	32.6
Rural	6,393	8,706	11.2	18.8
New York				
Central city	6,755	11,474	6.2	19.4
Suburbs	6,803	10,891	7.3	13.6
Rural	6,300	9,159	6.1	5.4

Source: Betsy Levin and others, *Public School Finance: Present Disparities and Fiscal Alternatives*, A Report Prepared by the Urban Institute for the President's Commission on School Finance (The Commission, 1972), Vol. 1, pp. 97, 100, 103.

Another cost variation arises from the differences in the physical environment and history of school districts. While these factors affect expenditures, they may have little to do with the quality of schooling and thus vitiate the usefulness of expenditures as a substitute measure of educational quality. In cold climates such as New Hampshire, resources must be devoted to heating the schools and shoveling snow from the sidewalks— expenses that are minimal in San Diego. Inner city schools must spend more to protect themselves: vandalism cost the New York City school system $3.7 million in 1971, while Newark spent an equivalent of $26 per pupil just to guard its school buildings. In rural or low density districts the costs of vandalism may be negligible, but transportation costs per pupil are often higher than elsewhere. The cost of school plant operation and maintenance tends to be greater in the older school buildings of cities than in the modern, efficiently designed plants found in many new suburbs. Similarly, older communities, with stable or shrinking enrollments, have higher teacher costs, because salaries rise with the number of years on the job, and the proportion of the teaching force in such communities that has been working in the school system for a long time is higher than in the rapidly expanding new suburbs.

Even if all school districts were equally efficient and had equivalent amounts of real resources per student, the children would still receive schooling of equal quality only if the educational task faced by each district were roughly the same. This is clearly not the case. Some types of educational programs are more expensive than others, and the children who need high cost programs are not evenly distributed among the school districts of each state. While the relative costs of various educational programs have not been determined with any precision, the National Educational Finance Project (NEFP) has made some approximations based on current notions of "good practice" (see Table 4-2). Among its findings was that "good practice" programs spent more for older children than for younger ones, because they made greater use of specialized teachers and

Table 4-2. Ratios of Mean Current Operating Expenditures per Pupil by Program, Grade Level, and Type of School District to Mean Expenditure per Pupil in Basic Programs, Grades 1-6, 1968-69 School Year[a]

Program and grade level	Cities (12 districts)	Suburbs (8 districts)	Independents (8 districts)
Basic			
Grades 1-6	1.000	1.000	1.000
Grades 7-9	1.177	1.174	1.135
Grades 10-12	1.446	1.219	1.454
Mentally and physically handicapped			
Grades 1-6	2.397	2.436	2.821
Grades 7-9	2.098	1.878	2.113
Grades 10-12	2.220	1.752	2.111
Socially maladjusted			
Grades 1-6	2.954	2.499	0.000
Grades 7-9	2.880	1.368	0.000
Grades 10-12	2.432	1.567	0.000
Remedial and compensatory			
Grades 1-6	1.805	1.702	2.354
Grades 7-9	2.940	1.996	2.157
Grades 10-12	1.718	1.962	1.616
Vocational-Technical			
Grades 7-12	1.915	1.680	1.781
Prekindergarten	1.133	1.047	1.499
Kindergarten	1.298	1.110	1.199

Source: William P. McLure and Audra May Pence, "Early Childhood and Basic Elementary and Secondary Education," in Roe L. Johns and others, *Planning to Finance Education* (Gainesville, Florida: National Educational Finance Project, 1971), p. 26.

a. Ratios should not be compared across types of school district.

equipment in higher grades.[8] Students with severe physical or mental handicaps require still more expensive programs. Vocational and technical courses of study also tend to be relatively costly, and children from low income or deprived homes who learn less from their families and peers need costly compensatory programs to teach them in school what middle class children learn at home.

Children who require expensive special programs tend to be concentrated in certain districts. Central cities and rural areas have more than a proportionate share of students needing costly programs, while suburban jurisdictions, on the whole, have a low cost mix of pupils (Table 4-3). Using the NEFP measures, one would calculate that for an equivalent educational program New York City would have to spend $1,334 per pupil to provide the schooling that would cost the nearby wealthy suburban school district of Edgemont (Scarsdale) $1,000.

It is probably true in general that interstate and urban-rural expenditure disparities overstate the differences in both the real resources devoted to education and the quality of schooling provided. Cost differences alone are likely to explain a significant portion of the gap in per pupil educational spending between the industrial states of the North and the more rural states of the deep South. On the other hand, a comparison of expenditures probably masks the real differences between cities and suburbs within the same region. The high expenditure levels found in central cities should be discounted considerably to reflect the greater costs of running a school system in the central city and the greater numbers of city children requiring special high-cost programs.

The Magnitude of Expenditure Disparities

Despite all the pitfalls inherent in using expenditure differences as even a crude measure of the quality of schooling, they remain the only index available for all jurisdictions. From Table 4-4 it is clear that the resources devoted to education—as measured by dollars spent per pupil—differ immensely both among and within states. School districts in New York spend on the average more than twice as much as the average district in nine other states. Within states the expenditure variation among school districts is usually even greater. In many cases, however, the districts with

---

8. A growing number of educators have started to question this practice; they reason that since learning is a cumulative process more resources should be devoted to the earlier than to the later school years. See Benson, *Final Report*, p. 75.

Table 4-3. Percentage of Total Elementary and Secondary Public School Enrollment in Need of High-Cost Programs, Selected New York Districts, 1971[a]

			Program			
School district	Handi-capped students	Voca-tional[b]	Reading disadvan-taged	ESEA,[c] Title 1	High school	Pre-school
Large city districts						
Albany	3.5	8.0	34.0	27.6	17.5	9.4
Buffalo	3.8	18.8	46.0	39.8	21.4	8.1
New York City	1.0	8.2	46.0	36.1	24.9	8.6
Syracuse	7.9	40.7	34.0	32.4	18.6	10.0
Yonkers	2.5	3.4	27.0	19.8	22.0	9.9
Suburban districts						
Baldwinsville	2.6	13.5	14.0	4.0	18.5	7.7
Briarcliff	0.7	1.2	4.0	0	31.6	7.5
Cheektowaga	2.4	6.3	13.0	2.1	14.5	7.3
Edgemont (Scarsdale)	0.7	0	8.0	0	24.7	6.9
Herricks	0.4	2.5	9.0	0.5	29.4	4.8
Kenmore	1.3	6.3	16.0	0	27.2	5.9
Manhasset	0.6	2.8	13.0	6.4	24.9	7.1
Massapequa	1.0	5.5	9.0	0	25.5	6.1
Mount Vernon	2.2	20.2	33.0	37.6	20.4	10.1
New Rochelle	1.8	13.3	20.0	6.8	22.6	8.6
Vestal	0.9	3.6	7.0	1.0	22.5	6.4
Rural districts						
Homer	2.4	9.6	17.0	7.0	18.5	6.2
Ogdensburg	1.9	11.1	21.0	8.2	24.4	6.7
Wayland	0.9	6.0	13.0	5.5	19.7	6.8

Source: Authors' survey, except for figures under reading disadvantaged, which are from "Revising School Finance in New York State," Final Report Prepared for New York State Commission on the Quality, Cost and Financing of Elementary and Secondary Education (Syracuse University Research Corporation, August 1971; processed), App. C-1.

a. The same student may be counted as in need of more than one program.

b. Percentage of students in grades 7–12 enrolled in vocational-technical programs.

c. Elementary and Secondary Education Act of 1965.

extremely high expenditures are either isolated jurisdictions with small numbers of students or special districts devoted to educating children with physical handicaps or learning disabilities. Yet even if such districts are removed from the comparison by ignoring the highest expenditure districts containing 10 percent of each state's students, the expenditure disparities among the remaining districts are considerable; their magnitude is demonstrated by a comparison of the second and third columns of Table 4-4.

If the special cases we have just mentioned are excluded, the districts with the highest expenditure levels in any state tend to be found in the wealthiest suburban areas. Central cities, which on the whole spend well above the statewide average, usually exceed by a slight amount the expendi-

Table 4-4. Elementary and Secondary Public School Expenditures per Pupil, by State, 1969–70 School Year

Dollars

State	High district	Ninetieth pupil percentile[a]	Low district	Fiftieth pupil percentile[a]
Alabama	580	473	294	407
Alaska	1,810	1,254	480	994
Arizona	2,900	991	410	713
Arkansas	1,005	512	294	407
California	3,187	918	402	747
Colorado	2,801	853	444	694
Connecticut	1,311	1,002	499	772
Delaware	1,081	1,081	633	741
Florida	1,036	824	582	722
Georgia	735	706	364	516
Hawaii	851	851	851	486
Idaho	3,172	904	483	664
Illinois	2,295	1,129	390	892
Indiana	961	729	373	619
Iowa	1,166	912	591	752
Kansas	1,572	798	489	646
Kentucky	885	576	344	462
Louisiana	922	730	499	655
Maine	1,966	660	215	551
Maryland	1,036	1,037	634	795
Massachusetts	4,243	963	454	732
Michigan	1,275	888	409	734
Minnesota	1,492	777	373	650
Mississippi	825	541	321	453
Missouri	1,929	808	213	667
Montana	8,515	1,358	467	900
Nebraska	3,417	786	274	621
Nevada	1,678	929	746	838
New Hampshire	1,356	739	280	594
New Jersey	2,876	1,009	484	772
New Mexico	1,183	645	477	520
New York	7,241	1,193	633	1,077
North Carolina	732	675	467	590
North Dakota	1,842	776	327	649
Ohio	1,684	881	412	648
Oklahoma	2,565	662	309	557
Oregon	4,941	914	431	798
Pennsylvania	4,230	1,102	535	845
Rhode Island	1,206	1,045	531	736
South Carolina	610	562	397	511
South Dakota	6,012	750	175	607
Tennessee	774	629	315	491
Texas	11,096	668	197	540
Utah	1,514	630	533	568
Vermont	1,517	905	357	687
Virginia	1,159	776	441	606
Washington	3,993	981	433	831
West Virginia	721	706	502	601
Wisconsin	1,391	849	408	747
Wyoming	14,554	1,146	617	706

Source: *Review of Existing State School Finance Programs*, Vol. 2: *Documentation of Disparities in the Financing of Public Elementary and Secondary School Systems—By State*, A Commission Staff Report Submitted to the President's Commission on School Finance (The Commission, 1972), pp. 19 ff., with corrections.

a. The ninetieth pupil percentile is the expenditure level at which 10 percent of the students in a state have more spent on them than that level; at the fiftieth percentile, half of the state's students have more spent on their education and half have less.

ture levels of the average district in their suburbs.[9] At the bottom of the spectrum are the school districts in nonmetropolitan areas, which spend considerably less per student than those in urbanized regions.

Sources of Expenditure Variations

The variations among districts in expenditure levels are primarily the result of differences in the amounts of money each raises from its own resources; on the whole, state aid tends to moderate expenditure disparities.[10] In turn, differences in the amounts local districts raise are related both to the varying ability of districts to generate revenues and to their willingness to do so. Although there are great disparities in the relative revenue raising ability or wealth of various districts, the appropriate measure of a school district's fiscal capacity is not so obvious. The courts and most state equalization programs have relied on the value of taxable property per pupil as the proper index, because virtually all local revenues are raised from property taxes. By this measure, some districts in a state have 10,000 times the fiscal capacity of others, and even within narrow confines of a metropolitan area there are variations of ten or fifteen to one (see Chapter 3, Table 3-10). The highest values of property per pupil are found in industrial enclaves and in the few exclusive suburbs of any metropolitan area. Central cities exhibit property values per pupil well above the average for their states, and in many instances property values per pupil are higher in central cities than in their suburbs. The primary cause for this apparent wealth is not that cities contain a disproportionate share of property within their boundaries, but that, in comparison with the suburbs, a smaller fraction of the population is enrolled in public schools[11] (see Table 4-5). Al-

9. Current expenditures per pupil in 1969–70 were higher in the central city than in the surrounding areas in 46 of the nation's 70 largest metropolitan areas. See Seymour Sacks and Ralph Andrew, with Tony Carnevale, "School State Aid and the System of Finance: Central City, Suburban and Rural Dimensions of Revenue Sharing" (Syracuse University, no date; processed), Table 2.

10. Betsy Levin and others, *Public School Finance: Present Disparities and Fiscal Alternatives*, A Report Prepared by the Urban Institute for the President's Commission on School Finance (The Commission, 1972), Vol. 1, p. 47.

11. Netzer found that in twenty of the thirty-two metropolitan areas for which data were available the value of taxable property per capita was greater in the suburbs than in the central city. Dick Netzer, *Economics of the Property Tax* (Brookings Institution, 1966). For additional data on the variations in property values per pupil among different types of districts, see Roe L. Johns and James A. Burns, "Comparison of Revenues for Different Population Classifications of School Districts," in Roe L. Johns and others (eds.), *Status and Impact of Educational Finance Programs* (Gainesville, Florida: National Educational Finance Project, 1971), p. 197; Levin and others, *Public School Finance*, Vol. 1, pp. 54, 61, 65.

Table 4-5. Fiscal Capacity and Public School Enrollment Ratios for Selected Cities, Suburbs, and Rural Areas, 1969–70 School Year

Money amounts in dollars

Area[a]	Equalized property value		Personal income		Public school enrollment as percentage of total population
	Per pupil	Per capita	Per pupil	Per capita	
Boston	20,661	3,120	20,345	3,099	15
Suburbs	32,520	6,775	18,715	3,899	21
Rural Massachusetts	53,144	12,315	14,021	3,249	23
New York City	47,625	6,546	27,270	3,736	14
Suburbs	37,640	8,131	22,421	4,843	22
Rural New York	20,582	5,139	10,296	2,574	25
Newark	19,815	4,089	11,344	2,498	22
Suburbs	48,443	8,909	25,936	4,629	18
Rural New Jersey	45,780	10,523	14,086	3,238	23
Philadelphia	24,057	3,549	20,614	3,041	15
Suburbs	26,952	5,246	20,085	3,909	19
Rural Pennsylvania	14,279	3,397	10,632	2,529	24
Wilmington	27,899	5,142	16,081	2,964	18
Suburbs	19,165	4,481	15,881	3,713	23
Rural Delaware	12,222	3,009	11,174	2,751	25
Baltimore	15,727	3,331	13,624	2,886	21
Suburbs	19,674	4,080	19,117	3,965	21
Rural Maryland	13,010	3,239	8,925	2,222	25
Cleveland	30,281	6,043	14,276	2,849	20
Suburbs	52,057	9,972	23,004	4,406	19
Rural Ohio	23,788	5,444	8,839	2,023	23
Detroit	16,808	3,271	16,920	3,227	19
Suburbs	15,644	3,990	15,785	4,026	26
Rural Michigan	11,032	3,033	8,977	2,468	27
Chicago	20,798	3,618	19,662	3,420	17
Suburbs	18,381	4,157	19,228	4,348	23
Rural Illinois	21,870	5,399	11,189	2,762	25
Milwaukee	30,875	5,671	17,445	3,204	18
Suburbs	40,176	8,822	18,694	4,105	22
Rural Wisconsin	21,989	5,433	9,519	2,352	25
Minneapolis-St. Paul	14,851	2,349	22,027	3,484	16
Suburbs	10,021	2,719	14,828	4,024	27
Rural Minnesota	8,746	2,276	8,799	2,290	26
St. Louis	15,314	2,825	15,025	2,772	18
Suburbs	14,260	3,024	19,081	4,046	21
Rural Missouri	10,290	2,249	10,143	2,217	22
Denver	13,255	2,474	19,055	3,557	19
Suburbs	7,068	1,920	13,791	3,747	27
Rural Colorado	8,738	2,272	9,554	2,484	26
San Francisco	24,108	3,056	33,832	4,289	13
Suburbs	13,955	3,042	21,307	4,644	22
Rural California	16,991	3,844	13,450	3,043	23

though most nonmetropolitan school districts have the smallest amount of taxable property per student, this is by no means universally true. Some rural areas such as Cape Cod, Massachusetts, have large amounts of vacation real estate to tax, and other districts may have valuable farmland in their tax base.

As the previous chapter pointed out, property values per pupil may be a relatively poor measure of the comparative ability of school districts to raise money, even though the districts rely almost exclusively on property taxes for their locally generated revenues. The basic defect is that at least some of the tax advantages or disadvantages of living in a school district with extremely high or low property values per pupil may be reflected in house values and rents. Thus, for example, two neighboring suburbs of Boston—Lexington and Belmont—house families of roughly equal incomes, yet Belmont's per-pupil property value is about double Lexington's. It is difficult to maintain that Belmont has twice the capacity to pay for its schools—if that were true, people would be flocking from Lexington to buy houses in Belmont. It is more likely that Belmont's homeowners have paid relatively high prices for their residences in part because they knew they could support good schools with a low tax rate, while Lexington's paid less for equivalent houses knowing that their property tax rates would have to be higher to support an equivalent level of school spending. In short, of the many considerations reflected in the value of property, at least one is the relative tax burden that must be placed on a house to raise one dollar per student for education. Of course, in a program of state aid to education the state is concerned primarily with the welfare of children in communities with low tax bases. The fact that Lexington homeowners have lower mortgage payments than Belmont's doesn't necessarily do the school children of Lexington any good. However, in developing state assistance programs, the relative financial capacities of different school districts must be taken into account, and property values per pupil will

---

Footnotes to Table 4-5:

Sources: Total equalized property values are from published and unpublished data of the respective State Board's of Equalization; population and income data are from U.S. Bureau of the Census, Census of Population, 1970, General Social and Economic Characteristics, Final Report PC(1)-C, volumes for the respective states; pupil enrollment is from reports from respective State Departments of Education or from Census of Population, 1970, PC(1)-C reports.

a. Suburbs included are the following: Boston—remainder of standard metropolitan statistical area; New York City—Nassau and Westchester counties; Newark—remainder of Essex County; Philadelphia—Bucks, Delaware, and Montgomery counties; Wilmington—remainder of New Castle County; Baltimore—Baltimore County; Cleveland—remainder of Cuyahoga County; Detroit—Macomb and Oakland counties and remainder of Wayne County; Chicago—Du Page County and remainder of Cook and Lake counties; Milwaukee—remainder of Milwaukee County: Minneapolis-St. Paul—remainder of Hennepin and Ramsey counties; St. Louis—St. Louis County; Denver—Arapahoe and Jefferson counties; San Francisco—Marin and San Mateo counties.

Rural is defined as follows: of the counties in each state with populations over 10,000, the three counties with the highest percentages of rural population.

fail to measure the relative abilities to pay whenever residential values have built into them the tax differences among districts.

Family or personal income is an alternate measure of fiscal capacity that avoids some of the problems of the per-pupil property value index. In the first place, it does not exhibit such unrealistic variations in school district capacities. It also avoids the problems arising from the possible capitalization of tax advantages into housing costs because it assumes that if two neighboring districts house families of similar incomes they will have equal fiscal capacities irrespective of their property tax bases.

Although income per pupil is highest in the wealthy suburbs, income per pupil in central cities is on the whole higher than in the average suburb; this is not because income per capita is high but because the fraction of the cities' population that is enrolled in public schools is low. On a per-capita basis, most cities are poorer than their suburbs (see Table 4-5). By the income measure, rural districts generally have the least in the way of revenue raising ability.

It is important to note that the criterion by which fiscal capacity is measured may alter the relative rankings of some districts. In many states the correlation between the property values of a district and the income of its residents is weak. Districts that seem wealthy by the property value measure often seem poor when ranked by income. One reason for this is that many communities with large concentrations of nonresidential property house predominantly low and lower middle income families. Some central cities fall into this category, as do such industrial enclaves as Lackawanna, New York, Emeryville, California, and River Rouge, Michigan. But whatever measure of wealth or income one chooses as the most appropriate, it is clear that there are tremendous disparities among school districts in the ability to raise local revenues. This means that to raise an equivalent amount of revenue per pupil different communities have to exert vastly different tax efforts.

Of course the amount of local resources a district devotes to education depends on its willingness to tax itself as well as on its capacity to do so, and the degree of willingness may differ greatly among jurisdictions. The residents of some communities place great emphasis on education and are willing to tax themselves heavily to ensure that their children receive a good education. A community's taste for education may be influenced by its values and by the structure of its population. Districts with few school-age children, or with large proportions of retired or single voters, or with high parochial school attendance, may put education fairly low in their priorities for local public expenditures. Willingness to spend on education also depends on the alternative demands on a community's funds. Central cities confronting problems such as crime, congestion, or poverty may not accord the same priority to education as a tranquil middle class suburb. The voters of both districts may have identical feelings about education, but face radically different sets of public expenditure alternatives. This fact has led to the argument that cities should be compensated for "municipal overburden," or for the necessity of providing public services that are not needed elsewhere.[12]

Finally, the willingness of the voters of a community to support education may depend on who pays the final bill. In a school district consisting solely of owner occupied houses, every dollar locally raised for education comes out of the pocket of the resident taxpayer-voter, while in communities with large concentrations of nonresidential property local voters may pay for only a fraction of each additional school dollar; since industry pays for the rest, the residents may be more willing to increase the local contribution.[13]

The interaction of differences in the ability and willingness of school districts to raise local revenues for education results in widely disparate tax rates. In general the districts that tax themselves the most heavily are those with the lowest property values per student. As Table 4-6 shows, of a

12. Those who would like to compensate selected school districts for what they regard as municipal overburden will have to solve a number of difficult conceptual problems, which include:

(1) How does one distinguish "municipal overburden" from a community's greater taste for public goods?

(2) How does one adjust for the fact that in some jurisdictions certain services such as fire protection, sanitation, and even schooling are largely provided privately, while in others these are provided publicly?

(3) How does one account for the alternatives to public service costs incurred by those living in uncongested areas? The city dweller may pay taxes for police protection, but the suburban commuter pays for equivalent protection by driving two hours a day to get to and from an area inaccessible to criminals.

(4) Should society compensate or subsidize persons who choose to live in jurisdictions with excessively high social costs? Some part of the high public service costs of cities may simply reflect the inefficiencies of too dense concentrations of population. The cities will never thin out if these excess costs are subsidized by higher levels of government.

These issues are raised in Harvey E. Brazer and others, "Fiscal Needs and Resources: A Report to the New York State Commission on the Quality, Cost and Financing of Elementary and Secondary Education" (November 1971; processed), Chap. 5.

13. The local voters' zeal to get contributions from local industry is, of course, tempered by a fear of driving the industry away. Nonresidential property owners have been known to make their prospects for moving clear to voters before property tax elections.

Table 4-6. Relation of School District Wealth to Tax Rates, Local Revenue per Pupil, and Total Expenditures per Pupil, 110 Texas School Districts, 1966–67 School Year

Market value of taxable property per pupil (dollars)	Number of school districts	Equalized tax rates per $100 valuation (dollars)	Local revenue per pupil (dollars)	Total expenditure per pupil by local, state, and federal governments (dollars)
Above 100,000	9	0.31	610	856
100,000–50,000	26	0.38	287	610
50,000–30,000	29	0.55	224	529
30,000–10,000	41	0.72	166	546
Below 10,000	5	0.70	63	441

Source: Joel S. Berke, Affidavit, U.S. District Court, Western District of Texas, San Antonio Division, Civil Action 68-175-SA (1971), Tables 2 and 5.

representative sample of 110 Texas school districts, the wealthiest tax themselves at less than half the rate of the poorer jurisdictions and raise more per pupil. State and federal aid do little to reduce these local disparities, except at the extremes of the distribution. The relationships among the disparities in expenditures, wealth, and tax effort were the basic evidence upon which the courts based their decisions in the school finance cases.

The Court Decisions and the Educational Responsibility of the State

In eight states courts have ruled that the disparities described in the previous section are unacceptable because they violate the equal protection clause of the Fourteenth Amendment to the Constitution. This clause, which reads, "No state shall . . . deny to any person within its jurisdiction the equal protection of the laws," has been interpreted as precluding discrimination on the basis of "suspect classifications" in cases where "fundamental interests" are involved. Exceptions to this rule are permitted only when a state can establish that it has a "compelling interest which justifies" discriminatory treatment and "that the distinctions drawn by the [state's] law are *necessary* to further its purpose."[14]

All the lower court decisions closely followed the California ruling's logic with respect to the application of the Fourteenth Amendment to the issue of school finance. The California decision first reaffirmed previous court findings that wealth, like race, was a "suspect" characteristic upon

14. *Serrano* v. *Priest*, p. 18.

which to condition the access to fundamental rights. They then found that the California system of school financing as a whole resulted in a classification on the basis of wealth, because the quality of education received by each child appeared to be largely a function of the wealth of the school district in which he happened to live. In other words, the local property tax base determined how much local money each district could raise, and state aid did little to offset the differences arising from the disparate revenue raising capabilities of the districts.

The California court then went on explicitly to define education as a "fundamental interest"—comparable to voting rights or the criminal defendant's right to counsel—the access to which could not be conditioned upon the "suspect classification," wealth. The court's judgment, which broke new legal ground, was based on the overriding importance of education both to the recipient and to society. It argued: "First, education is essential in . . . preserving an individual's opportunity to compete successfully in the economic market place. . . . Second, education is universally relevant. . . . Every person . . . benefits from education. . . . Third, . . . few other government services have such sustained, intensive contact with the recipient. Fourth, education is unmatched in the extent to which it molds the personality of the youth of society. . . . Finally, education is so important that the state has made it compulsory. . . ."[15] Thus, according to the California court, education is a fundamental interest.

The last step in the court's reasoning was that the great disparities permitted by the California financing system were not needed for any "compelling state interest." While the defendants had argued that the existing system was necessary "to strengthen and encourage local responsibility for control of public education," the court reasoned that "no matter how the state decides to finance its system of public education, it can still leave . . . decision-making power in the hands of local districts."[16] It also rejected the argument that there was a compelling state interest in allowing each local district the choice of determining how much it wanted to spend on education. In a poor jurisdiction, the judges argued, "such fiscal free-will is a cruel illusion," because it "cannot freely choose to tax itself into an excellence which its tax rolls cannot provide."[17] In fact, the court argued, only rich districts were truly free to decide how much they wished to spend.

15. *Ibid.*, pp. 42–44.
16. *Ibid.*, pp. 45, 46.
17. *Ibid.*, p. 47.

The constitutional logic of the school finance decision of the lower courts represents one way of looking at the equity of the educational system and at the responsibility of the state in providing this important service. It is a fiscal approach focused on the relation between the prices (tax rates) paid by the residents in different communities and the services (per-pupil expenditures) they receive for those prices. The decisions in California, Texas, and elsewhere held that any system was unfair—or unconstitutional —if the quality of education provided by school districts was a "function of wealth, other than the wealth of the state as a whole."[18] In other words, it was the responsibility of the state to ensure that communities that paid the same tax rates or extended equivalent efforts in behalf of education received services of an equal quality.

An alternative view of the state's responsibility in the area of elementary and secondary education would focus on educational results rather than on fiscal equity. Under this approach the function of the state is to ensure that all children receive an "equal" education, or at least that educational resources are distributed among school districts according to their relative educational need.[19] The quality of schooling each child receives, it is argued, is too important to be influenced by either the wealth of the local school district or by the tastes and preferences of its voters. Why should a child living in a community with a large retired population be penalized if his neighbors do not want to support a school system of high quality but prefer an elaborate set of services for senior citizens? Whatever the social merits of basing education on need, the courts have found themselves unable to deal with such a fuzzy concept.

A third way of looking at the states' constitutional responsibility for education and at the fairness of the present system stresses the minimum provision of educational services. This approach argues that it is the responsibility of government "to protect against certain hazards which are endemic in an unequal society."[20] This is the foundation of most of our

18. *Rodriguez* v. *San Antonio Independent School District*, Per Curiam Order of December 23, 1971, p. 5.

19. This argument, made in the early school finance cases, raises the difficult problems of deciding what "equal" education means and of measuring educational "need." See *McInnis* v. *Shapiro* and *Burruss* v. *Wilkerson*.

20. Frank I. Michelman, "Foreword: On Protecting the Poor Through the Fourteenth Amendment," *Harvard Law Review*, Vol. 83 (November 1969), pp. 13–16, and, for the quotation, p. 9. See also Harvey E. Brazer, "Federal, State, and Local Responsibility for Financing Education," in Roe L. Johns and others (eds.), *Economic Factors Affecting the Financing of Education* (Gainesville, Florida: National Educational Finance Project, 1970), pp. 247–49.

public assistance legislation, which can be understood as saying that our society has decided to insure citizens against the chance that they will have too little money to buy the necessities of life. In the case of education, the hazard against which the state must protect its citizens is the possibility that a child may be deprived of the schooling necessary to function in a modern society because he lives in an impoverished school district. Just how one determines the minimum level of schooling is unclear, but presumably enriched schooling can be regarded as a luxury, access to which the state has no obligation to guarantee or equalize. Thus, the minimum protection approach to the constitutional question would focus on the spending levels only of those districts that fail to provide a satisfactory minimum.

Although the basic education aid programs of most states have acted to guarantee a certain minimum level of educational support for all children, in many instances the floor is far below the level required to ensure that an individual will be able to function adequately in today's society. In a number of the largest states, the district with the lowest expenditure per pupil expends only slightly more than half of the statewide average (see Table 4-4).

It is not clear that a popular consensus regarding the state's responsibility in the area of school financing has yet been reached. Nor is it clear what line of argument the Supreme Court will find persuasive in its review of the Texas case (*Rodriguez* v. *San Antonio Independent School District*). It could, of course, accept the constitutional logic and prescription offered by the lower courts, or it might reject the line of reasoning and reverse the decision. Such a reversal might be based on the denial that education was a "fundamental interest," a position that would in turn lead to the rejection of the applicability of the equal protection clause to school finance. If this happened, most of the lower court decisions of 1971 and 1972, which were based on constitutional logic similar to that of the Texas case, would be nullified. The same issue was not raised in New Jersey (*Robinson* v. *Cahill*), where the arguments hinged on the language of the state constitution. It is possible that new legal challenges based on the provisions of state constitutions would be successful; since such decisions would not come under the review of the United States Supreme Court, they could renew the legal pressure for reform. Finally, the court might overturn the existing school financing systems on new grounds: the high court might, for example, accept the minimum provision approach and find that states had not fulfilled their responsibility to guarantee that all children within their boundaries receive the education necessary to function in a modern society. While the court's decision may define the characteristics of school financing systems that are constitutionally tolerable, it will almost certainly not designate a single acceptable method of school finance.

Alternative Paths to Reform

There are many methods available for reducing the disparities and inequities inherent in current state systems of school finance. Some of these alternatives would meet a strict interpretation of the lower court's requirements for new school financing plans; they would eliminate completely the role local school district wealth now plays in determining expenditure levels. Other reforms would only reduce the existing wealth-related disparities. Since the magnitude of the differences in the expenditure levels, wealth, and tax rates among districts appeared to influence the thinking of the courts, it is possible that such a reduction would satisfy a less stringent interpretation of the constitutional requirements for school finance systems. Compliance with judicial rulings is of course only one criterion by which to evaluate alternative methods of financing schools; the total amount spent on education, as well as the distribution of the burden of raising it, would vary with the type of reform selected. The alternative reforms also would have vastly different consequences with respect to both the locus of educational decision-making power and the future of the public school system as we know it today.

Larger State Equalization Programs

Strengthening and expanding the basic state aid programs that are currently in operation would require the least fundamental change. Where the basic state aid program consists of a flat grant whose size is unrelated to a district's fiscal capacity, the grant would have to be increased. In states with foundation programs, the level of the foundation guarantee would have to be raised. In other states, the range over which percentage equalizing plans or guaranteed tax base programs are applicable would have to be expanded. Modifications such as these would leave the basic structure of school finance unchanged: the ultimate power to decide on the level of resources would still rest with the local school district, although the minimum permissible level would be raised along with state taxes.

It may be that minor modifications in existing state programs would substantially reduce the wealth-related expenditure disparities that now exist. Existing programs have so far had little impact, not because of flaws in their basic design but as a result of their size and of the constraints on their operation created by state political and budgetary pressures. On the whole, flat grants have been small in relation to the total amount spent per student by the average district. Similarly, foundation levels have been unrealistically low, and equalization programs have had to operate over very limited expenditure ranges. The stipulation that all districts must receive a positive grant has further crippled the operation of many equalization programs.

If existing state aid programs were strengthened and expanded, many states might reasonably argue that they had fulfilled their responsibility for providing their citizens with a minimum level of schooling. States such as North Carolina and Delaware, whose basic grants are large in relation to the average level of expenditure, may well be meeting the obligation already. If the expanded state aid programs significantly reduced the magnitude of the wealth-related expenditure disparities, it is also conceivable that such moderate reforms would meet a loose interpretation of the courts' objections to the existing systems.

Full State Financing

A more stringent interpretation of the court rulings would require that the influence of community wealth on educational expenditure be eliminated altogether. There are two basic ways this could be accomplished. The first is to remove the local community from the school financing decision process by making the state (or federal) government responsible for raising all the public moneys devoted to education. But centralizing the fiscal responsibility for education would not answer the important questions of how the revenues collected by the state would be distributed, and to whom.

One approach to full state financing of schools is the assumption by the state of the administrative and operational responsibility for providing education. Teachers, principals, and other school district workers would then become state employees. Only in Hawaii is education now a state service. Many Americans fear that a unitary state school system would necessarily be insensitive to local needs and problems, overbureaucratized, and of mediocre quality; the fear may well preclude complete state governance of schools even if states assume the full fiscal responsibility.

A less extreme alternative would be for the state to distribute the revenues it collects to local school districts, which, with the exception of revenue raising, would retain all the prerogatives they have today: in states where they currently have these powers, they would continue to hire and fire teachers, and set salary schedules, classes, textbooks, and curriculum. Under such a system, the nature of schooling might vary considerably among districts.

The most radical form of school governance compatible with the state's assuming the responsibility for raising all *public* money is the voucher system.[21] Under such a program the family, rather than the state or the local school district, would become the basic decision-making unit. Parents would receive a state educational voucher for each of their children.[22] The voucher could be used to purchase schooling from any private or government-operated institution that had met certain minimal requirements set by the state. The schools would collect the vouchers from the parents, redeem them for a cash payment from the state, and use the proceeds to operate. Parents who wanted their children to receive a more enriched education than a school could provide using only the receipts of the vouchers would be free to supplement the voucher with an additional tuition payment. Such a system would probably foster a good deal of educational diversity. While it would eliminate community wealth as a determinant of educational quality, in all likelihood family wealth would take its place, since richer parents would be more likely to supplement the voucher.

This possibility could be circumvented if schools that accepted vouchers were prevented from charging supplementary tuitions. Children whose parents desired a higher quality of schooling than could be provided through the basic voucher would be forced into institutions outside the system, and their parents would have to bear the full cost of the superior schooling just as parents of nonpublic school students do today. An alternative method of reducing the influence of family wealth on educational opportunity in a simple voucher system would be to provide parents with supplementary vouchers whose value would be keyed to both the family's

21. The first modern proposal for educational vouchers was made by Milton Friedman, *Capitalism and Freedom* (University of Chicago Press, 1962), Chap. 6. For a comprehensive discussion of the various voucher proposals, see Center for the Study of Public Policy, "Education Vouchers: A Preliminary Report on Financing Education by Payments to Parents" (Cambridge, Massachusetts: The Center, 1970).

22. A program of educational tax credits would be similar to a voucher plan. Tax credits are discussed in Chapter 6.

income and the tuition charged by the school attended by their children.[23] The state could equalize the ability of parents to afford supplementary tuition charges by ensuring that families that made the same effort—devoted the same fraction of their disposable income to education—had similar resources with which to pay the added charges. For example, the supplementary voucher schedule could guarantee that every family that devoted 1 percent of its income to educating a child had $500 in supplementary tuition benefits. To send a child to a school charging an added tuition of $500, a family with an income of $20,000 would have to pay $200, while the family with an income of $5,000 would be required to spend only $50 of its own income; the supplementary voucher would pay for the rest. Unlike the plan that would preclude supplementary tuitions, this alternative would result in a system of publicly supported schools that devoted varying amounts of real resources to educating each student, but the influence of family wealth on the choice of schools would presumably be eliminated. Income-related vouchers are analogous to existing state equalization schemes, except that the family rather than the school district decides on the levels of educational quality.

For the most part, voucher systems have been advocated, not as a means of improving the equitability of the existing systems of school finance, but because they would introduce more competition into the educational system. Competition, it is hoped, would lead to an improvement in the quality of education, a greater diversity in types of schooling available, and an increase in parents' control over and satisfaction with their children's education. Many, however, consider the introduction of the forces of the private marketplace into a field as traditionally "public" as education too radical a change. Vouchers might threaten the dominant position of the government as the major supplier of educational services. While public agencies could own and operate schools under such a system, they would be equal competitors with nonpublic schools. Some feel that in such an environment the public educational sector would rapidly shrink. Those who regard the "publicness" of education as a goal in itself have thus objected to voucher systems. Teachers, school administrators, and the educational establishment, all of whom have a vested interest in the maintenance of the existing system, have also bitterly opposed even modest

23. See John E. Coons, William H. Clune III, and Stephen D. Sugarman, "Educational Opportunity: A Workable Constitutional Test for State Financial Structures," *California Law Review*, Vol. 57 (April 1969), pp. 321–22.

experimentation with vouchers.[24] Still others have objected to voucher schemes out of a fear that they will result in increased school segregation. Unless precautions are taken to ensure that institutions do not discriminate in their admission policies against minority children, the poor, the hard to educate, problem pupils, or less able students, an increase in racial or socioeconomic segregation could well accompany a movement toward a voucher system. Another cause of antagonism is the belief that taxpayer support for such a system would shrink.

Many have expressed apprehension that full state assumption of the responsibility for raising public educational revenue will lead to simplistic resource distribution that will preserve existing inequities and create new ones. For example, the "one scholar, one dollar" method, in which every school received the same amount per student, or every voucher was of equal value,[25] would lead to inferior education for pupils who required expensive educational programs and for pupils living in high-cost school districts.

Recent court decisions have not precluded distributing resources on the basis of costs or needs. Nor have they ruled out voucher systems in which the value of the voucher varied with the educational need of the child, more valuable vouchers being given to handicapped children, those in vocational education programs, and pupils from disadvantaged homes. In fact, in the New Jersey ruling, Judge Theodore I. Botter argued that an unequal distribution of resources that could be justified on the basis of "educational need" was acceptable, but that the courts were not the body to measure or define such need.

Analysis of the forces working on state politics often arouses apprehension over the way a state will allocate funds.[26] Many state legislatures are dominated by rural and suburban interests that, while willing to shed a few tears in behalf of the inner cities' plight, have not been eager to provide government resources for these hard-pressed areas. It is possible that an equal division of the states' educational revenues among pupils might help

24. During the past half decade, the Office of Economic Opportunity has attempted to induce school districts in a number of states to experiment with vouchers. A limited demonstration was begun by the Alum Rock Union Elementary School District in San Jose, California, in the fall of 1972.

25. Several of the reform programs considered by the California legislature in 1972 would have distributed resources in this manner. See Betsy Levin and others, *Paying for Public Schools: Issues of School Finance in California* (Urban Institute, 1972), Chap. 4.

26. Joel S. Berke and John J. Callahan, "Serrano v. Priest: Milestone or Millstone for School Finance," *Journal of Public Law*, Vol. 21, No. 1 (1972).

both rural and suburban areas at the expense of the cities. Suburbs could maintain their educational superiority because of their lower costs and less expensive mix of pupils, while for the rural districts an equal per-pupil division of the state resources would, in all likelihood, represent a large increase over the amount of money they now spend on education. Inner cities, on the other hand, with their high costs, expensive mix of students, and high expenditure levels, might find themselves, under full state assumption and an equal per-pupil distribution of resources, with less revenue for education. It is worth noting that some states are not insensitive to the problem. For example, the existing state aid formulas in New Jersey and Minnesota provide substantial extra amounts of money for children of welfare recipients.

Full state assumption would undoubtedly mean an increase in the total amount of resources devoted to education. Political pressures at the state level are such that the average expenditure per pupil in a state-financed school system would probably have to be close to the amount now spent in the state's high expenditure districts. If the voucher system of school governance were selected, the average voucher would also have to be at this level. The alternative of choosing a lower level of expenditure, or one closer to the existing state average, would involve cutting back the quality of schooling enjoyed by a substantial fraction of students, most of whom are the children of the more powerful and influential citizens of any state. If the level were too low, many families would quit the public school system, and the traditional support education has had in state legislatures might begin to decline.

Table 4-7 provides estimates for 1969–70 of the cost to each state of bringing the average expenditure level up to that enjoyed by the state's ninetieth percentile student; the aggregate increase in educational spending would have been of the order of $7 billion, a figure that has probably grown to $8.2 billion for 1972. For some states, state assumption at this level would necessitate a very substantial rise in state taxes, as the last column of Table 4-7 shows. Equalization to the eightieth, seventieth, and fiftieth percentile levels would have cost approximately $5.2 billion, $3.6 billion, and $2.0 billion, respectively, in 1972.

It is difficult to say what effect full state assumption for the responsibility of raising school revenues would have on the education tax burden borne by various classes of persons. As the previous chapter pointed out, much would depend upon the particular mix of taxes that was used to raise the additional money. It is safe, however, to assume that a voucher system

Table 4-7. Cost of Equalizing School Expenditures to the Ninetieth Pupil Percentile, by State, 1969–70 School Year

State	Total cost (millions of dollars)	Cost per pupil (dollars)	Cost as a percentage of 1970 state taxes
Alabama	44.2	57	6.7
Alaska	11.3	198	13.2
Arizona	96.7	242	20.4
Arkansas	40.9	101	11.6
California	828.1	177	15.1
Colorado	72.0	144	15.3
Connecticut	141.3	213	19.0
Delaware	34.8	296	17.8
Florida	132.1	101	9.3
Georgia	177.1	174	18.8
Hawaii	9.6	53	2.8
Idaho	36.5	214	23.4
Illinois	457.0	220	15.9
Indiana	129.2	116	12.9
Iowa	93.9	144	14.9
Kansas	76.1	153	17.7
Kentucky	63.1	97	9.0
Louisiana	61.1	79	7.3
Maine	26.2	108	12.6
Maryland	190.8	221	17.6
Massachusetts	259.1	228	18.6
Michigan	364.1	169	15.5
Minnesota	120.7	122	11.8
Mississippi	45.7	88	9.4
Missouri	125.8	140	15.3
Montana	68.5	422	53.2
Nebraska	54.8	167	21.0
Nevada	9.1	80	6.1
New Hampshire	19.6	131	20.7
New Jersey	317.7	216	23.8
New Mexico	27.3	100	10.0
New York	610.2	182	10.0
North Carolina	95.0	86	8.0
North Dakota	19.5	134	16.0
Ohio	518.9	216	30.5
Oklahoma	61.5	110	12.2
Oregon	62.7	136	14.6
Pennsylvania	504.3	220	18.2
Rhode Island	49.5	279	21.6
South Carolina	32.3	54	5.9
South Dakota	22.8	137	20.2
Tennessee	99.5	119	14.5
Texas	292.7	121	14.8
Utah	14.5	50	5.8
Vermont	24.1	208	17.8
Virginia	145.1	146	15.2
Washington	121.2	153	11.8
West Virginia	34.1	92	8.9
Wisconsin	101.6	109	7.6
Wyoming	29.1	341	34.4
All states, total	6,973.0	160	14.5

Sources: Cost and enrollment data from *Review of Existing State School Finance Programs*, Vol. 2, Report Submitted to the President's Commission on School Finance, pp. 22 ff. (cost data include an estimate of the cost associated with the lowest 5 percent of students); state tax data from Bureau of the Census, *State Government Finances in 1970*, GF70 No. 3 (1971), p. 19.

that permitted supplemental tuition would shift some of the burden for financing education to parents and away from taxpayers.

Capacity Equalization

The second basic approach to eliminating the influence of school district wealth on the quality of education in each community is for the state to act to equalize the fiscal capacity of all districts. Under this approach, the ultimate power to determine the quality of education in each locality would continue to rest with the voters of each school district.

The most direct manner of accomplishing such equalization would be for states to redraw school district boundaries in such a way as to make the per-pupil fiscal capacity of each the same. While this would be the least expensive manner of conforming to a strict interpretation of the lower court's requests for new systems of school finance, it is the least realistic from a political standpoint, because in most states the only way to equalize the resource bases of all school districts would be to make them rather large geographic units. Rural areas, because of their low wealth, would have to be joined with districts in urbanized areas. Some central city districts with little fiscal capacity, such as Newark, would have to be merged with some of the districts in their suburbs.

The reaction in the Detroit and Richmond areas to suggestions of a metropolitan-wide school system has shown this approach to be highly unpopular. Part of this response may be due to the fear that larger districts would be administratively unwieldy and unresponsive to the special needs of some of the pupils that they served. But much of the opposition stems from the fact that there have been several successful court suits compelling a school district to allocate resources equally between races and among schools.[27] Consolidating school districts may also entail an increase in busing for the purpose of achieving racial balance, and a substantial redistribution of resources among individual schools. A subsidiary problem with equalizing school district resources by redrawing boundaries is that district lines would have to be changed periodically to reflect the normal ebb and flow of children and of wealth in various neighborhoods. Families living on the fringe of a school district would never know for sure what school district they would be in during the next year, and property values in border areas would soon come to reflect the uncertainty. The modifica-

27. See, for example, *Hobson* v. *Hansen*, 269 F. Supp. 401 (1967).

tion of district lines might well become a politicized process in which educational considerations played only a minor role.

An alternative method of equalizing the fiscal capacity of all school districts would be for the state to guarantee that districts that made the same tax efforts on behalf of education would receive equivalent amounts of resources per student. State aid programs with such varied names as "district power equalizing," "percentage equalizing," and "guaranteed tax base" all reflect this notion. Under such plans the state would establish a schedule showing the level of tax effort (tax rate) required of all districts to support various levels of expenditure per pupil. Each district would choose the amount of expenditure it wished to devote to educating each of its students. It then would obtain from the state schedule the required effort or tax rate that must be imposed on its local tax base. If at this rate the local tax base generated less revenue per student than the guarantee, the state would make up the difference. On the other hand, if the local tax base produced more than the guaranteed amount, the district would be required to turn the surplus over to the state, which would presumably use the receipts to pay poorer districts.

The schedule establishing the effort a district must make to achieve a certain level of resources per pupil can be constructed in a number of ways. It might be proportional: if a district wanted to double the resources it devoted to schooling, it would have to double its effort (example *A* of Figure 4-1). Alternatively, the returns to greater effort might vary over the schedule, being greater than proportional at low levels and less than proportional beyond a certain point. Such a schedule, depicted in example *B* in Figure 4-1, would discourage districts from devoting excessively small or large amounts of resources to educating their children. If it were thought desirable to have most districts devote roughly an equivalent amount of resources to each child's education, a discontinuity could be inserted in the schedule (example *C*).[28] Most districts would then select the level at which the discontinuity occurred, since greater effort would give a district only marginally higher expenditures for a big increase in taxes, while if a district were below the level of effort at which the discontinuity occurred, a slight increase in taxes would result in a major rise in the resources available for education.

Equalization schemes such as these have the advantage that they do not disturb the boundaries or powers of existing school districts. District lines need not be redrawn, nor is the ultimate power to determine the quality

28. This is one of the alternatives suggested in Benson, *Final Report*, Chap. 4.

Figure 4-1. **Examples of Alternative Capacity-Equalization Schedules for School Districts**

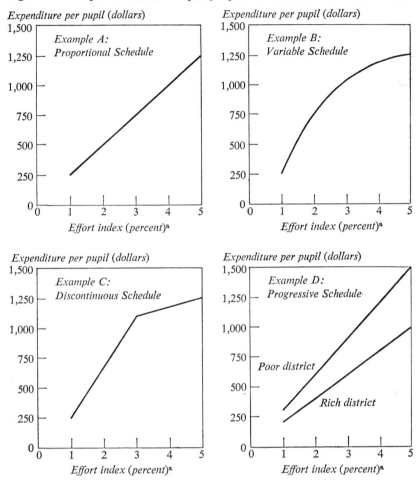

a. If the value of property per pupil is chosen as the measure of local fiscal capacity, the effective school property tax rate is the corresponding index of effort; if income per pupil is chosen as the measure of ability to pay, school tax revenues divided by income is the appropriate index of effort.

of education taken away from the local community. All the plans do is to equalize the tax prices various communities must pay to obtain an equivalent amount of resources per pupil.

A number of difficulties and problems, however, arise in the attempt to implement capacity equalizing programs. A major problem is the choice of appropriate measures of district fiscal capacity and effort by which the state would calculate the amount it either owed to or should receive from each community. Although most analysts have advocated the use of property values per pupil and effective property tax rates as indexes, there are reasons to believe that these measures would be biased because tax advantages and disadvantages may already be reflected, at least in part, in property values.[29] Personal income per pupil offers an alternative measure of school district wealth; the corresponding index of effort would be school tax collections as a fraction of personal income. Because of the low correlation between income and property values, the choice of the measure of district wealth will have a major impact on the relative gains of various districts. Some communities that would receive money from the state under one measure would pay into the state equalization fund under another.

Another problem that might arise with the implementation of a capacity equalization scheme is that entire wealthy districts may attempt to withdraw from the public school system or, if this is illegal, to operate their systems at minimal levels. This would occur if the state schedule relating tax efforts to permissible expenditure levels were far inferior to the existing relation in wealthy communities between local tax rates and the revenue per pupil generated by these rates. Consider, for example, the case of a rich district that with a 1 percent tax effort can raise $1,000 per pupil in local revenue, which it adds to the $500 it receives in state aid. If it were faced with a state schedule that required that a 10 percent effort be exerted to maintain a $1,500 expenditure level, the district would be forced to raise $10,000 per pupil from its local tax base to maintain its expenditure level. Of this amount, $8,500 would go into the state equalization fund. Rather than tax themselves at this rate just to maintain an unchanged quality of public schooling, the residents of this district may collectively decide it is cheaper to send their children to private schools where a $1,000 tuition payment gets them $1,000, rather than $150, worth of services. While the possibility that wealthy communities would withdraw from the public school system can be reduced by making the effort-benefit schedule for all districts similar to that now faced by the richest community, an immense drain on the state budget would result, because all districts would receive state supplements and none would pay into a surplus fund.[30] An alter-

29. After a number of years property values would, of course, adjust, but those living in high property wealth districts would face both significant capital losses and excessively high school tax payments during the transitional period.

30. The state's cost would be lowered if the range of disparities in the tax bases of school districts were reduced. Redrawing school district boundaries in such a way as to merge the few richest districts with their poorer surroundings is one way of accomplishing this; another approach is to remove commercial and industrial property from the local school tax base.

native solution would be to combine a capacity equalizing scheme with a universal flat grant provided by the state. If the grant were large—say, $700 per student—even rich districts would have an incentive to stay in the system, because the residents of such districts would have to pay the state taxes needed to support the basic grant program in any event, and they would give up $700 in benefits if they sent their children to private schools.

Incorporating adjustments for the varied educational needs and costs faced by different school districts is a third problem that would arise with the implementation of capacity equalization programs. One method for making such compensatory adjustments is to use a "weighted pupil" concept in determining each district's wealth or permissible expenditure level. For example, by the National Educational Finance Project's ratings presented in Table 4-2, a handicapped child in a city school system would count as 2.397 normal elementary school students, while a disadvantaged elementary school student in the central city would be worth 1.805 pupils. Although two districts might each have 1,000 enrolled students and an equivalent aggregate local tax base, if one had more high-cost students than the other it would have a higher "weighted pupil" enrollment, and would thus receive, at any level of effort, more money from the state than the other district. If states could develop cost indexes for various regions in the state, a similar adjustment could be made.

Another problem of capacity equalization schemes is that they may not fulfill the legal requirement that the correlation between local wealth and the quality of education be substantially reduced. It may be that richer communities, even when faced with the same effort-benefit schedules as other districts, will still be willing to spend a higher fraction of their resources on their children's schooling. A possible explanation is that those living in property-rich communities are themselves more highly educated and have developed a "taste" for education. Another possibility is that children from wealthy homes gain more earning power from an increment in the quality of their education than do others; the "payoff" for schooling would therefore be greater for these children. The correlation between wealth and the quality of education desired by a community may also continue because equalizing the tax prices people must pay for the service may not really equalize the burden of buying education. A 1 percent property tax rate in a property-poor community may be harder to bear than the same rate in a property-rich area. One percent of a poor man's income may be more burdensome than an equivalent fraction taken from a millionaire; this is, at least, the presumption behind the progressive income tax. If this is so, "capacity equalization" might still result in a positive relation between wealth and the quality of education received by children. One way of avoiding this would be to have a progressive set of capacity equalization schedules, in which the guaranteed return for any level of effort would be related inversely to the level of wealth of the district or its inhabitants. This is shown in Figure 4-1, example *D*, in which the poor community would be accorded a more generous effort-benefit schedule than the rich community.[31]

The level and shape of the effort-benefit schedule selected by the state and the response of school districts to the schedule would determine whether a capacity-equalizing scheme would cause the total amount of resources devoted to education to rise or fall. If the state guaranteed all districts the revenue raising ability of its richest community, the total amount spent on education would almost certainly rise, because every district but the richest would face a lower "tax price" for education than it does today, and in response all would choose to increase their expenditure levels. (Of course, residents of some districts might face much larger state tax bills to support the equalization fund; their incomes, and in turn their education spending, would consequently be reduced.) On the other hand, if the effort-benefit schedule chosen were inferior to that currently enjoyed by a substantial number of districts, the aggregate amount spent on schooling could fall. Wealthier districts would face a rise in their "tax prices" and as a result would cut back their levels of expenditures. The drop could more than offset the increased expenditure that would occur in the low wealth areas.

These relationships are illustrated in Figure 4-2. Line *R* shows the effort-benefit schedule for the richest district in a state under existing state-financing plans. It is assumed that the rich district receives $200 from the state and can add to the state allocation by taxing itself along line *R*. For example, the rich district might tax itself at 2 percent, raising $1,000 in local funds, for a total expenditure of $1,200 (point R_1). The poorest district's effort-benefit line, under existing plans, is shown by line *P*. It receives $300 from the state and, if it taxed itself at 3 percent, would be able to spend a total of $900 (point P_1). If the state were to adopt a capacity-equalizing financing program in which all school districts could choose to tax and spend along line *R*, the poorest school district would face a substantially more favorable price for education. If the poorest district responded to the new system by keeping its old tax rate of 3 percent, it would be allowed to spend $1,700 (point P_2). Alternatively, if it wanted

31. See Benson, *Final Report*, p. 84.

Figure 4-2. Capacity-Equalization Schedules for Expenditures Devoted to Education

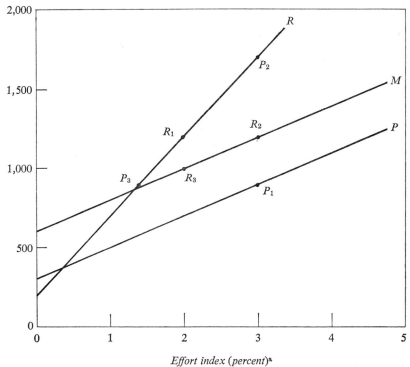

Expenditure per pupil (dollars)

*Effort index (percent)*ᵃ

Lines *R* and *P* represent the relation between effort and expenditure in the richest and poorest districts in the state, respectively; line *M* represents a hypothetical capacity-equalization plan that provides a state grant of $600 per pupil.

a. If the value of property per pupil is chosen as the measure of local fiscal capacity, the effective school property tax rate is the corresponding index of effort; if income per pupil is chosen as the measure of ability to pay, school tax revenues divided by income is the appropriate index of effort.

to continue to spend $900, it would be able to reduce its tax rate by more than half (point P_3). Most districts would choose some intermediate position, taxing themselves at a lower rate than before but spending more than under the existing system. On the other hand, if capacities to spend were equalized across all districts by a schedule such as line *M* in Figure 4-2, it is difficult to predict the outcome of capacity equalization on spending. Poor districts would probably raise their expenditures somewhat, for the reasons just stated, but the rich districts would now face less favorable opportunities. The district whose spending was previously governed by line *R* now finds that in order to maintain expenditures of $1,200 it must raise local tax rates by more than 50 percent (point R_2). Or it can maintain its previous tax rate and spend about $200 less per student (point R_3). It is most likely to respond by increasing its tax rate by an amount insufficient to prevent some expenditure reduction.

How large the expenditure disparities among communities would be if states undertook to equalize school district capacity by redrawing district boundaries or through a capacity-equalized grant system, it is impossible to say. Little is known either about the possible responses of school districts to changes in their educational "tax price" or about the determinants of expenditure levels other than district wealth.[32] To be sure, state grants that equalized fiscal capacity would probably cause poor districts to increase their expenditure levels while reducing their tax efforts, and cause the reverse to occur in wealthy areas. But how great the resulting changes in educational expenditure would be is open to conjecture. Similarly, even if school district boundaries were redrawn so as to make them all of equal fiscal capacity, expenditure disparities would persist because of differences in tastes.

Hybrid Solutions

The various approaches to reforming existing school finance systems are by no means mutually exclusive. Hybrid plans that blend components of the different approaches are not only possible but probable. For example, a state might reform its school financing system by enforcing a high minimum level of expenditure in each district financed by state revenues and at the same time instituting a program of capacity-equalized local supplementation. Limits could be placed on the permissible local supplementation, or else beyond a fixed expenditure level local districts might be set free to raise their revenues without the aid of the capacity-equalizing program. In short, the various programs can be combined in a great number of ways to produce school financing systems that offer varying degrees of equality and local autonomy or diversity.

The variety of proposals currently being considered in some states illustrates the wide range of approaches to the reduction of current school financing disparities and inequities. Some emphasize the role of the state. In New York, the Fleischmann Commission has recommended full state

---

32. The lone attempt to examine these issues at the school district level empirically is David S. Stern, "The Effects of Alternative State Aid Formulas on the Distribution of Public School Expenditures in Massachusetts" (Ph.D. thesis, Massachusetts Institute of Technology, 1972).

assumption of the responsibility for raising all educational revenues.[33] A statewide property tax would be used to raise most of the money now raised by local taxes, but future growth in the state's education budget would be financed out of the state income and sales tax receipts. After a transition period, the state funds would be distributed on the basis of enrollment. Although extra weight would be given to pupils who did poorly on state achievement tests, no differentiation would be made on the basis of grade levels.[34] Full state funding is also one of the alternatives suggested by the consultant staff to the California Senate Select Committee on School District Finance. Under its plan, basic resources would be distributed among school districts in accordance with "weighted pupil" enrollment. Both this proposal and that of the Fleischmann Commission envision that local school districts would retain all the prerogatives they now have, except the financial control.

Other school financing reform proposals have advocated a basic state-financed school system with a system of local supplementation. For example, Minnesota's Governor Wendell Anderson, the ACIR, and the President's Commission on School Finance all advocate that states assume the main part of the responsibility of raising school revenues.[35] All, however, would allow local districts to supplement from local revenues the amount provided by the state, as long as the "add on" did not exceed 10 percent of the basic state grant. The Minnesota proposal would require that local districts that supplemented the state grant raise $2 for every $1 they wanted to spend: to spend at a level 10 percent higher than the basic grant, the community would have to raise an amount equivalent to 20 percent of the states' allotment. Turning over to the state 50 percent of the amount raised locally is likely to reduce the desire of the districts to supplement the state grant.

Capacity-equalizing grant programs have been the heart of several proposals. New Jersey Governor Cahill's reform suggestions called for a basic state grant for each school district. The size of the grant per pupil would be

---

33. *Report of the New York State Commission on the Quality, Cost and Financing of Elementary and Secondary Education* (The Commission, 1972), Vol. 1, Chap. 2.

34. Both the Fleischmann Commission and the consultants to the California Senate Select Committee reached the conclusion, in the words of the California group, "there is no real educational justification" for allocating "more money to students at higher grade levels." Benson, *Final Report*, p. 75.

35. See Advisory Commission on Intergovernmental Relations, *Who Should Pay for Public Schools?* (1971), pp. 1, 20–23; President's Commission on School Finance, *Schools People, & Money: The Need for Educational Reform*, Final Report (1972), pp. xii, xiii.

sufficient to provide an adequate education for each child and would be adjusted to reflect regional differences in wage scales and costs of living.[36] But districts that desired to spend more on education than the basic state allotment would be free to raise additional revenue from their local tax base. A capacity-equalizing state grant would allow low wealth jurisdictions to face the same "tax prices" as richer areas if they chose to supplement the basic state support level. This equalization scheme, however, would cease to apply to expenditure levels per pupil in excess of 133 percent of the basic state grant. According to this plan the revenue to pay for the increased educational role of the state would come from a statewide property tax and a new income tax.

A capacity-equalizing scheme combined with a basic grant of $500 per pupil was also suggested for California by the consultant committee to the California Senate Select Committee. Unlike the New Jersey proposal, however, the plan put no upper limit on the effort a district could exert and still take advantage of the plan.

A great number of the plans being considered at the state level represent modification of existing systems. In California, the Greene bill and a proposal put forward by the California State Board of Education would use the revenues from a new state property tax to raise the basic level of state school support but would leave local districts free to use their own property tax bases to raise as much supplementary money as they wanted.[37] In New York, the Regents proposed raising the operating ceiling of the state percentage equalization program from $860 per pupil to $1,037 and giving extra weight in the state aid formula to handicapped children, those in vocational programs, and those scoring below the minimum competency level on the state evaluation tests.[38] They also suggested that limits be placed on the future rate of increase in expenditure per pupil; high spending districts could raise expenditures by no more than 6 percent a year while low spending ones could raise their outlays by as much as 15 percent.

The Watson amendment, which was defeated by the voters of California in 1972, would have altered the existing school financing system by removing the school district from the revenue raising picture entirely. Rather

36. See William T. Cahill, "A Master Plan for Tax Reform" (address to the New Jersey Legislature, May 18, 1972; processed), pp. 37–44.

37. Levin, *Paying for Public Schools*, pp. 33–34, provides a good description of the strengths and weaknesses of the proposals being considered in California.

38. University of the State of New York, State Education Department, "Financing Public Elementary and Secondary Education, 1973–74: Regents Legislative Proposal, FY 1973–74" (SED, November 1972; processed).

than shifting financial responsibility to the state, the county would have become responsible for financing the local contribution to education. In a number of other states there are also proposals that would make larger units of local government than school districts bear the local burden for raising local educational revenues; administrative matters, however, would remain the province of the existing districts.

States, of course, are considering many other proposals for school financing. This account should be sufficient, however, to bring out the variety of ideas voters and legislators are likely to be facing in the next few years. The basic questions that will have to be answered in designing a more equitable school finance system are: How high should the basic state educational program be set? Will the differing educational needs and costs of various districts be taken into account? Should local districts be allowed to supplement the basic state program, and if so by how much? If local districts are allowed to supplement the state program, will the state make adjustments for the varying abilities of school districts to raise the supplemental revenues? Finally, what kinds of taxes should states use for their increased share, and how should the districts' ability to pay be measured?

Whatever method is chosen to reduce the disparities and inequities of the existing systems of school financing, it is likely to have at least three important effects on American society. In the first place, the residential patterns in metropolitan areas may be significantly affected. If, as most persons feel, decisions about residential location are strongly influenced by the quality of schooling available in various areas, equalizing the quality of education will make central cities and other areas with poor schools more attractive places to live and the exclusive suburbs relatively less desirable. Second, public schools that now provide a heterogeneous mix of youth services are likely to change rather profoundly, at least in wealthy areas. In order to circumvent any loss of their relative educational superiority, such school districts are likely to withdraw support from as many ancillary services now provided by schools as they can. High school athletic teams may become clubs sponsored by local civic organizations, the school library may be merged with the town facility, and community French and science clubs may spring up. Such cooperative efforts would allow the school district to spend all the basic state grant or all the revenues raised from the equalized tax base on instructional items. Finally, efforts to equalize educational quality among districts will quite probably lead to major shifts in nonpublic school enrollments. Some families residing in districts that now have superior public schools may become dissatisfied either because of a loss in their children's relative educational advantage or because of the local taxes they would have to pay under a capacity-equalizing scheme to maintain this advantage. Their major alternative would be to enroll their children in nonpublic schools, and to move into communities with lower local taxes. On the other hand, parents of nonpublic school children who reside in communities with inferior public schools may respond in the opposite way: if they notice an improvement in the quality of their local public schools, they may take their children out of the nonpublic institutions. Such shifts would have important repercussions on the nonpublic sector, whose fiscal problems are the subject of the next chapter.

chapter five **Public Aid and Nonpublic
Schools**

From 1965 to 1971 nonpublic school enrollment de-
clined by 1.6 million students, or by more than one-fifth. Nonpublic school
teachers and administrators, parents affected by school closings, and taxpayers worried about the added burdens placed on public schools have all
expressed concern over the continuation of this decline. At both the state
and federal levels, politicians have responded with promises of new programs to aid nonpublic schools. Yet at present there is little understanding
either of what is causing the enrollment decline or what public policy can
do about it. There is considerable controversy over the extent to which government resources should be used to bolster the nation's nonpublic schools,
especially at a time when many feel that public education is in the throes of
a fiscal crisis.

This chapter attempts to clarify the issues surrounding public aid to nonpublic schools. It considers first the enrollment and financial situation of
the nonpublic sector and then the general factors that have affected the
availability of and demand for nonpublic education in recent years. Next
it surveys the arguments for and against public aid to nonpublic schools,
the evidence that supports them, and the legal constraints on public aid.
The final section of the chapter deals with possible solutions to problems
facing nonpublic schools.

The Nature of the Problem

Some 5 million students, or 10 percent of the nation's school children, are
enrolled in nonpublic schools. Such aggregate statistics, however, are mis-
leading, for they mask the relative importance of nonpublic schools in

95

some areas of the country. Nonpublic school enrollment is highly concentrated; in six states, more than one child in six attends nonpublic schools, while in six others the figure is less than one in twenty-five (Table 5-1). The industrial states, especially those in the northeast, tend to have high non-

Table 5-1. Nonpublic School Enrollment as Percentage of Total Enrollment, Selected State and Local Governments, 1970–71 School Year

State or local government	Percentage of total school enrollment in nonpublic schools
States with a high fraction of students in nonpublic schools	
Rhode Island	19.3
Pennsylvania	19.2
New York	18.8
New Jersey	18.3
Wisconsin	18.2
Illinois	16.9
Massachusetts	16.3
States with a low fraction of students in nonpublic schools	
Alabama	4.0
Georgia	3.1
Alaska	2.8
Arkansas	2.7
Oklahoma	2.5
North Carolina	2.4
Utah	2.0
Cities with a high fraction of students in nonpublic schools	
Albany, New York	47.2
Philadelphia, Pennsylvania	35.5
Pittsburgh, Pennsylvania	34.9
St. Paul, Minnesota	32.7
Buffalo, New York	29.4
Boston, Massachusetts	28.1
New York, New York	25.9
New Orleans, Louisiana	25.2
Chicago, Illinois	25.2
Milwaukee, Wisconsin	23.8
San Francisco, California	22.3
Cincinnati, Ohio	21.8
Cleveland, Ohio	17.8
Southern counties with a high fraction of students in nonpublic schools	
Noxubee County, Mississippi	21.8
Yazoo County, Mississippi	17.9
Sunflower County, Mississippi	16.8

Source: U.S. Bureau of the Census, *Census of Population, 1970, General Social and Economic Characteristics,* Final Report PC(1)-C, volumes for the respective states.

Table 5-2. Distribution of Public and Nonpublic School Enrollment, by Location, Fall 1970

Percent

Location	Public school enrollment	Total nonpublic school enrollment	Catholic school enrollment	Nonpublic enrollment as a percentage of total school enrollment
Central city	24.5	39.2	52.6	16.4
Suburbs	36.6	40.2	29.7	11.9
Small town and rural	38.9	20.6	17.7	6.1
All schools	100.0	100.0	100.0	10.9

Sources: Public and nonpublic enrollment from Bureau of the Census, *Current Population Reports*, Series P-20, No. 222, "School Enrollment: October 1970" (1971), Table 4, p. 20; Catholic data from National Catholic Educational Association, Research Department, *A Report on U.S. Catholic Schools, 1970–71* (Washington: NCEA, 1971), pp. 8–11.

public school enrollments, while the southern and mountain states generally have the fewest nonpublic school students in relation to their total enrollments.

In most states nonpublic school enrollment is disproportionately concentrated in large cities. This is particularly true of Catholic schools, as Table 5-2 shows. In many large urban centers, more than a quarter of the children attend nonpublic schools; in Albany, New York, the figure is close to one-half. In a few southern communities, where "white academies" have been established to circumvent the integration of public schools, private institutions also educate a substantial fraction of the school children.

The geographic distribution of nonpublic school enrollments is largely a reflection of the distribution of Catholics in the nation, because more than four-fifths of all nonpublic school enrollment is accounted for by Catholic institutions (Table 5-3). Although the Lutheran, Jewish, Seventh-Day Adventists, and a host of other religious denominations also operate schools, their efforts, in comparison with the Catholics', appear minor; none accounts for more than 4 percent of the total nonpublic enrollment. The diverse institutions without religious affiliation account for only 7 percent of all nonpublic school enrollment. In effect, this means that the view that public aid to nonpublic schools is really aid to religious, and especially to Catholic, schools is not far from the truth. Such aid is also concentrated in a limited group of states and localities.

Table 5-3. Distribution of Enrollment in Nonpublic Schools, by Church Relationship, 1970–71 School Year

Percent

Church relation and denomination	Percentage of total nonpublic school enrollment
Affiliated	93.0
Catholic	83.0
Lutheran	3.9
Seventh-Day Adventist	1.0
Jewish	1.3
Episcopal	1.0
Christian (National Union)	0.9
Baptist	0.5
Friends	0.2
Methodist	0.1
Presbyterian	0.1
Other	1.0
Nonaffiliated	7.0

Source: President's Panel on Nonpublic Education, *Nonpublic Education and the Public Good*, Final Report to the President's Commission on School Finance (1972), p. 7.

Table 5-4. Enrollment in Nonpublic Elementary and Secondary Schools, Fall 1960–71

Thousands

Year	Total enrollment in nonpublic schools	Enrollment in Catholic schools	Enrollment in other nonpublic schools	Nonpublic as percent of total school enrollment
1960	5,969	5,254	715	14.0
1961	6,011	5,370	641	13.7
1962	6,003	5,494	509	13.5
1963	6,397	5,591	806	13.9
1964	6,732	5,601	1,131	14.3
1965	6,953	5,574	1,379	14.3
1966	6,671	...	...	13.5
1967	6,489	5,198	1,291	12.8
1968	6,145	4,941	1,204	12.0
1969	5,711	4,658	1,053	11.1
1970	5,655	4,367	1,288	10.9
1971	5,378	4,027	1,351	10.4

Sources: Total nonpublic enrollment from U.S. Bureau of the Census, *Current Population Reports*, Series P-20, No. 234, "School Enrollment in the United States: 1971" (1972), p. 3, and preceding issues for 1960–64; Catholic data from National Catholic Educational Association, *A Statistical Report on Catholic Elementary and Secondary Schools for the Years 1967–68 to 1969–70* (NCEA, 1970), pp. 5, 8; NCEA, *Report on U.S. Catholic Schools, 1970–71*, p. 10; and, for 1971, NCEA, "Data Bank Bulletin No. 36," September 27, 1972.

Table 5-5. Percentage Change in Nonpublic School Enrollment, by Region and Church Affiliation, 1961–62 to 1970–71

Region	Catholic	Other religiously affiliated	Nonaffiliated
North Atlantic	−14.5	44.0	28.7
Great Lakes and Plains	−21.8	26.4	110.7
Southeast	−5.6	167.7	242.4
West and Southwest	−18.0	39.6	80.5
U.S. total	−17.0	48.9	92.9

Source: U.S. Department of Health, Education, and Welfare, National Center for Educational Statistics, *NCES Bulletin*, No. 12 (June 7, 1972), pp. 2, 4.

Falling Enrollments

Since 1965 nonpublic enrollment has been steadily declining. The decline is accounted for almost entirely by a drop in Catholic school enrollments (Table 5-4), which had expanded even more rapidly than public schools during the 1950s and early 1960s. Since 1964, however, the number of children attending Catholic institutions has fallen by roughly 200,000, or more than 4 percent, a year. Most of the decline has taken place in the elementary schools, whose enrollments are down more than one-fourth from their peak of 4.5 million; at the same time secondary enrollment dropped by 15 percent.

The drop in Catholic school enrollments has been accompanied by school closings. In the four years 1967–71 there was an average decline of 343 elementary and 107 secondary schools annually. For the most part, Catholic school closings have been concentrated in suburban and rural areas. While 11 percent of all Catholic schools shut down between 1967 and 1970, only 8 percent of the central city schools closed.[1]

In nonpublic schools other than Catholic ones, however, aggregate enrollment has gradually increased in recent years. In every region of the country there has been a significant rise in the last decade in the number of pupils attending nonaffiliated schools and institutions associated with non-Catholic religious denominations (Table 5-5). This is not to say that all categories of non-Catholic nonpublic schools have experienced enrollment increases. Boarding schools, military academies, Lutheran elementary

1. In rural areas, many school closings have resulted from the consolidation of smaller schools and do not therefore necessarily imply enrollment decreases. National Catholic Educational Association, Research Department, *A Report on U.S. Catholic Schools, 1970–71* (Washington: NCEA, 1971), pp. 8–9.

schools, and Mennonite institutions, to name a few, have recently been faced with shrinking student bodies.[2]

While there are no data to show exactly where the growth in non-Catholic nonpublic school enrollment has occurred, it is possible that much of it has taken place in the nation's largest cities. In such places as New York City, where many residents feel that the public schools have deteriorated, non-Catholic private school enrollment has grown at a fairly rapid pace,[3] as it has in some parts of the South with the appearance of segregated "white academies." Although a sizable fraction of the children attend white academies in some southern rural counties (see Table 5-1), the overall significance of these institutions should not be overestimated. In Mississippi, the 15,000 to 20,000 students that are estimated to have left the public systems in the last three years to attend private academies represent only 3 percent of the state's total school population.[4]

In summary, the reduced enrollment in the nonpublic sector has been concentrated in a few categories, the Catholic schools accounting for most of the decline. On balance, other religious schools' enrollments have grown, and nonsectarian institutions have grown very rapidly.

The Causes of the Enrollment Decline

Although falling enrollments have not been confined exclusively to the Catholic schools, most of the problem lies with them. An explanation of the causes of the decline of enrollment in Catholic schools will thus explain the shrinkage of the nonpublic sector as a whole. This is true not only

2. Al H. Senske, "Lutheran Elementary School Statistics, 1971–1972," Board of Parish Education, Lutheran Church–Missouri Synod (St. Louis: The Board, 1972; processed); National Association of Independent Schools, *NAIS Report*, No. 39 (January 1972), p. 2; for a breakdown of the changes in nonpublic school enrollment in New York by institutional affiliation, see Louis R. Gary and associates, "The Collapse of Nonpublic Education: Rumor or Reality?" The Report on Nonpublic Education in the State of New York for the New York State Commission on the Quality, Cost and Financing of Elementary and Secondary Education (The Commission, 1971; processed), Vol. 1, Table I-2, p. I-6.

3. See New York Department of City Planning, "Three Out of Ten: The Nonpublic Schools of New York City" (Department of City Planning, City of New York, March 1972; processed), p. 18.

4. Southeastern Public Education Project, American Friends Service Committee, "Survey of Private Schools Started in Mississippi Since the Passage of the 1964 Civil Rights Act," in *Equal Educational Opportunity: Part 3A—Desegregation Under Law*, Hearings before the Senate Select Committee on Equal Educational Opportunity, 91 Cong. 2 sess. (1970), pp. 1196–98.

because the rest of the nonpublic school sector is expanding but also because most types of non-Catholic nonpublic institutions that are declining are being affected by many of the factors that influence Catholic school enrollments.

COST INCREASES. It is no easy task to sort out the various forces influencing Catholic school enrollments; rising costs, changing tastes, and demographic factors have all played their part. The force that has received by far the most attention is rising costs. In the 1967–68 to 1970–71 period costs per pupil in Catholic elementary schools rose by two-thirds, while secondary school costs went up by 58 percent (Table 5-6). By way of contrast, public school expenditures per pupil increased by "only" 31 percent during the same three-year period.

Three factors are usually cited as the major causes of the rapid growth in Catholic school costs: the steady shift from religious to lay teachers, the rise in faculty salaries, and the decline in pupil-teacher ratios. The shift to lay teachers has been forced on the schools by a fall in the number of nuns and brothers in teaching orders and by the broadening of the missions of the teaching orders to include social welfare activities. In the 1967–70 pe-

Table 5-6. Comparison of Costs per Pupil, Teachers' Salaries, and Pupil-Teacher Ratios, Catholic and Public Schools, 1967–68 and 1970–71 School Years

Money amounts in dollars

Item	1967–68	1970–71	Percent change, 1967–68 to 1970–71
Per-pupil cost			
Catholic elementary	145	241	66.2
Catholic secondary	335	529	57.9
Public elementary and secondary	621	812	30.8
Average teacher salary			
Catholic elementary (lay)	4,246	5,575	31.3
Catholic secondary (lay)	6,034	8,047	33.4
Catholic elementary and secondary (religious)	1,285	1,995	55.3
Public elementary	7,280	9,021	23.9
Public secondary	7,692	9,568	24.4
Pupil-teacher ratios			
Catholic elementary	33.4	28.0	−16.2
Catholic secondary	20.0	18.5	−7.5
Public elementary	26.2	24.8	−5.3
Public secondary	19.5	18.9	−3.1

Sources: Catholic data from National Catholic Educational Association, *A Statistical Report on Catholic Elementary and Secondary Schools for the Years 1967–68 to 1969–70*, pp. 14, 19, and NCEA, *Report on U.S. Catholic Schools, 1970–71*, pp. 9, 16, 24, 31; public school data from National Education Association, Research Division, *Estimates of School Statistics, 1971–72* (NEA, 1971), pp. 5, 9, 10, 13, 16, 21.

Table 5-7. Increase in Costs per Pupil of Catholic Elementary and Public Elementary and Secondary Schools, by Source, 1967–68 to 1970–71 School Years

Cause of increase	Amount of increase (dollars per pupil)		Increase as percentage of total		Increase as percentage of cost per pupil, 1967	
	Catholic schools	Public schools	Catholic schools	Public schools	Catholic schools	Public schools
Higher proportion of lay teachers	12.66	...	13.2	...	8.7	...
Rise in faculty salaries	34.35	75.28	35.8	39.4	23.7	12.1
Lower pupil-teacher ratios	17.18	16.72	17.9	8.8	11.8	2.7
Rise in prices, and provision of more materials and services	31.81	99.00	33.1	51.8	21.9	15.9
Total	96.00	191.00	100.0	100.0	66.2	30.8

Sources: Developed from data and sources in Table 5-6, from price increase data in U.S. Bureau of the Census, *Statistical Abstract of the United States, 1971* (1971), p. 339, and from public school data in U.S. Office of Education, *Projections of Educational Statistics to 1979–80*, 1970 Edition (1971). Figures are rounded and may not add to totals.

riod alone, the percentage of lay teachers in the elementary schools rose from forty-one to fifty-three, and in the secondary schools from thirty-eight to forty-eight. As Table 5-7 shows, however, the changing mix of teachers accounts for less than one-seventh of the increase in elementary school costs.

The rapid rise in salaries appears to have been the principal source of rising costs. Salaries of both lay and religious teachers in Catholic schools have increased even more rapidly than those of public school teachers. No doubt the same factors that are responsible for the escalation of public school teachers' wages have been at work in the parochial school sector as well. For example, in some areas Catholic school administrators have been faced with union problems and strikes. In New York and San Francisco, where lay teachers are now represented by unions affiliated with the AFL-CIO, as well as in other archdioceses, teachers have struck for higher salaries and better working conditions. Lay teachers have also fought to have their salary schedule related to that of the local public school system; in many cases they have succeeded in obtaining 90 percent parity or more. Although some Catholic school systems have attempted to mitigate the tremendous cost of such agreements, by hiring teachers with less experience and fewer academic credentials, the average salary paid has risen dramatically.

Falling pupil-teacher ratios, the third factor, have accounted for slightly less than a fifth of the recent cost increase. In part, the drop in the ratios was involuntary, occurring when schools, unable to fill their classrooms, were forced to operate at less than capacity. In part, however, it reflected a desire of school administrators to reduce class size or the workload on teachers. Despite the recent reduction, pupil-teacher ratios in Catholic elementary schools still exceed those in the public sector.

Taken together, the three factors—all of which contribute to the per-pupil cost of instructional personnel—are responsible for two-thirds of the total increase in cost in Catholic elementary schools. The balance of the increase was the result of rising prices and the provision of additional materials and services. As in the public sector, parochial school expenditures are being pushed up both by inflation and because more textbooks and school supplies are being provided for each student.

INCREASED CHARGES. Unless they are covered by increased church subsidies, gifts, or government assistance, rising costs necessitate higher tuitions and fees, which in turn act to reduce the number of parents able and willing to send their children to parochial schools. In recent years the tuitions and fees charged by such institutions have increased even more rapidly than school expenditures (Table 5-8). The rapid escalation of tuition

Table 5-8. Income per Pupil, 1970–71 School Year, Catholic Elementary and Secondary Schools, by Source, and Change from 1967–68 School Year
Money amounts in dollars

Source of income	Amount of income, 1970–71	Percent of total	Percent change, 1967–68 to 1970–71
Elementary			
Tuition	58	24.1	81.2
Fees	12	5.0	33.3
Parish subsidy	129	53.5	48.3
Diocesan subsidy	3	1.2	50.0
Other	39	16.2	160.0
Total	241	100.0	66.2
Secondary			
Tuition	314	59.4	72.5
Fees	40	7.6	90.5
Parish subsidy	50	9.5	11.1
Diocesan subsidy	34	6.4	54.5
Other	91	17.2	40.0
Total	529	100.0	57.9

Sources: National Catholic Educational Association, *A Statistical Report on Catholic Elementary and Secondary Schools for the Years 1967–68 to 1969–70*, pp. 20, 79, 80; and NCEA, *Report on U.S. Catholic Schools, 1970–71*, pp. 10, 24. Figures are rounded and may not add to totals.

has in part been forced on Catholic schools by the slow growth of parish income, the source of more than half the revenue of the elementary schools.[5]

Although the percentage rate of growth in tuition and fees has been rapid, the absolute rise has been moderate, and hence charges at Catholic schools remain extremely low. During the 1967–68 to 1970–71 period, average tuition and fees in Catholic elementary schools rose by only $28 per pupil reaching a level of $70 in 1970–71. Even if all the contributions made by the parish to its elementary school are derived from parents of Catholic school children, the total family payment per child was under $200 in 1970–71 and had risen only $71 in the three preceding years. Compared to the growth in the average family's income during the same period, the increase in the cost of Catholic elementary schools was very small.

Secondary school tuitions and fees are considerably higher than those levied on elementary school pupils because the institutions are generally run by the diocese and thus do not benefit from large parish subsidies. Although secondary school charges rose by some $150 during the 1967–68 to 1970–71 period, at around $350 they remain far below the fees charged by most other nonpublic secondary schools.

For the increases in tuitions and fees to have affected enrollment enough to have created a "cost crisis," the demand for Catholic education would have had to be highly responsive to changes in student charges. A number of analyses of the situation in various localities have suggested that this is not the case. After noting that enrollment declines were proportionally greatest in suburban areas where tuitions were the lowest and family incomes the highest, the Fleischmann Commission Report concluded that in New York "there is no evidence . . . that tuition increases have significantly affected enrollment."[6] A similar judgment was made by the Gurash Committee in Philadelphia, which pointed out, "There is no evidence of a strong relationship between changes in tuitions (or student fees as proxy tuitions) and declines in enrollment. To the contrary, evidence to date, and at the levels of tuitions now charged, seems to indicate that the demand for Catholic school education is insensitive to current tuition lev-

5. See John T. Gurash (chairman), *The Report of the Archdiocesan Advisory Committee on the Financial Crisis of Catholic Schools in Philadelphia and Surrounding Counties* (Philadelphia: The Committee, 1972), pp. xvii and 14 (hereafter referred to as the Gurash Committee Report); and *Report of the New York State Commission on the Quality, Cost and Financing of Elementary and Secondary Education* (The Commission, 1972), Vol. 1, p. 5.35 (hereafter referred to as the Fleischmann Commission Report).

6. Fleischmann Commission Report, p. 5.23.

els."[7] However, after reviewing the evidence from a number of similar investigations, a study for the President's Commission concluded that the price elasticity for demand for Catholic elementary education lay somewhere in the range of -0.05 to -0.15;[8] that is, for every 10 percent tuition rise, enrollments would fall by between 0.5 percent and 1.5 percent. In view of the tremendous percentage increases in tuitions and fees that occurred over the past few years (Table 5-8), these figures imply that between one-fifth and one-half of the fall in elementary school enrollments during the 1967–68 to 1970–71 period could be attributed to price increases; one-third is probably a realistic figure. In other words, rises in tuition and fees have caused about 85,000 elementary students a year to transfer to the public school system.

Enrollment decreases have secondary repercussions. As children drop out of Catholic schools, either because tuitions are rising or for other reasons, some schools are forced to close. When nearby parochial schools are not available, such closings may force into public schools some children who would otherwise have stayed in the system. The magnitude of such involuntary enrollment reductions is hard to estimate with precision. Between 1967 and 1970, there was a net drop of 984 Catholic elementary schools and 291 secondary schools which had previously enrolled, respectively, 197,000 and 70,000 students.[9] Not all these losses, however, can be attributed to cost-related school closings. In the first place, some of the closings represented school consolidations, which did not produce net reductions in the number of places available.[10] Second, another group of schools that closed charged no tuition at all; tuition cannot have been the cause of their demise.[11] Third, some of the students attending schools that

7. Gurash Committee Report, p. xx.
8. Kenneth M. Brown, "Enrollment in Nonpublic Schools," in Frank J. Fahey (director), *Economic Problems of Nonpublic Schools*, Submitted to the President's Commission on School Finance by the Office for Educational Research, University of Notre Dame (The Commission, 1972), p. 178.
9. Brown, "Enrollment in Nonpublic Schools," pp. 164–65.
10. National Catholic Educational Association, *Report on U.S. Catholic Schools, 1970–71*, pp. 5–7. For example, although the number of parish elementary schools declined from 9,817 to 8,676, the number of interparochial and diocesan elementary schools rose from 169 to 358. In Buffalo, New York, when ten poorly attended schools were closed, the diocese made sure that all the children would be accommodated in other institutions in the diocese. George R. La Noue, "Parochial Schools and Public Policy," in Gary and associates, "Collapse of Nonpublic Education," Vol. 2, p. 2.
11. In New York, for example, thirty of the seventy-six elementary schools that shut their doors charged no tuition. See La Noue, "Parochial Schools and Public Policy," Vol. 2, pp. 2–4.

closed would have left anyway, just as they left schools that remained open. When adjustments are made for this fact and for consolidations and closings clearly unrelated to tuition increases, it is likely that some 45,000 to 60,000 students were forced out of the system by school closings attributable to rising costs in the period from 1967–68 to 1970–71. These figures represent 6 to 8 percent of the decline in Catholic elementary school enrollments. In total, therefore, the direct effects of tuition increases and the enrollment reductions of associated school closings probably accounted for about 40 percent of the total decline in elementary enrollment in recent years.

Comparable figures for the secondary schools are harder to estimate, and are much less important, since only 10 percent of the drop in Catholic school enrollment occurred in secondary schools. The data, however, suggest that the percentage attributable to increased student charges is much higher, probably around two-thirds of the total.[12] When this decline is added to that in Catholic elementary schools, probably no more than 45 percent of the fall in Catholic school enrollment can be said to be related to higher tuitions and fees.

DEMOGRAPHIC AND PREFERENCE CHANGES. In addition to rising tuition and fees, several other factors have contributed to declining enrollments in Catholic schools. The prime cause has been the declining preference of Catholics for parochial education. For a number of reasons, the public schools have become an attractive alternative for ever-growing numbers of Catholic parents. Catholic schools were originally established in this country in the late nineteenth century because of the strong Protestant bias in the public schools. Because the bias has become much weaker, Catholic parents are much less apprehensive about sending their children to public schools. Moreover, as the incomes of Catholics have caught up with those of the rest of the nation, parents have become more and more conscious of the quality of their schools; they are no longer satisfied with the large classes, the high fraction of teachers without advanced training, and the lack of physical facilities and special activities necessitated by the very tight budgets of many Catholic schools.

The Second Vatican Council, which created a more liberal atmosphere within the church, has tended to reinforce the trends. The council empha-

12. Increases in tuitions and fees of Catholic secondary schools account for about a 5 percent decline in enrollment, or one-half of the total. Although estimating the impact of school closings is difficult because the attendance zones of secondary schools are not as clearly defined as those of parish elementary institutions, a 1 or 2 percent decline in enrollments can probably be attributed to school closings.

sized that parents are principally responsible for the religious education of their children. As Catholics have become better educated, and hence better equipped to assume the responsibility, they have found it less necessary to turn to church schools. Younger parents, who are likely to be more attuned to new church teachings, and better educated parents, enroll their children in Cathlic schools at a lower rate than do older and less educated parents.[13] Some parish priests have encouraged this shift away from parochial schools as a means of revitalizing the parish community. Conscious of the emphasis the Second Vatican Council placed on lay participation, they have reasoned that the parish should place less emphasis on its role as a supplier of educational services and more on involving the adult community in church activities.[14] To some extent, the changes in attitudes of Catholic parents merely reflect the diminishing role of formal religion among all Americans. Church attendance has fallen off considerably in the last decade; if fewer American parents are actively involved in organized religion, it is likely that they also consider it less important for their children to have a church-related education.[15]

Demographic factors are another important reason for declining Catholic school enrollments. As more and more Catholics have reached middle and upper income levels they, like their non-Catholic counterparts, have moved to the suburbs. Such suburbanization has depopulated a number of inner city parishes, forcing them to close their schools for lack of children. The choice facing the Catholic parent who has reached the suburbs is no longer one between a strife-torn, deteriorating public institution and a nearby parochial school but between a good neighborhood public school that offers much in the way of sports programs, extracurricular activities, and attractive physical facilities, and a possibly distant Catholic school with few such "frills." A number of studies have shown that suburban Catholics consider the public schools to be academically superior to Catholic schools, particularly at the elementary level.[16] In fact, over the last few years the

13. Dennis J. Dugan, "The Determinants of Enrollment in Catholic Schools: An Empirical Analysis of the Archdiocese of St. Louis," in Fahey, *Economic Problems of Nonpublic Schools*, pp. 388–445.

14. For a discussion of this, see George Elford, "School Crisis — or Parish Crisis?" *Commonweal*, Vol. 93 (January 29, 1971), pp. 418–20.

15. Between 1964 and 1971, the percentage of adults attending church on an average Sunday fell from 45 to 40. In this period Catholic church attendance has fallen from 71 to 57 percent. See *The Gallup Opinion Index*, Report 79 (Princeton, N.J.: GOI, January 1972), p. 24.

16. See Frank J. Fahey and Richard G. Kiekbusch, "Attitudes Toward Nonpublic Education," in Fahey, *Economic Problems of Nonpublic Schools*, pp. 1–154.

Table 5-9. Estimates of Catholic Elementary School Age Population and Enrollment
Rates, Selected Years, 1955–77

Year	Catholic school-age population (thousands)	Enrollment rate
1955	6,688	0.530
1957	7,258	0.531
1959	8,008	0.535
1961	8,713	0.511
1963	9,385	0.486
1965	10,121	0.444
1966	10,250	0.426
1967	10,378	0.396
1968	10,539	0.366
1969	10,656	0.338
1970	10,720	0.313
1971	10,720	0.287
1972	10,603	...
1973	10,397	...
1975	9,741	...
1977	9,254	...

Sources: Kenneth M. Brown, "Enrollment in Nonpublic Schools," in Frank J. Fahey (director), *Economic Problems of Nonpublic Schools*, Submitted to the President's Commission on School Finance by the Office for Educational Research, University of Notre Dame (The Commission, 1972), p. 160, except 1971 enrollment rate, which is estimated from P. J. Kenedy and Sons, *The Official Catholic Directory, 1971* (Kenedy, 1971), and 1977 population, which is estimated by authors.

fraction of suburban Catholic children enrolled in parochial schools of the St. Louis area has declined by about 15 percent, while in the central city the fraction of Catholic children attending Catholic schools has actually risen by 8 percent.[17] Thus, while rising incomes enable more parents to afford nonpublic schooling, increased incomes also allow families to move to areas where the parochial schools may be less accessible and the public schools with which they must compete are of high quality. This probably explains why a higher fraction of suburban than of central city parochial schools have closed their doors in recent years.

Increases in tuitions and fees, changes in parents' preferences, and demographic factors have all contributed to a decline in the rate at which Catholics send their children to parochial schools. As Table 5-9 indicates, this decline is not a new phenomenon but a trend that is more than a decade old. As long as the number of school age Catholic children expanded rapidly, Catholic school enrollments were shielded from its full impact.

17. Brown, "Enrollment in Nonpublic Schools," p. 172.

But since the mid-1960s there has been a marked slowdown and then halt in the growth of the potential Catholic school population. This change and the decline that will occur over the 1971 to 1977 period is the result of a recent drop in Catholic birth rates which was even greater than those experienced by other religious groups.[18]

Although the sources of reduced enrollment in the Catholic schools are in some respects unique, there is evidence that the Lutheran, Mennonite, and other nonpublic schools that have suffered recent enrollment declines have been affected by similar basic forces. In Illinois, many of the Lutheran elementary schools located in ethnic neighborhoods of the central cities have closed their doors, because their clientele has moved to the suburbs where the children now attend public schools.[19] In other instances rural communities with strong parochial school traditions have had to discontinue their schools because the general rural to urban population shift has depopulated the community. Disenchantment with the established churches, decreasing numbers of infant baptisms, and increased competition from the public schools have also acted to reduce their enrollments. Pressure to increase teachers' salaries, which are extremely low in some Protestant denominational schools, has also been an important factor pushing up tuition and reducing enrollments. Changes in parental and student preferences are probably a major factor in the reduction of the student bodies of military academies and single sex boarding institutions.

The Future

Barring any radical changes in parental preferences or government policy, the nonpublic school sector is likely to continue to contract over the next decade. One obvious reason is that there will be a shrinking pool of children for both nonpublic and public schools to educate. The decline will be particularly precipitous among the potential clientele of the Catholic elementary schools, and this factor alone could cause enrollments in these institutions to drop by 15 percent or one-half million students by 1977, even if the current decline in the rate at which Catholic parents send their children to parochial schools is halted. The shrinking pool of school age chil-

18. See Jack Rosenthal, "Study Shows Catholics Having Smaller Families," *New York Times*, May 30, 1972, pp. 1, 5. (The study referred to is the 1970 national fertility study submitted to the Commission on Population Growth and the American Future.)

19. Donald A. Erickson and others, "Crisis in Illinois Nonpublic Schools," Final Research Report to the Elementary and Secondary Nonpublic Schools Study Commission, State of Illinois (The Commission, 1971; processed), p. 4-20.

dren could also cause enrollments in the non-Catholic nonpublic schools to fall by some 6 percent or 80,000 students by 1977 if there is no change in the rate at which parents send their children to these schools.

Altered preferences and living patterns will undoubtedly cause the rates to change; but the direction and magnitude of such changes is a matter of conjecture. A point that should be made, however, is that it is not necessary for past trends and relationships to continue. For example, while a general disenchantment with formal religion undoubtedly hurt church affiliated schools during the 1960s, the process could reverse itself. If an increasing number of parents become dissatisfied with the secularization of the public schools, they might react either by enrolling their children in existing church affiliated schools or by establishing new religiously oriented institutions.[20] Similarly, the traditional reluctance of parents to withdraw their children from public schools could be eroded if racial tensions and class conflicts worsen in these schools, or if a growing number of parents become convinced that the public schools are failing in their educational mission. Such a change in attitude has already taken place in some large cities; if extended, it could markedly boost the rate at which parents enroll their children in nonpublic schools.

Tuition increases necessitated by rising costs will also act to reduce nonpublic school enrollment during the next decade. In all likelihood outlays will go up fastest in Catholic, Lutheran, and other religiously affiliated institutions, for two reasons. First, the ability of these institutions to maintain low expenditure levels partially through reliance on the "contributed services" of their teachers seems to be ending. For example, a shortage of people entering religious vocations will force Catholic schools to turn increasingly to lay teachers, who are likely to continue to seek wage parity with their public school counterparts.[21] Second, church affiliated institutions have been insulated from competition with the public sector by the religious allegiances that tied their clientele to their schools. That bond may

20. An example of the latter was reported in "Missouri Parents Set Up Own School to Counter an Anti-Christian Philosophy," *New York Times*, October 2, 1972, p. 28. Also see "Statement of the American Association of Christian Schools" (testimony before the House Committee on Ways and Means, August 1972; processed).

21. For the nation, the total number of teachers from religious orders is projected to decline from 80,312 in 1970 to 42,812 in 1975 and 20,142 in 1980. Ernest J. Bartell, "Costs and Revenues of Nonpublic Elementary and Secondary Education: The Past, Present, and Future of Roman Catholic Schools," in Fahey, *Economic Problems of Nonpublic Schools*, pp. 218, 563, 565. In New York the number of religious order teachers is projected to decline from 12,542 in 1969–70 to 1,375 in 1980–81. Gary and associates, "The Collapse of Nonpublic Education," Vol. 1, p. II-11.

be weakening. If so, competition from the public sector will place pressure on Catholic and other low-spending schools to improve their physical facilities and strengthen the quality of their educational programs. Shrinking student bodies will also tend to push up unit costs. Bartell's study for the President's Commission on School Finance estimated that, depending upon the degree to which Catholic schools consolidate, their expenditures per pupil at the elementary level will range between $500 and $841 by 1975, and those at the secondary level between $912 and $1,169.[22] These figures imply roughly a doubling of expenditures per pupil in five years. While expenditures will also increase in the rest of the nonpublic school sector, the rise will probably not match the rate of increase in the Catholic or Lutheran schools, because many of the remaining institutions receive little in the way of "contributed services" that could be eliminated, and most already have relatively small classes and better paid faculties.

Tuition increases in the nonpublic schools will have to match expenditure increases unless the institutions are able to sustain large deficits, or unless they receive substantial amounts of new public or private moneys. Church subsidies, a major source of income for the Catholic and Lutheran schools in the past, are not expected to grow significantly in the future. Nor will it be possible to increase significantly the fraction of church revenue devoted to maintaining educational institutions, because 55 to 60 percent of parish income is already devoted to this purpose. What this implies is that in the absence of public subsidy Catholic elementary school tuition and fees would have to rise between 1970 and 1975 by about $390, or 560 percent, if no new source of revenue were found and if a deficit were to be avoided. Under the same assumptions, secondary school tuition and fees would have to be $500, or 160 percent, higher.[23] Increases of this order of magnitude would reduce Catholic school enrollments substantially, and the reduction would undoubtedly dominate any enrollment changes in the remainder of the nonpublic school sector.

Thus the number of children attending nonpublic schools is likely to shrink considerably over the next decade, both because of the decrease in the size of the school aged population and because rising costs will push up tuition charges, which in turn will make parents less able or willing to send their children to nonpublic schools. A continued growth in the preference parents have exhibited for secular education would further depress

22. "Costs and Revenues," p. 256.
23. These are rough approximations based on the partial consolidation model provided in Bartell, *ibid.*, p. 256, and assuming his projections of increased church subsidies.

nonpublic school enrollments, since more than nine-tenths of these institutions are now affiliated with churches. A further suburbanization of clientele now served by the nonpublic schools would have a similar effect.

The total number of students attending nonpublic institutions is expected to decline by 2.4 million, or 46 percent, by 1980, according to the following estimate of future nonpublic school enrollment made for the President's Commission on School Finance:[24]

Type of school	1970	1975	1980
Catholic elementary	3,359,311	2,150,500	1,407,900
Catholic secondary	1,008,463	822,245	690,100
Other nonpublic	914,793	845,300	763,900
Total	5,282,567	3,818,045	2,861,900

In considering this decline, the nation is faced with two questions: Should government attempt to come to the aid of the nonpublic school sector? If so, what types of public support could achieve the objectives of public policy?

The Pros and Cons of Public Aid to Nonpublic Schools

The question of whether additional public aid should be given to nonpublic schools is a matter of considerable debate.[25] President Nixon has come out strongly in favor of such aid. In April 1972 he told the convention of the National Catholic Educational Association, "America needs her nonpublic schools. Those nonpublic schools need help. Therefore, we must and will find ways to provide that help."[26] The President's Panel on Nonpublic Education concurred with this position, concluding that "public interest requires *the Federal Government to take major initiatives* toward a solution of the financial crisis in nonpublic education."[27] The leadership in Congress, the Democratic standard bearers in the 1972 presidential elec-

24. Brown, "Enrollment in Nonpublic Schools," pp. 193, 195, 208.

25. See *Tax Credits for Nonpublic Education*, Hearings before the House Committee on Ways and Means, 92 Cong. 2 sess. (1972), Pts. 1, 2, 3.

26. "Remarks of the President to Sixty-ninth Annual Convention, National Catholic Educational Association" (speech delivered at Philadelphia, April 6, 1972; processed), p. 7.

27. President's Panel on Nonpublic Education, *Nonpublic Education and the Public Good*, Final Report to the President's Commission on School Finance (1972), p. 33.

tion, and a number of governors and state legislators have also taken this position. Leaders from a number of religious denominations including the Catholics and Lutherans, and some nonpublic school administrators, have also expressed the opinion that public aid to nonpublic schools is both urgently needed and in the national interest.

There are others, however, who disagree. Some legal scholars and others, notably the Committee for Public Education and Religious Liberty (PEARL), Protestants and Other Americans United for Separation of Church and State (POAU), and the American Civil Liberties Union have objected to such aid for constitutional reasons. A few religious denominations, including the Baptists and the Unitarian-Universalists, have also opposed aid to nonpublic schools because in their view it would undermine religious liberty and the separation of church and state, and be a divisive policy. Some fundamentalist denominations have shied away from public support for nonpublic schools because they fear that government regulations and controls will come with such aid. The National Education Association has consistently opposed additional aid to nonpublic schools, primarily on the grounds that public revenues should first be devoted to meeting the unmet needs of public schools. The AFL-CIO has also raised its voice against such aid, at least as it has been proposed so far.

On the whole, public opinion seems to be split on this issue; according to a Gallup poll made in 1970, 48 percent favored public aid to nonpublic schools, 44 percent opposed such assistance, and the remaining 8 percent had no opinion.[28]

The Economic Argument

A number of arguments have been marshaled to support public aid. President Nixon, his Panel on Nonpublic Education, and others who feel that the public interest requires such aid have reasoned that public aid is economical. Nonpublic schools save the taxpayers money; if they collapse, a significant new load will be placed on public educational systems and the taxpayers who support them. The additional burden would be concentrated in those states and cities where nonpublic enrollments are the largest; many of these governments already have a great deal of difficulty balancing their budgets. As President Nixon has argued, "If the nonpublic schools were ever permitted to go under in the major cities in America, many pub-

28. *The Gallup Opinion Index*, Report 66 (December 1970), p. 15.

lic schools might very well go under with them, because they simply couldn't undertake the burden."[29]

While it is certainly true that the collapse of the nonpublic school sector would place an additional burden on state and local taxpayers, the magnitude of the burden is a matter of debate. A study made for the President's Commission suggests that the additional costs that would result from the sudden disappearance of all nonpublic schools might be by no means as large as some have claimed. The study estimates that closing all nonpublic schools would add from $1.35 billion to $3.18 billion to the current operating costs of public schools, an increase of from 3 to 6 percent over present levels.[30] Another sum, from $4.7 billion to $9.9 billion, would be needed for capital outlays, but these expenditures would be spread over several years or might never occur if existing facilities were used more intensively, or if vacated nonpublic schools were rented. In New York, the state that would be most adversely affected by a complete shutdown of nonpublic schools, current public school expenditures would have to be increased by from 8.5 to 14 percent,[31] an increase only slightly greater than the state's recent yearly growth in school expenditures.

Since it is difficult to envision a cataclysm that would bring the entire nonpublic school system crashing down, it is more realistic to look at the added costs that would be imposed on the public school system by a continuation of the present gradual decline in nonpublic school enrollments. Using estimates of the marginal costs of transferring a student from the nonpublic to the public sector, and assuming a shift of roughly 300,000 pupils a year, we find that current public school expenditures would have to be increased each year by between $72 million and $165 million to accommodate the newly transferred students.[32] This is an annual increase of 0.2 to 0.4 percent in current public school spending. Although the grad-

29. "Remarks of the President to Sixty-ninth Annual Convention," p. 5.

30. See Thomas R. Swartz, "The Estimated Marginal Costs of Absorbing all Nonpublic Students into the Public School System," in Fahey, *Economic Problems of Nonpublic Schools*, pp. 301–50.

31. Swartz, "Estimated Marginal Costs," pp. 309–19; and National Education Association, Research Division, *Estimates of School Statistics, 1971–72* (NEA, 1971), p. 36.

32. These national aggregates are based on state-by-state estimates of the marginal cost of transfers of students from the nonpublic to the public sector, in Swartz, "Estimated Marginal Costs," pp. 324–28; and on state-by-state estimates of the number of nonpublic elementary and secondary school pupils likely to shift to the public sector, derived from Brown, "Enrollment in Nonpublic Schools," pp. 192–95.

The high figure is based on Swartz's "low excess capacity" formula and the low figure on his "high excess capacity" formula. These formulas differ mainly in their assumptions about pupil-teacher ratios and the extent to which existing public schools are utilized. On a per-pupil basis the marginal costs may appear surprisingly low. One reason for this

ual shift of pupils from nonpublic to public institutions may also require increased capital for new construction, such outlays would in all likelihood be very low since in many communities the students transferring from nonpublic schools could be absorbed by the spaces left vacant by the decline in the school age population.[33]

Although the national aggregate figures do not suggest that continued decline or even collapse of the nonpublic school sector would be catastrophic from the fiscal standpoint, in specific localities where nonpublic school enrollment is substantial there might be serious adjustment problems. Much would depend on mobility patterns and state aid formulas. If the students from nonpublic schools were suddenly to transfer en masse to their local public schools, many big cities that are already in financial distress would be hard hit. Estimates for Philadelphia, where more than a third of the school children now attend nonpublic schools, indicate that if all the Catholic school students were transferred to the public system the city's school district budget would have to rise by about $150 million, or some 40 percent, in 1972–73.[34] In the more likely event that 10 percent of the Philadelphia Catholic school enrollment were transferred each year, costs would rise by $11.5 to $12.4 million in 1972–73, requiring a 3 to 3.5 percent increase in the school budget—a not insubstantial rise for a system that had an operating deficit of $30 million in 1971–72.

Estimates such as these are probably on the high side because they do not take into account residential mobility. What evidence there is suggests that, when inner city parish schools close their doors, not all the students transfer to the city's public school system; many of the affected families move to the suburbs, distributing themselves among the numerous surrounding school districts and easing the fiscal pressure on the city.[35] Furthermore,

---

is that the decline in the school age population has left many school districts with some excess capacity. Thus nonpublic school transfers just fill up seats that would otherwise be empty. Another reason is that a portion of public school expenditures represents fixed costs that need not be increased when the student body is increased by transfers of pupils from nonpublic institutions.

33. See Fleischmann Commission Report, p. 5.51.

34. See Tables 5-8 and 5-9 of the Gurash Committee Report.

35. Wilbur J. Cohen (project director), *The Financial Implications of Changing Patterns of Nonpublic School Operations in Chicago, Detroit, Milwaukee and Philadelphia*, A Report Submitted to the President's Commission on School Finance by the School of Education, University of Michigan (The Commission, 1972), pp. 92, 100. Swartz's estimates of the marginal cost of absorbing nonpublic school children in the public school system might prove low if a significant number of nonpublic school students moved to the suburbs, because much of the excess capacity in the public sector is concentrated in central city school districts.

not all the increased cost of such a transfer would fall on the shoulders of the beleaguered city taxpayers; some would be paid by higher state aid. If a state instituted a "capacity equalizing" state aid system of the type described in the previous chapter, the transfer of nonpublic students to the public system would not imply higher local taxes. The district would be able to maintain its previous level of per-pupil expenditures, without changing its tax rate; the state, in effect, would pay for the newly transferred students. Even under existing state aid formulas that depend on enrollments or per-pupil property values, or both, the state would bear part of the burden. In Philadelphia between one-half and three-quarters of the increase in expenditures created by the transfers mentioned above would be covered by expanded state aid; in New York state, more than half the burden of students transferring from the nonpublic schools to the public schools would be borne by state rather than local taxpayers.[36]

The relatively low cost of absorbing nonpublic school children into the public system raises the question whether the economic argument for aid to nonpublic education is sound. To be economical from the taxpayer's standpoint, a program of public aid to nonpublic schools must cost less than the aggregate expense of a public school education for all those who were kept in or attracted to the nonpublic schools *because* of the subsidy. It is not obvious that this would be the case. As was pointed out earlier, it will cost the taxpayers of the nation somewhat less than $200 million to absorb the approximately 300,000 children who are expected to transfer each year from the nonpublic to the public schools. Would a subsidy of $200 million to nonpublic schools or their pupils avoid a net outflow of 300,000 students from this sector? If the $200 million could be concentrated on those families who are most sensitive to tuition charges or on those nonpublic schools that are on the brink of closing, the answer is clearly positive. A subsidy of nearly $700 per student is implied by a $200 million program designed to entice 300,000 students to enroll or stay in the nonpublic sector. There is no conceivable public aid program, however, that could target funds on just those whose enrollment behavior would be most affected.

36. Gurash Committee Report, Table 5-9, p. 119, and Andre L. Daniere and George F. Madaus, "Impact of Alternative Patterns of Catholic School Student Transfers to the Public Schools on Public Budgets in the State of New York," in Gary and associates, "Collapse of Nonpublic Education," Vol. 2, pp. C-8 and C-9. If some existing state aid formulas were left unchanged, districts with few nonpublic school students would bear part of the cost of transfers of students to the public school system in districts with large nonpublic school enrollments, because they would lose state aid since their tax base would rise in relation to the state average per-pupil property value.

Any realistic program must offer aid to some categories of eligible pupils or schools, many of whom would have remained in or transferred to the nonpublic sector without the aid. If the $200 million were spread equally over all nonpublic schools, it would amount to only $40 per student. Whether this level of subsidy per student is large enough to halt the net transfers to the public sector is doubtful.[37]

If a subsidy to nonpublic schools would in the end save taxpayers money, and if this is sufficient reason for a subsidy program, then the question becomes, which level of government should support the program of aid to nonpublic schools? A good case can be made for state and local, rather than federal, support, because it is the state and local areas that reap the fiscal gain. The taxpayers of Albany and of New York state now benefit because they do not have to support the education of the 47 percent of Albany's school children who are enrolled in nonpublic schools. These taxpayers should thus finance any system of public aid to the nonpublic schools of Albany. To do otherwise—that is, to finance the program federally—would be to give a federal subsidy to those living in areas with large nonpublic school enrollments. Take the extreme example of the two states, Utah and Rhode Island. In Utah, 98 percent of the children are educated in public schools, while one-fifth of those in Rhode Island attended nonpublic institutions; school taxes in Rhode Island are "abnormally" low because so many children are in the nonpublic sector, but private expenditures on education are "abnormally" high. A federally financed system of aid to nonpublic schools would provide a net subsidy to the parents of nonpublic school children and taxpayers of Rhode Island, because it would act to keep nonpublic school tuition low, thus benefiting the parents, and help maintain the size of the nonpublic school sector, which in turn keeps educational taxes down. While taxpayers in Rhode Island would pay federal taxes to support the program, so would those in Utah; but the latter group would receive virtually no benefit from the program, and would in effect subsidize the low state and local taxes in Rhode Island. Thus, if the economic rationale for aid to nonpublic education is accepted, it implies that such aid should be financed at the local and state levels only.

37. A study of the situation in Massachusetts concluded that it would cost less to absorb the nonpublic student transfers to the public system over the 1971–75 period than to furnish any form of state assistance that could successfully halt such transfers. (Massachusetts Commission to Study Public Financial Aid to Nonpublic Primary and Secondary Schools and Certain Related Matters, *Summary Report* [1971], as reported in Richard F. Halverson, "Other State Commissions Studying Aid to Nonpublic Schools," in Gary and associates, "Collapse of Nonpublic Education," Vol. 2, pp. C-84 to C-88.)

Nonpublic Schools and the Inner City

A second major argument that is often used in defense of public aid to nonpublic schools is that it is in the national interest to maintain such schools in the inner city. President Nixon, his Commission, and the Panel on Nonpublic Education have reasoned that nonpublic schools keep working class and middle class whites in central cities, which improves the cities' tax base, helps maintain stable integrated neighborhoods, and keeps cities from becoming minority ghettos. Furthermore, it is argued, inner city nonpublic schools constitute "beacons of hope" for the underprivileged because they offer a good education in "poor and racially isolated communities which need them most."[38]

There can be no doubt that the availability of nonpublic schools has been a major factor that has kept many middle and upper income families from leaving central cities. In some cities such as New York and Washington, D.C., almost all the upper income families send their children to private schools. Without these institutions most would move to the suburbs, further weakening their city's tax base. Nonpublic schools have also helped to maintain some semblance of socioeconomic and racial diversity in the nation's largest cities. Catholic schools have been a factor that has preserved many ethnic neighborhoods in such cities as Chicago, Milwaukee, Philadelphia, and Boston. However, there is only fragmentary evidence that nonpublic schools are important forces maintaining stable integrated neighborhoods in central cities. Data from Detroit, Chicago, and New York indicate that there are Catholic schools that seem to play a stabilizing role in some integrated neighborhoods.[39] However, in many instances, the existence of a neighborhood nonpublic school has not been a strong enough influence to preserve an integrated community.

Finally, it is doubtful that inner city nonpublic schools are a real "beacon of hope," or a viable educational alternative for a significant number of minority or disadvantaged children. Nationally, the nonpublic schools serve a much "whiter" population than do the public schools (Table 5-10). Moreover, no more than 3 percent of Catholic schools, which are virtually the only nonpublic institutions located in the urban slums, serve the pre-

---

38. "Remarks of the President to Sixty-ninth Annual Convention," p. 5.

39. Cohen, *Financial Implications*, pp. 24–30; New York Department of City Planning, "Three Out of Ten," pp. 41–44.

Table 5-10. Ethnic Composition of Public and Nonpublic Schools, Fall 1970
Percent

Type of school	White	Minority[a]
Public		
Elementary	77.4	22.6
Secondary	79.7	20.3
Nonpublic: Catholic		
Elementary	88.6	11.4
Secondary	92.1	7.9
Nonpublic: non-Catholic		
Elementary	87.0	13.0
Secondary	92.8	7.2

Sources: Estimated from Bureau of the Census, *Current Population Reports*, Series P-20, No. 222, Table 4; Bureau of the Census, *Census of Population, 1970, General Social and Economic Characteristics*, Final Report PC(1)-C1, *United States Summary* (1972), Table 88; National Catholic Educational Association, *Report on U.S. Catholic Schools, 1970–71*, p. 36; and Department of Health, Education, and Welfare, "HEW News," HEW–A66 (June 18, 1971).
a. Minorities include Negroes, American Indians, Orientals, and Spanish-surnamed Americans.

dominantly disadvantaged clientele of city poverty areas,[40] and low in-come minority students probably make up no more than 3 percent of Catholic enrollments. Most non-Catholic nonpublic schools do far less for inner city students from disadvantaged, minority backgrounds. There are exceptions, such as the Ebenezer Lutheran School in Chicago,[41] the ghetto street academies that have sprung up in some of the larger cities, and the few expensive private schools that have recently increased their enrollment of scholarship children from poor and minority homes. But fewer than 1 percent of inner city minority school children attend either Catholic or non-Catholic nonpublic schools.

While no one can doubt that strengthening the tax bases of central cities, fostering socioeconomic and racial integration, and improving the educational opportunities of disadvantaged ghetto children are worthwhile objectives, one can question whether aid to nonpublic schools is the most efficient means of attaining them. Strengthening the tax base of cities by keeping the upper and middle class in residence may be attempted through a wide variety of means, such as providing the groups with the noneducational public services they desire, or even, paradoxically, by lowering some

40. National Catholic Educational Association, *A Report on U.S. Catholic Schools, 1970–71*, p. 27. Although 13 percent of all Catholic schools are located in the inner city poverty areas, only one-fourth of these schools have student bodies of which 60 percent or more come from low income families.
41. Erickson and others, "Crisis in Illinois Nonpublic Schools," pp. 4-20 to 4-23.

of the taxes they pay. In education, it can be argued that since a much larger pool of potentially mobile middle class residents send their children to public schools, these institutions should have first priority in public aid. Finally, if aid is to be given to the nonpublic school sector for the purpose of averting an exodus of middle class families to the suburbs, aid should be restricted to those families who are most likely to leave without aid and to those who bring the most to the city's tax base. On balance, it would seem that an aid program for city residents in nonpublic schools that excluded the poor (who contribute little to the tax base) and the rich (whose decision to move is probably independent of nonpublic school aid) would be best suited to the goal. General aid to all nonpublic schools is too blunt an instrument for this rather narrow purpose.

The goal of fostering socioeconomic and racial integration through nonpublic school aid also suggests several alternative approaches by government. First, it is clear that the ability of nonpublic schools to make a significant contribution toward integration of the city is presently limited because the sector is so small. This suggests either that the public schools should receive more government aid for this purpose or that the nonpublic sector should be improved and expanded in a way that directly contributes to integration. An example of the second approach would be a program of special grants to nonpublic schools that serve racially mixed neighborhoods and student bodies. Most existing nonpublic schools would of course not qualify, but new schools might develop in response to such a program.

Finally, approaching the objective of improving the education of disadvantaged city children through general aid to existing nonpublic schools makes little sense. Since a minuscule number of such children presently attend the nonpublic system, 99 percent of a general aid program would fail to aid the disadvantaged. The public aid programs that merit serious consideration in pursuit of this goal are either those that provide educational services to disadvantaged children (such as Title I of the Elementary and Secondary Education Act), or programs of education vouchers to allow educationally needy children to buy supplementary services. Although both of these programs would in fact provide aid to nonpublic schools, they would affect only those schools that served needy children.

The arguments for aid to the nonpublic sector discussed in this section imply a highly varied assortment of assistance programs, ranging from subsidies limited to poor families to subsidies that would explicitly exclude the poor. In general, however, the social ills that are addressed are far too complex to be attacked through the existing nonpublic school sector. If nonpublic education is to be used as a vehicle for preserving the cities, fostering integration, and providing choice for the disadvantaged, a conscious choice of a major expansion and redirection of nonpublic education is necessary.

Diversity and Competition

A third popular line of argument in support of the case for aiding nonpublic schools is that these institutions offer a useful alternative to the public system, that education is of such importance that people ought to have a choice. Furthermore, its proponents argue, the nonpublic schools are a source of innovation, and competition is necessary to keep the public sector on its toes. President Nixon has emphasized these points both in his messages to Congress and in speeches. In his Philadelphia address he lauded the diversity and richness of the existing mixed system and concluded that it would be intolerable that a "single school system" should "ever gain absolute monopoly over the education of our children."[42]

It is certainly true that the nation's educational system is richer and more diverse with its nonpublic schools than it would or could be without them. But the nonpublic schools are not the only source of diversity and competition; the nation's public schools are far from a homogeneous group. There are almost 17,000 different operating local public school districts, which range in size from fewer than 10 students to more than one million, and in expenditures from $175 to $14,554 per pupil. Even in a limited geographic area there is generally a large number of public school systems, offering parents a broad choice of educational alternatives. Residents of some metropolitan areas have more than 100 school districts from which to choose (Table 5-11); while each school system may not offer a distinctive educational environment, some variation in educational offerings can usually be found. It should be noted, however, that the choice is open only to those who are both willing and able to move. Many families, for economic, racial, or other reasons, may be unable to live in the school district or neighborhood they would like. For them, nonpublic schools may offer the only alternative to their local public school.

For many parents who find themselves in this situation, however, it is easy to overemphasize the choice offered by the nonpublic schools, which

42. "Remarks of the President to Sixty-ninth Annual Convention," p. 8.

Table 5-11. Number of Public School Districts in Selected Metropolitan Areas, 1969–70 School Year

Metropolitan area	Number of school districts
East	
Philadelphia	218
New York	192
Pittsburgh	134
Paterson-Clifton-Passaic	97
Midwest	
Chicago	325
St. Louis	108
Kansas City	105
Detroit	97
South	
Dallas	67
Houston	58
Tulsa	56
Oklahoma City	47
West	
Los Angeles-Long Beach	96
San Francisco-Oakland	83
Phoenix	69
San Bernardino-Riverside-Ontario	67

Source: Seymour Sacks and Ralph Andrew, with Tony Carnevale, "School State Aid and the System of Finance: Central City, Suburban and Rural Dimensions of Revenue Sharing" (Syracuse University, no date; processed), Table 1.

may in fact be severely limited by religious, ethnic, and economic constraints. In some localities the only nonpublic schools that are readily available are Catholic institutions, to which non-Catholic parents may be reluctant to send their children because of the religious values that are incorporated in the educational process. Furthermore, where spaces are at a premium, Catholic school administrators generally give preference to the children of fellow Catholics. This is not surprising, since a large fraction of the cost of parochial schools is borne by church subsidies. Nor is it unique; other sectarian schools discriminate on a religious basis, and state laws have been written to permit the practice. Where they exist, nondenominational schools and religiously affiliated institutions that do not stress theistic values may also fail to provide a realistic alternative for many families, because competition for the few available spaces is tight and tuitions are often extremely high.

The competitive and innovative value of existing nonpublic schools may also be overstated. As the Fleischmann Commission concluded, "by and large, public and nonpublic schools are very similar with respect to methods of teaching and the substance of what is taught."[43] When this is true, competition among public school districts may be a more important force than competition between the public and the nonpublic sectors. Moreover, most nonpublic schools do not have the financial margin needed to be innovative; Catholic and Lutheran schools are generally run on such tight budgets and at such low expenditure levels that they have little left over for innovative or experimental programs. While there are a number of progressive and dynamic nonpublic schools in the nation, it is not always clear that new methods and practices developed in small, high expenditure elite classrooms can be duplicated economically in public schools.[44] Furthermore, some contend that the innovations arising in these institutions have limited value because "there are no effective links between the public and nonpublic sectors to allow for the dissemination of information on innovative techniques, so that to consider nonpublic schools as models for public schools is not valid."[45] Finally, there is a good deal of experimentation now going on in many of the nation's public school systems.[46] On the other side of the argument it is worth pointing out that there are certain types of innovations and educational experiments that can be executed only in the private sector because of the political, bureaucratic, and union constraints on public schools. But for the most part innovative and experimental nonpublic schools will survive with or without a program of government aid to the nonpublic sector.

If real pluralism and a genuine choice are to be offered the American parent, and if significant competition is to be generated between the nonpublic and public sectors, more is needed than the preservation of the existing mixed educational system; public aid sufficient for a large-scale expansion of the nonpublic sector would be called for. A voucher system such as one of those mentioned in the previous chapter might serve this end. If nonpublic schools are to be aided because of their innovative influence, the most sensible approach, which is already being undertaken on a small scale, would be to provide special government grants for innovation rather than general aid to all nonpublic schools or pupils.

43. Fleischmann Commission Report, p. 5.21.
44. Henry M. Brickell and others, *Nonpublic Education in Rhode Island: Alternatives for the Future*, A Study for the Rhode Island Special Commission to Study the Entire Field of Education (The Commission, 1969), p. 17.
45. Fleischmann Commission Report, p. 5.21.
46. U.S. Office of Education, *Experimental Schools Program: 1971 Experimental School Projects; Three Educational Plans*, DHEW(OE) 72–42 (1972).

The Double Burden Argument

Another argument that is sometimes used to defend public aid for nonpublic schools is that the parents who send their children to such schools bear a double burden for what is basically a public good. They pay taxes to support public schools, and tuitions to the nonpublic institutions. By sending their children to nonpublic schools they also reduce the burdens on others who pay taxes to support the public schools. But at least in part the education of their children produces benefits to society at large. Are they not therefore entitled to some public subsidy? If the complaint were simply that parents of nonpublic school children support a public service from which they receive no direct benefits, it would be easily dismissed. All public services, with the exception of those completely financed through user charges, are supported in part by some persons who do not receive direct benefits. Childless and aged persons pay taxes to the public school system, and few who contribute to the financing of the welfare system ever receive a welfare check.

But the argument is more complex: the tuition payments produce an educated child, who supposedly indirectly benefits the nation as a whole, just as public schools indirectly benefit families that do not have children enrolled in the public system. Thus, if society values the general benefits that arise from elementary and secondary education, it should support the activity no matter who runs the school. While this is a valid argument for providing a public subsidy for nonpublic education, it hardly settles the question of the level of aid or the priority to be attached to this particular public good.

First of all, nonpublic schools already receive a considerable subsidy from the public purse. (This point is discussed in detail later in this chapter.) Advocates of increased public aid for nonpublic schools must show that the additional public good produced by larger subsidies to nonpublic education should be valued by the nation more than the attendant cost.

Second, it is worth noting that citizens have many opportunities to avail themselves of a service publicly provided or to purchase the same service privately. In such circumstances, those who substitute private purchases receive no subsidies. The man who buys a burglar alarm for his house may reduce the need for public spending on police, but has to pay for the alarm system without public aid. Families who go away for the summer, reducing the strain on the town's public recreational facilities, generally buy their

Table 5-12. Catholics as a Percentage of Population in 1971 in the States with the Eight Highest Numbers of Presidential Electoral Votes in 1972

State	Catholics as percentage of total population
California	21
New York	36
Pennsylvania	31
Illinois	32
Texas	18
Ohio	21
Michigan	27
New Jersey	43

Sources: Bureau of the Census, *Statistical Abstract of the United States, 1971*, p. 352; *Official Catholic Directory, 1971*, insert following Pt. 4.

own plane tickets. A line has to be drawn at some point in the matter of goods and services that are supplied by both public and private agencies; the double burden on the nonpublic school family is by no means unique.

The Political Factor

The reason for which many have advocated public aid to nonpublic schools is not often mentioned explicitly in the debate, even though it is probably the compelling force behind most of the recent proposals. This is the political factor. By giving federal or state aid to nonpublic schools, it is argued, one can win the political allegiance of a very important segment of the American electorate—Catholics—without offending any other groups. In the view of some political analysts, the traditional allegiance of Catholic voters to the Democratic party has become weaker. Until recently, large numbers of Catholics supported the Democratic party because of its economic philosophy, but many have now become attracted to the Republican party's approach to social problems and foreign policy.[47] Since in many politically important states Catholics represent a large fraction of the electorate, shifts in their voting behavior would be of immense political significance (Table 5-12).

47. See Kevin P. Phillips, *The Emerging Republican Majority* (Arlington House, 1969), pp. 169–75; Louis R. Gary and K. C. Cole, "The Politics of Aid—and a Proposal for Reform," *Saturday Review*, Vol. 55 (July 22, 1972), pp. 31–33; and "Vital Voting Bloc Defects to Nixon," *Washington Post*, October 8, 1972.

Table 5-13. Percentage Distribution of Public and Nonpublic Elementary and Secondary School Students, by Family Income Class, Fall 1970

Family income (dollars)	Elementary		Secondary	
	Public	Nonpublic	Public	Nonpublic
Under 3,000	8.5	2.4	6.8	0.5
3,000–4,999	13.0	4.9	11.2	4.6
5,000–7,499	20.3	15.3	18.2	10.7
7,500–9,999	21.2	23.1	19.3	20.7
10,000–14,999	24.9	32.1	27.5	31.0
15,000 and over	12.1	22.2	17.1	32.6

Source: Bureau of the Census, *Current Population Reports*, Series P-20, No. 222, Table 15, p. 40. Data do not include kindergarten enrollment. Percentages may not add to 100 because of rounding.

The Redistributive Argument

The case against public aid for nonpublic schools rests on three major arguments. The first is that such aid would represent a perverse redistribution of income, since subsidies would flow into the pockets of the wealthy. Data on the family incomes of public and nonpublic students show that for the nation as a whole, students attending nonpublic schools come from higher income families (Table 5-13); thus a national aid program would tend to benefit relatively wealthy students. Some of the national difference between the family incomes of public and nonpublic school pupils, however, is attributable to the concentration of nonpublic schools in regions of the country that have higher than average incomes, notably in the urban Northeast. This could mean that a state program of aid to nonpublic schools would not have a perverse distributional impact, but the possibility cannot be readily assessed because family income comparisons between public and nonpublic students within states or local areas are extremely rare. Although one survey of New York City, which contains 10 percent of the nation's nonpublic school students, showed that median family incomes of Catholic students were slightly below those of the city as a whole, only 2 percent of the families of Catholic school students were on welfare, while the proportion in the public schools was more than ten times as great.[48] The other nonpublic schools in New York, most of which have extremely high tuition, presumably enroll children from much wealthier than average families. Dugan's study of the archdiocese of St. Louis found that in St. Louis city the median income of Catholic families was slightly above the citywide median income for all families, while both in St. Louis County

48. New York Department of City Planning, "Three Out of Ten," p. 75.

and in the outlying areas of the diocese, the median income of Catholics was slightly below the general median.[49]

The redistribution case against public aid for nonpublic schools is relatively easy to overcome by directing assistance to low income children, much as is done in means-tested college scholarship programs. Of course if few such children were currently enrolled in nonpublic schools, and if few poor families responded to subsidies by transferring their children to nonpublic schools, the total amount of assistance would be small.

Shared Experience, Equal Opportunity, and Integration

A second line of argument against public aid to nonpublic schools appeals to the importance of preserving the social goals that are allegedly fulfilled through the public school system. The public sector, some argue, provides all children with both a shared common experience and a set of values that are vital for the development of citizens. Nonpublic schools, because of their particularistic emphasis on religion, ethnicity, or elitism, do not represent the same type of experience and do not inculcate the same common values; aid to these institutions, to the extent that it weakens the public school system, is wrong and divisive. Furthermore, it is argued, nonpublic schools undermine equal educational opportunities. They often enroll only the better students, leaving the less able and problem pupils concentrated in the public institutions. Where nonpublic school enrollments are large, voter support for public educational spending is undermined, and with it the chance for many low income students to better themselves.

Much of this reasoning is based on assertions rather than facts, and the weight one gives to the argument depends mostly on one's values. The "divisiveness" and uniqueness that some argue should exclude nonpublic schools from public support are regarded by others as diversity and as the source of alternatives that should be preserved and expanded through government aid. If common values are essential to society, the major impli-

49. The value of the New York and St. Louis information is reduced because in the first case the comparison is made between the incomes of families with children in nonpublic schools and those of all families, not just of those with children in public schools; and in the second case the incomes of all Catholics, not just those with children in parochial schools, are compared to those of all families. See Dugan, "The Determinants of Enrollment in Catholic Schools," pp. 428, 433, 438, and U.S. Bureau of the Census, *Census of Population, 1970, General Social and Economic Characteristics*, Final Report PC(1)-C27, *Missouri* (1972), Tables 89, 124, 135.

Table 5-14. Percentage of School Children Attending Public and Nonpublic Elementary
and Secondary Schools, by Race, Selected Cities, 1970

	Black and Spanish-surnamed		White and other[a]	
City	Public	Nonpublic	Public	Nonpublic
New York	92	8	61	39
Washington	93	7	52	48
Boston	93	7	64	36
Philadelphia	91	9	44	56
~~Newark~~	95	5	66	34
Detroit	95	5	64	36
Cleveland	96	4	69	31
Chicago	91	9	57	43

Source: Bureau of the Census, *Census of Population, 1970, General Social and Economic Characteristics*, Final Report PC(1)-C, volumes for the respective states, Tables 83, 91, and 97 in each volume.
a. "Other" includes Orientals and American Indians, who constitute only a minuscule fraction of the total.

cation for public policy would seem to be that governments, in chartering educational institutions, should ensure that these common values are part of the program of all institutions; that done, the question of whether to give public aid still remains. Similarly, the charge that they skim the cream of the student crop is better leveled against exclusive suburbs than against nonpublic schools.

The allegation that aid to nonpublic schools would increase racial segregation is difficult to evaluate. As we have noted, the nonpublic sector enrolls a much lower proportion of minority children than do the public schools. The difference between the two sectors is so dramatic in many major cities (see Table 5-14) that it is not unreasonable to conclude that majority children have enrolled in nonpublic schools for the purpose of "fleeing" minority children in the public system. Even if this conclusion is accepted,[50] the relevant question is how an expanded program of public aid to nonpublic schools would affect segregation. To the extent that public support would hold down tuition increases in the nonpublic sector, it can be argued that the group most likely to be retained in that sector is the minorities. If over the next few years tuition increases of the magnitude suggested earlier in this chapter take place, it is virtually certain that minority groups, who can least afford tuition, will be priced out of the nonpublic market, since one can assume that scholarships would not rise sufficiently to offset tuition increases. On the other hand, part of the reason that

50. The data are also compatible with the explanation that relatively few minority students are Catholic or are able to afford nonpublic tuition fees.

minorities are now enrolled in Catholic schools, which enroll most of the minorities in the nonpublic sector, is that as white Catholics have left, the parochial schools have made a significant effort to fill their vacant seats with non-Catholic children from disadvantaged minority backgrounds.[51] If a new program of public aid made Catholic schools more attractive to the white parish clientele, there is little reason to doubt that they would displace the minorities.

It is clear that little desegregation has taken place in either the public or the nonpublic sector in northern cities.[52] The marginal effect that a program of aid to nonpublic schools would have on desegregation is likely to be slight. Irrespective of what is done about aiding nonpublic schools, the progress of desegregation in the North will depend on court orders and political leadership.

In the South a more clearcut analysis can be made of the impact of nonpublic school aid programs on segregation. Many of the "white academies" that have developed to preserve school segregation are in precarious financial positions. Some analysts fear that nonpublic school aid will shore up these academies and make them a permanent part of the southern landscape. Restrictions might of course proscribe support for schools that discriminated, but such restrictions would be very hard to enforce, especially if the aid were in a general form such as tax credits. Furthermore, if all types of discrimination were prohibited, denominational institutions that discriminate on the basis of religion would not be eligible for assistance. If religious discrimination were tolerated, it could be used to preserve racial exclusiveness as well, because the membership of many denominations or churches is almost exclusively from a single race.

The Constitutional Issue

Since most of government aid to nonpublic schools would benefit church-related institutions, a major argument against such assistance has been that it would violate the United States Constitution. The First Amendment to the Constitution provides that "Congress shall make no law respecting an establishment of religion, or prohibiting the free exercise

51. One-third of the non-Catholics in Catholic schools or 50,000 pupils are non-Catholics from disadvantaged neighborhoods. See National Catholic Educational Association, *Report on U.S. Catholic Schools, 1970–71*, Chap. 4.

52. Segregation has in fact been getting worse in the northern public schools in the last three years. See U.S. Department of Health, Education, and Welfare, "HEW News," January 13, 1972.

thereof," and, according to opponents of nonpublic school aid, this provision proscribes most forms of aid to sectarian nonpublic schools.[53]

Over the past quarter of a century, the Supreme Court has decided a number of cases involving aid to parochial schools. Out of these rulings there has evolved a legal doctrine defining the types of assistance that are constitutionally permissible.[54] In 1947 the constitutionality of tax-supported transportation for nonpublic school pupils in New Jersey was upheld.[55] In its decision the court ruled that while direct aid to nonpublic schools was illegal, aid in the form of public services for individuals was permissible. In 1968 the court upheld a New York law that provided secular textbooks for nonpublic students, on the grounds that since the law had a secular purpose it did not aid religion.[56] Two years later the court upheld tax-exempt status for church properties on the grounds that it avoided "excessive government entanglement."[57]

Finally, in 1971, the court pulled together and more clearly defined the criteria on which the constitutionality of public aid to nonpublic schools was to be determined. It did this in a decision dealing with Pennsylvania and Rhode Island laws, which granted salary supplements to teachers in nonpublic schools. Before ruling that these laws violated the First Amendment, the court reiterated that some types of relationships between church and state were acceptable under the Constitution; that there was no "wall" of separation, but rather a "blurred, indistinct, and variable barrier depending on all the circumstances of a particular relationship." The decision cited "fire inspections, building and zoning regulations, and state requirements under compulsory school attendance laws [as] examples of necessary and permissible contacts."[58] The court then went on to reaffirm its previous position that certain forms of state financial aid to sectarian schools were

53. Many state constitutions contain more explicit prohibitions on aid to church-related schools. The Blaine amendment (Article XI, Section 3) to the New York state constitution is a prime example: "Neither the state nor any subdivision thereof shall use its property or credit or any public money, or authorize or permit either to be used, directly or indirectly, in aid or maintenance, other than for examination or inspection, of any school or institution of learning wholly or in part under the control or direction of any religious denomination, or in which any denominational tenet or doctrine is taught, but the legislature may provide for the transportation of children to and from any school or institution of learning" (as quoted in the Fleischmann Report, p. 5A.2).

54. A good summary of this court history can be found in Charles M. Whelan and Paul A. Freund, *Legal and Constitutional Problems of Public Support for Nonpublic Schools*, Submitted to the President's Commission on School Finance (The Commission, 1972), pp. 26–40 and 66–80.

55. *Everson* v. *Board of Education*, 330 U.S. 1 (1947).

56. *Board of Education* v. *Allen*, 392 U.S. 236, 243 (1968).

57. *Walz* v. *Tax Commission*, 397 U.S. 664, 674 (1970).

58. *Lemon* v. *Kurtzman*, 403 U.S. 602, 614 (1971).

permissible. For example, states were allowed "to provide church-related schools with secular, neutral, or nonideological services, facilities, or materials."[59] The court outlined a threefold test of constitutionality for new legislation in this area: "First, the statute must have a secular legislative purpose; second, its principal or primary effect must be one that neither advances nor inhibits religion . . . ; finally, the statute must not foster 'an excessive government entanglement with religion.' "[60] The court laid great stress on the latter test and went to some length to explain that any statute that involved even a minimum of government supervision would probably be found in violation. Because of the supervision that would be required to ensure that teachers taught secular subjects and not religion, the salary supplementation laws were found to violate the criterion.

What will happen next is not clear. During the next few years the Supreme Court will probably have to deal with two separate types of aid: new forms of secular categorical aid, and general aid in the form of vouchers or tax credits. Although lower courts have overturned much legislation in these forms, there is no clear indication of how the Supreme Court will view the programs.[61] In refusing to review the lower courts' decisions that rule out tuition reimbursement grants, the Supreme Court has made it

59. *Ibid.*, at 616.
60. *Ibid.*, at 612, 613.
61. The following have been ruled out by lower courts: (a) laws providing nonpublic schools with reimbursement for the costs incurred in connection with keeping health, enrollment, and other state required records and for the expenses involved in administering state tests and requirements (*PEARL* v. *Rockefeller*, decision by the federal Southern District Court of New York, April 27, 1972); (b) laws providing state assistance for the maintenance and repair of nonpublic school buildings (see discussion in *New York Times*, October 3, 1972, of reiteration by the federal court of an earlier ban of such assistance in a challenge by PEARL of a 1972 New York law); (c) laws reimbursing nonpublic schools for the expenses involved in providing secular educational services (*Johnson* v. *Sanders*, decision of June 30, 1971, and *Committee for Public Education and Religious Liberty* v. *Levitt*, decision of federal court in New York, January 11, 1972); (d) laws providing parents of nonpublic school children with a cash reimbursement for tuitions, fees, or charges made to nonpublic schools (*Lemon* v. *Sloan*, where on April 6, 1972, a federal court denied a motion to dismiss a challenge, and *Wolman* v. *Essex*, decision of Ohio federal district court, April 17, 1972); and (e) laws permitting local school districts to lend teachers, textbooks, and other services to parochial schools and receive state reimbursement for part of the cost (*Americans United* v. *Oakey*, No. 6393, 40 U.S.L.W. 2597, D. Vt., decided March 6, 1972).

The Supreme Court has agreed to review lower court decisions involving (a) a Pennsylvania law that provided parents $75 for each child enrolled in a nonpublic elementary school and $150 for each child enrolled in a nonpublic secondary school; (b) a New York law that provided state reimbursement to nonpublic schools for the cost of pupil testing and record keeping required by state law; and (c) a New York law that provided tuition grants for low income families, tax credits for taxpaying families with incomes below $25,000, and state aid for the maintenance and repair of nonpublic schools in deprived neighborhoods.

clear that direct cash grants to parents of students in nonpublic schools are not tolerable.

For policymakers searching for constitutional means of aiding nonpublic schools, three characteristics of any proposed program would seem relevant: (1) whether the *objective* of the program is to abstain from taxation or to give aid that requires an appropriation; (2) whether the *form* of the aid is money or services, equipment, facilities, and materials; and (3) whether the *channel* of the aid is the parent, the student, the teacher, or the school.[62] Some legal scholars believe that the most constitutionally viable form of support would be aid in the form of tax relief to the parents of nonpublic school students.

Constitutional objections to aid to nonpublic schools would not arise if the aid were limited to nonsectarian schools. But such schools now comprise only 7 percent of the nonpublic enrollment and are probably the most prosperous both financially and in enrollment growth. It is thus likely that the constitutional question of the relation of church and state will have to be resolved by the Supreme Court before any major program of aid to nonpublic schools is undertaken.

Alternative Approaches to Aiding Nonpublic Schools

If on balance the arguments favoring aid for nonpublic schools prevail, some difficult issues must still be dealt with. First, the objective of government assistance must be defined. Should a program be aimed primarily at slowing or halting the decline in nonpublic school enrollments, or at greatly expanding the size of the nonpublic sector? Should such a program provide general aid benefiting all nonpublic institutions, or should it target the aid on low income children, schools serving integrated neighborhoods, on innovative institutions? Second, there is the question of what types of policies could achieve the desired ends. In view of the importance that such nonfinancial factors as suburbanization, falling birth rates, and parental preferences have played in the decline of nonpublic school enrollments, it may be that a renewed growth or even stabilization of the nonpublic sector is an unobtainable objective. Alternatively, such objectives may be attainable only with unrealistically high subsidies that would divert public funds from higher priority programs, or through a radical restructuring of the public school sector. Similarly, government subsidies to low income parents may provide little added stimulus to enrollment of their

62. See Whelan, "The Constitution and Public Assistance to Education in Nonpublic Schools," in Whelan and Freund, *Legal and Constitutional Problems.*

children in nonpublic schools, and grants for experimentation may fail to generate any useful innovations. Third, there is the ever present problem of constitutionality—of what types of program will be ruled out by the courts. As long as the nonpublic sector is dominated by religiously affiliated schools the problem will continue. It is these institutions that policymakers would most like to help and that are most in need of assistance.

While these are difficult questions, some insight into the probable objectives, effectiveness, and constitutionality of various approaches to aiding nonpublic schools can be gained by looking at the existing ways in which these institutions are supported by government programs.

The Existing System of Public Aid

Most people are not aware of the magnitude and variety of public programs currently providing assistance to nonpublic schools. Such institutions are helped both by indirect government subsidies and by direct government expenditures (see Table 5-15). Some aid goes to the schools themselves, while some is channeled through the students and their parents.

Indirect government subsidies usually take the form of tax exemptions or deductions; nonpublic schools generally do not pay local property taxes, and contributions made either to churches or directly to such schools can be deducted from the portion of a family's income subject to state and federal income taxation. These subsidies are often overlooked because the government does not list them as expenditures, nor do the schools count them as income. Yet since they do tend to reduce total operating costs and lower the tuition charged by nonpublic schools, such tax exemptions and deductions should be considered as a form of government aid. Moreover, the general public seems recently to have become more aware of indirect subsidies. A 1971 survey found that more than half the citizens in nine of the ten cities sampled favored removal of the tax-exempt status of nonpublic schools.[63]

It is difficult to estimate the exact value of indirect subsidies. Calculations based on the average plant value of a sample of nonpublic schools and the average property tax rate suggest that the value of local property tax exemptions was about $207 million in 1970–71.[64] If the incomes of

63. "City Taxes and Services: Citizens Speak Out," *Nation's Cities*, Vol. 9 (August 1971), p. 9.

64. This assumes the following average plant values: Catholic elementary, $250,000; Catholic secondary, $600,000; private Catholic secondary, $800,000; other sectarian schools, $500,000; and nonsectarian schools, $1,315,000; as well as a tax rate of 2.5 percent—approximately the average in the urban Northeast.

Table 5-15. Public Aid Received and Total Income of Nonpublic Schools, and Aid as a Percentage of Income, Fiscal Year 1971

Millions of dollars

Aid and income items	Amount	Aid as percentage of total income
Federal		
Direct expenditures	99.4	4.0
Income tax deductions	126.3	5.1
Total	225.7	9.2
State		
Direct expenditures	207.7	8.5
Income tax deductions	6.3	0.3
Total	214.0	8.7
Local		
Direct expenditures	2.1	0.1
Property tax exemptions	207.4	8.4
Total	209.5	8.5
Federal, state, and local		
Direct expenditures	309.2	12.6
Tax deductions and exemptions	340.0	13.8
Total	649.2	26.4
Total income plus non-reported public aid and subsidies	2,455.7	...

Sources: Direct expenditures are from *Public Aid to Nonpublic Education*, A Staff Report Submitted to the President's Commission on School Finance (The Commission, 1972). Local expenditures are estimated as 1 percent of state expenditures. For estimation of tax subsidies, see text. State income tax is estimated as 5 percent of federal income tax. Total income is derived from Table 2-6 above; National Catholic Educational Association, *Report on U.S. Catholic Schools, 1970–71;* and NCEA, *A Statistical Report on Catholic Elementary and Secondary Schools for the Years 1967–68 to 1969–70.* Figures are rounded and may not add to totals.

those who donated money either directly to nonpublic schools or through churches were similar to those of the parents of nonpublic school students, subsidies resulting from the deductibility of gifts from federal taxable income amounted to another $126.3 million in 1970–71.[65] Similar reductions in state income tax liabilities added another $6.3 million, making the total of indirect government subsidies about $340 million (see Table 5-15).

65. On the basis of past Internal Revenue Service data (see U.S. Internal Revenue Service, *Statistics of Income—1969, Individual Income Tax Returns* [1971]) and existing tax rates, it was assumed that 75 percent of the donations were claimed as itemized deductions, and that the average applicable tax rate was 22 percent. It was assumed that all gift income was itemized, and that the applicable tax rate was 33 percent.

Most of the direct government expenditure for nonpublic schools is provided by state governments. Thirty-seven of the fifty states have one or more aid programs, and some states have as many as seven or eight. Estimating the total value of the expenditures is difficult because a single program frequently aids both public and nonpublic school students, and separate accounting records are not kept. However, using calculations based on a survey made by the staff of the President's Commission, one can estimate that in fiscal year 1971 state aid programs to nonpublic schools totaled approximately $208 million (see Table 5-15), $84 million of which was expended by New York state.[66] The largest single type of state aid program was in support of transportation services, which accounted for over one-fourth of the total. Assistance for handicapped children accounted for another fifth. The remainder was made up of a wide variety of programs including purchase of secular services, teacher salary supplements, administrative service reimbursements, tax adjustments, equipment grants, textbook aid, driver education, nutrition programs, and health services.[67] The purchase of secular services, salary supplements, and service reimbursements, which accounted for 30 percent of total state aid to nonpublic schools in 1970–71, have been declared unconstitutional in the state and federal decisions described above. Nevertheless, state appropriations increased for 1971–72 as more states added programs, existing programs were expanded, and states affected by the court decisions sought to rechannel funds into legal programs.

Most existing state programs are categorical. Those that seem to have withstood court tests best also resemble "child welfare" programs more closely than "educational" ones; that is, their principal focus is on the child's physical safety and welfare, not on direct aid to the educational process. In recent years, however, several states have initiated general aid schemes whose purpose is to reduce the effective tuitions paid by parents. For example, a law passed by the Connecticut legislature in 1972 would provide parents of nonpublic school pupils with reimbursements of $75 a year for the elementary grades and $150 a year for high school students. Pennsylvania and Ohio passed similar laws that were quickly declared

66. *Public Aid to Nonpublic Education*, A Staff Report Submitted to the President's Commission on School Finance (The Commission, 1972). Of the New York total, $24 million for an administrative services reimbursement program that has been declared unconstitutional by the state supreme court.
67. These services are often provided to nonpublic school students by local school districts, but the state reimburses the district for all or part of the costs.

unconstitutional. Both Hawaii and Minnesota provide state income tax credits and rebates to the parents of nonpublic school children.

Much of the direct local government assistance to nonpublic schools is similar to that of state governments, although it is much more scattered and irregular. But some local school districts also have formal cooperative arrangements with nonpublic schools that in effect form a very different type of public subsidy. Dual enrollment programs, which in 1970 could be found in some of the school districts of thirty-three states, are the most widespread of these arrangements.[68] Under dual enrollment arrangements a student concurrently attends both a public and a nonpublic school, taking some courses in each institution. The public school system usually provides specialized classes that require costly equipment, special facilities, or highly trained teachers.

Leased facility programs, under which a public school system rents classrooms from nonpublic schools in which it conducts the "public" part of a dual enrollment program, are another form of local subsidy for nonpublic schools. Shared facilities and services offer a third avenue of aid. Under such arrangements, the nonpublic school students might conduct their physical education classes in the public schools, or utilize the health services or psychological counseling provided by the public schools. There is thus a wide variety of ways in which local governments provide direct assistance to nonpublic schools, but there is little information with which to estimate the total amount of local government aid involved. It is generally believed to be only a small fraction of the sums administered by state governments; in Table 5-15 it is estimated as 1 percent of state expenditures.

Direct federal aid, on the other hand, does constitute a significant sum. The U.S. Office of Education estimated that it contributed about $100 million to nonpublic schools in fiscal year 1971 (see Table 5-15). Most of the federal aid for nonpublic schools was channeled through a few programs. Roughly 44 percent of all federal assistance was for aid to the disadvantaged under Title I of the Elementary and Secondary Education Act of 1965. Another third was for food programs. Most of the remainder went to aid for purchasing books, equipment, and supplementary services.

Altogether, public subsidies and aid to nonpublic schools amounted to almost $650 million in 1970–71 (see Table 5-15). Direct government as-

68. See "Local Cooperative Programs Between the Public and Nonpublic Schools," in Donald A. Erickson and George F. Madaus, *Issues of Aid to Nonpublic Schools*, Vol. 3: *Public Assistance Programs for Nonpublic Schools*, Submitted to the President's Commission on School Finance (The Commission, 1972), Chap. 4, p. 13.

sistance was about $310 million, or 13 percent of the income and aid received by the nonpublic school sectors. Indirect government assistance amounted to another 14 percent. Government already plays a very significant financial role in the nonpublic school sector.

*Methods of Strengthening the Fiscal Position
of Nonpublic Schools*

SELF-HELP. Although initiating new government subsidies to nonpublic schools is the route upon which public attention is currently focused, it is not the only way to fiscal salvation for these institutions. For the Catholic schools and other denominational schools, where most of the problem lies, the situation could be at least somewhat improved through self-help. In many areas, the Catholic school system is really a federation of nearly independent parish schools; better coordination or complete unification of the schools in each diocese could reduce costs. While most dioceses have administrative authority over the secondary schools, the elementary schools, which educate the bulk of the students, are largely under the control of the parish pastors. Many parishes and their pastors have been reluctant to combine their elementary schools with those of neighboring parishes. As a result numerous schools have been kept open, running inefficiently with half-filled classrooms. A diocese-wide plan for closing and consolidating schools would probably save the Catholic schools a considerable amount of money as well as improve the quality of the education provided. One estimate suggests that an extensive consolidation program might reduce total Catholic school costs by roughly $900 million, or by 35 percent of the amount that would be required in 1975 to operate an unconsolidated system.[69] The creation of single unified diocese-wide elementary school systems would also provide a vehicle for redistribution of parish resources. At present parish schools, as long as they do not run at a deficit, have virtual fiscal autonomy. Since parish officials set the levels of tuitions and parish subsidies, tuition and charges are often lower in wealthy neighborhoods than in poorer areas because the local parish is better able to subsidize the school.[70] A fiscally unified school system would redistribute resources from parishes that have no financial difficulties to those that are being forced to raise tuitions because of reduced parish income.

Higher tuitions and increased church subsidies may offer an additional

69. Bartell, "Costs and Revenues," p. 256.
70. Gary and associates, "Collapse of Nonpublic Education," Vol. 1, p. 4-12.

means of reducing the fiscal problems of both Catholic schools and institutions affiliated with some protestant denominations. Schools that charge little or no tuition could raise their fees significantly, since the evidence we have reviewed shows that enrollments would not be greatly affected. Of course, there are limits to this approach. If tuitions reached levels only the relatively wealthy could afford, the goal of making the parochial schools quasi-public institutions serving all the children of the congregation would be undermined. Furthermore, in some cases at least, higher tuition may not lead to a significant increase in available school resources. When tuition in the Catholic schools of Philadelphia was raised, parish collections tended to drop by an equivalent amount.[71]

In some instances increased church subsidies may not offer a reasonable alternative, in part because of the slow growth of the income of religious organizations. Catholic church collections have increased only slightly in recent years, and experts do not expect the situation to change with rising incomes, because the marginal propensity of families to contribute to the church appears to fall as family incomes increase.[72] Since well over half of parish income is already channeled into school subsidies, it is not likely that the fraction could be substantially increased. Some Lutheran congregations face a similar situation.

Attempts to reorganize the Catholic school system or to raise tuitions and church subsidies may run into considerable opposition.[73] Some parishioners and priests have come to regard school closings, even when part of a consolidation plan, as a manifestation of the collapse of the system, and have fought to keep their individual schools open at all costs. Furthermore, the public debate has convinced many that the religious denominations running schools are unable to provide more money for schools and that any rise in tuition, no matter how slight, will drive children from parochial institutions.

Another method by which nonpublic schools may be able to improve their fiscal situations, and at the same time maintain control of their programs, is to take full advantage of the existing federal programs of support. About 35 percent of the Catholic schools are now utilizing the school lunch program, and only about 60 percent take advantage of library services

71. Gurash Committee Report, p. 29.

72. *Ibid.*, p. xvii; Gary and associates, "Collapse of Nonpublic Education," Vol. 1, pp. 2-13, 2-14; Bartell, "Costs and Revenues," p. 249.

73. Gary and Cole, "The Politics of Aid"; and Gary and associates, "Collapse of Nonpublic Education," Vol. 1, pp. 2-14, 2-15.

grants for which they are eligible. The situation is similar with respect to the aid to the disadvantaged program (Title I, ESEA).[74] Although information is not available on other nonpublic schools, they probably make even less use of existing public aid programs. Of course, some of the blame for the low participation rates of nonpublic schools lies with public authorities, who often have thrown up obstacles to their fuller involvement in federal programs.

Nonpublic schools could also realize economies by participating more fully in dual enrollment and shared time programs. Legal opinion seems to agree that public schools would probably be required by the Constitution to accept "part time" students.[75] However, such programs are of limited use at the elementary level, where a single teacher is often the instructor for all subjects, few of which require special equipment or training. Furthermore, such enrollment programs might undermine the unique character that parochial and private education claims as its *raison d'être*, and thus prove self-defeating. Parents may understandably wonder why their children are enrolled in the nonpublic school. In Illinois it was found that nonpublic schools engaged in shared-time programs with public systems suffered much sharper enrollment drops than did similar institutions without such cooperative arrangements.[76]

Although there are a variety of steps nonpublic schools might take on their own to strengthen their fiscal position, the impact of these steps may be marginal. In fact, nonpublic school enrollments are likely to decline substantially even if these schools adopt all of the self-help strategies available to them. Public attention will thus continue to focus on increased government aid to these schools, and the debate will revolve around what form the aid should take.

EXPANDED GOVERNMENT PROGRAMS. For a variety of reasons, not all the methods currently used to support nonpublic schools offer feasible channels for expanding government aid. In the first place, some programs are already being used to capacity. For example, the property tax-exempt status of nonpublic schools cannot be increased, because virtually all of them now benefit from this form of government subsidy. Other programs such as noneducational "child support" services are incapable of providing

---

74. See S. P. Marland, Jr., "Public Policy and the Private Schools" (speech delivered to the National Catholic Educational Association, Philadelphia, April 3, 1972; processed), p. 6.
75. Fleischmann Commission Report, p. 5A-4.
76. Erickson and others, "Crisis in Illinois Nonpublic Schools," pp. 2-5, 2-6.

assistance in meaningful quantities. Even if the federal and state governments reimbursed schools for all such services they now provide, the total amount of aid would be small.

Certain other methods of aiding nonpublic education are ruled out because they are of dubious constitutionality. Direct cash assistance, it seems, would encounter the problem of "excessive entanglement" between church and state, because nonpublic schools would have to report to the government on the use of the funds, and the government would have to monitor the spending of public funds by the institutions.[77]

Still other methods may be ruled out because they are likely to have little impact on declining enrollments. An example of this is the proposal of the Panel on Nonpublic Education that a federal loan program assist in the construction of new nonpublic school facilities in areas where there are no nonpublic schools,[78] that is, in suburbs. Not only is it unlikely that such loans would withstand a constitutional challenge, because in many cases the buildings would be used at least partly for the teaching of religion,[79] but one can also question the extent to which a loan program would really stimulate nonpublic school enrollments. In the first place, the availability of parochial nonpublic schools in the new suburbs may hasten the exodus of Catholics, Lutherans, and others from the inner city, thus further depopulating the nonpublic schools in those areas. Second, as we have pointed out, Catholic schools are closing at a more rapid rate in the suburbs than elsewhere. A major cause of this trend is the parents' feeling that the education provided by the public schools is superior. A survey of the Catholic laity in the Indianapolis suburbs that asked whether the local public or Catholic school better prepared students for college and for a job found the following distribution of views (expressed as percentages of all respondents):[80]

77. State laws that attempt to circumvent the problem by specifying that the government funds may be used for the purchase of such "secular services" as instruction in mathematics, advanced sciences, physical education, and modern languages, for "salary supplementation" of those engaged in teaching secular subjects, for the maintenance and repair of the school building, or for services mandated by state education laws, have failed to pass the test in lower courts. See above.

78. *Nonpublic Education and the Public Good*, p. 42.

79. For this reason, most construction aid to parochial colleges and universities has been used for dormitories and laboratory construction. See *Tilton* v. *Richardson*, 403 U.S. 672 (1971).

80. Unpublished data collected as part of the 1968 Catholic Education Study directed by George Elford for the diocese of Indianapolis.

	Public school is better	Catholic school is better	No difference
Preparation for college	37.9	15.7	38.9
Preparation for a job	42.2	6.9	44.4

New buildings alone are not likely to change their evaluation. Third, a lack of physical facilities does not seem to have been an obstacle to the growth of nondenominational private institutions. Despite their high tuitions, enrollments in these schools have burgeoned in recent years.

Since some forms of categorical aid are incapable of further expansion, others are thought to be unconstitutional, and still others would have only a minor impact on the size of the nonpublic sector, most advocates of increased public support have focused on general aid that could be channeled to the families of nonpublic school students rather than directly to the schools. A number of types of aid programs fit the requirements. Since all provide a grant or subsidy to parents who pay nonpublic school tuitions, they would effectively reduce the cost of sending a child to nonpublic schools. The institutions could then presumably raise their tuition to generate needed revenue without adverse parental reactions. If the tuition increases were smaller than the subsidies, the cost of sending a child to nonpublic schools would actually decline.

Tuition reimbursement schemes or direct cash grants to parents with children in nonpublic schools are the most straightforward means of channeling money through parents to the nonpublic schools. The President's Panel on Nonpublic Education advocated creation of such a plan for low income families.[81] In recent years, New York, Illinois, Ohio, Pennsylvania, Connecticut, and Louisiana have passed legislation calling for cash payments to parents with children in nonpublic schools. Without exception, the plans have been declared unconstitutional by lower courts, and in refusing to review the Ohio case the Supreme Court has upheld the verdict.[82]

Educational vouchers, which were discussed in Chapter 4, represent a broader form of tuition reimbursement. Voucher plans would include all school children, and public as well as nonpublic institutions would charge tuitions. The universality of the plan has convinced some that a voucher

81. *Nonpublic Education and the Public Good*, p. 36.
82. See *New York Times*, October 11, 1972.

scheme could be designed that would pass judicial muster, in spite of the courts' lack of enthusiasm for limited tuition reimbursement grants. On the other hand, since the parent transmits the voucher to the school, which then cashes it with the government, it is difficult to see how vouchers could be considered anything but a direct payment from the government to the nonpublic school. If this were so, they too might be held unconstitutional; as the three-judge federal court reasoned in the Ohio tuition reimbursement case. "What may not be done directly may not be done indirectly. . . ."[83]

Although from the economic standpoint there is no difference between a cash payment from the government to an individual and an equal reduction in the individual's tax liability, some feel that from the legal standpoint the former involves more active government participation while the latter is merely a matter of definitions in the Internal Revenue Code.[84] For this reason, income tax credits for tuition payments made to nonpublic schools have received a great deal of attention in the search for an acceptable method of channeling substantial sums of public money to nonpublic schools.[85] Hawaii, Minnesota, New York, and California already provide state income tax credits that vary in size with the family's taxable income or the amount of tuition paid, or both, and the President's Panel on Nonpublic Education has recommended a similar program on a national scale.[86]

A number of objections to tax credits have been raised. In the first place, such credits would be of little use to low income families who have little or no tax liability. Although this situation could be remedied if a rebate were provided to those whose credit exceeded their liability, some feel that such a plan would transform credits into tuition reimbursements, which are unconstitutional. In the second place, many doubt that even without rebates income tax credits would be acceptable to the courts.[87] The general

83. *Wolman v. Essex*, Civil Action 71-396, U.S.D.C., S.D. Ohio, Eastern Div. (1972), Pt. 4.

84. See Boris I. Bittker, "Churches, Taxes and the Constitution," *Yale Law Journal*, Vol. 78 (July 1969), pp. 1285–1310.

85. A tax credit reduces the income tax liability of parents who pay tuitions; a full credit for the first $200 paid in tuition would reduce the tax liability of all families that paid $200 or more in tuition by $200; a 50 percent credit would reduce it by $100.

86. *Nonpublic Education and the Public Good*, p. 38.

87. Eight of the members of the President's Commission on School Finance, including its chairman, and the majority of the Fleischmann Commission in New York, concluded that tax credit schemes would not withstand judicial challenge. President's Commission on School Finance, *Schools, People, & Money: The Need for Educational Reform*, Final Report (1972), p. 97; Fleischmann Commission Report, pp. 5A.5 to 5A.10.

argument is that if credits were restricted to parents with children in schools that conformed to government regulations, "excessive entanglement" between church and state would arise when the government checked on the schools' compliance. On the other hand, if the credit were available without restrictions on the schools, there would be no assurance that public aid was not being used to support the religious component of sectarian school education.[88]

A number of experts who have disagreed with this view have argued that tax credits would be constitutional in that they represent aid to the parents, not to the school or to religious organizations.[89] Furthermore, they reason that if the credit is limited to a fraction of tuition paid, it can be said that only the secular portion of the education provided by denominational schools is being subsidized by public funds. In any event, the resolution of the constitutional issue of tax credits is far from clear.

Another method of channeling public money through parents to non-public schools would be to allow families to deduct tuitions when computing their taxable income, just as they now deduct charitable contributions. As Chapter 2 pointed out, some religiously affiliated schools have taken partial advantage of the current tax codes by maintaining low tuition rates while encouraging tax deductible contributions, either through special church collections or through "suggested" parental donations.[90] Making tuition tax deductible would thus allow all schools to do what some partially do already.

From the parents' standpoint, tax deductibility would reduce the real cost of nonpublic school tuition by an amount equivalent to the tuition deduction multiplied by the marginal income tax rate facing the family. It would thus give larger benefits to higher income taxpayers; the deductibility of a $500 tuition fee would reduce the tax liability of a family with taxable income of $25,000 by $180, that of a family with a taxable income of $8,000 by only $95. Moreover, only those who itemize deductions—mostly taxpayers with higher than average incomes—would gain.

88. In his dissent from the *Lemon* v. *Kurtzman* decision, Justice Byron R. White described this as the "insoluble paradox": "The State cannot finance secular instruction if it permits religion to be taught in the same classroom; but if it exacts a promise that religion not be so taught—a promise the school and its teachers are quite willing and on this record able to give—and enforces it, it is then entangled in the 'no entanglement' aspect of the Court's Establishment Clause jurisprudence." *Lemon* v. *Kurtzman*, at 668.

89. See Fleischmann Commission Report, pp. 5B.4 to 5B.10.

90. Erickson and others, "Crisis in Illinois Nonpublic Schools," pp. 4-31, 4-32.

Tax deductions also have the disadvantage that they cannot channel large amounts of resources to nonpublic schools that for social reasons want to keep tuitions relatively low. For example, estimates suggest that parents of children in Catholic schools will pay about $150 in tuitions in 1975.[91] This would leave the schools with a deficit of from $1.3 billion to $2.2 billion. Deductibility of tuition from taxable income would permit the schools to increase their charges by some $50 per child without raising the average cost to the parent.[92] Such an increase, however, would cover only from 10 to 28 percent of the expected deficit. Although tax deductions would allow the private schools that cater to children of wealthy families to raise their tuitions considerably without increasing the cost to parents, it is not these institutions that are having major financial problems.

While many think that a program of tax deductibility for tuitions paid to nonpublic institutions would be constitutional, there are others who feel that, unless broadly defined, deductions could raise constitutional problems.[93] This may appear strange since contributions to churches and schools have been permitted as deductible items, and the legality of property tax exemptions for religious buildings has been upheld by the courts. But in these cases, some legal scholars argue, the church-state issue was subordinated because of the broad nature of the programs. The law was not intended to benefit churches or religiously affiliated schools; these institutions benefited only by virtue of their classification as two of many types of nonprofit, charitable, or educational organizations. Such reasoning suggests that tax deductibility would have the brightest prospects for judicial acceptance if it were defined to include all types of parental payments for child development—tuition for after-school music, dance, arts and crafts, athletic, and religious lessons, as well as taxes paid for the support of public schools and nonpublic school tuition.

To summarize, a great many programs might be used to aid nonpublic schools. However, many of those that appear to be capable of providing significant amounts of public resources for these institutions are of dubious constitutionality. Those that have been accepted by the courts, on the other

91. Bartell, "Costs and Revenues."

92. If anything, this is an overestimate in that it assumes that all families with children in these institutions can take advantage of the deduction, and that the average marginal tax rate of the parents in 1975 will be that of a family with $13,000 taxable income.

93. For the former case, see Leo Pfeffer, "Aid to Denominational Schools Under Article XI, Section 3 of the New York Constitution," in Gary and associates, "Collapse of Nonpublic Education," Vol. 1, pp. 5-62 to 5-64.

hand, are not generally capable of channeling the amount of resources the schools appear to require to avoid substantial tuition increases.

Conclusion

The ultimate impact of any major program of public aid to nonpublic schools would depend on the magnitude and type of assistance provided. Merely to determine who would benefit most is not an easy task. Some of the problems are made obvious by an analysis of the effects of a tax credit. As long as the tuition in nonpublic schools did not rise by more than the amount of the credit, the parents would benefit, because the effective price they pay for nonpublic schools would be lower. Tuition increases induced by a tax credit might result in increased school expenditures, which would presumably improve the quality of education and would thus benefit primarily the pupils. In schools that depend heavily on church subsidies and gifts, the entire rise in tuition is not likely to result in increased expenditures; at least part would probably be absorbed by a compensating reduction in gifts and church subsidies. If this occurred, the parishes and congregations and their contributors would be the beneficiaries, and church resources would be freed for other uses.

The impact on nonpublic school enrollment of any of the proposals is also a matter of conjecture. Because of the limited role that rising charges have played in declining enrollment and the difficulty in targeting public subsidies on those who would respond most to them, only a very expensive program would lead to a dramatic growth in the number of nonpublic school students. In all likelihood, enrollments in Catholic and Lutheran institutions will continue to decline irrespective of public policy, but nondenominational schools may expand considerably under a policy of aid to nonpublic schools. The structure of the nonpublic sector may thus be changed through increased public aid.

Unless the variety of nonpublic schools in many communities increases considerably, the choice which these schools affords families will continue to be limited. Only those willing to send their children to a sectarian school will have a choice. The competitive pressure of nonpublic schools also will continue to be of minor importance unless that sector expands significantly.

Changes in the financing of public schools may well have a more profound effect on enrollment trends in the nonpublic sector than any constellation of government aid programs to the nonpublic sector. If increased state assumption of public school financing leads to a lowering of educational quality or to a diminution of choice, many parents may quit the public system to provide their children a better education. If, on the other hand, an improved public system results from reforms in education financing, nonpublic schools may be hard pressed to compete with the public sector, and their enrollment may be decimated despite any government program designed to aid them.

chapter six **The Federal Role
in School Finance
Reform**

The federal government has traditionally played a
minor role in elementary and secondary education finance. Recent court
decisions, and the alleged fiscal crisis in public and nonpublic schools, have
made it probable that the federal government's role will change in the near
future. As yet, the exact nature of the expanded federal role is far from
clear; this final chapter will examine a number of the alternatives currently
being discussed. A short review of the case for an increased federal role
precedes this analysis.

The Case for Federal Intervention

Two arguments are generally advanced in support of increasing the federal involvement in school finance. The first of these is based on society's
interest in having all its citizens moderately well educated, the benefits of
an educated electorate, a skilled and mobile labor force, and a system in
which class tensions are moderated by the belief that opportunities for economic and social advancement are relatively open. These social benefits are
not limited by the borders of school districts or states, but accrue to the
country as a whole, just as the entire nation bears the cost of failures of the
educational system. The poorly educated child of one state may migrate
and become the unemployed welfare recipient of another jurisdiction; if he
remains in the school district in which he was educated, resources from federal programs that all taxpayers support will be used in his behalf. Some
education programs, such as the desegregation of schools, may have widespread social effects. When we say that a program has "national purposes,"

147

we usually mean that its economic and social spillover effects are substantial. If the benefits and costs of education are shared by the nation as a whole, it stands to reason that the burden of raising a major share of public educational resources should be borne by the national government. Of course a similar case for federal involvement can be made for such other social programs as public assistance and certain kinds of health programs.[1]

The second argument advanced in behalf of a larger federal role is based on the superiority of the central government's revenue raising system. While states and localities worry about the effect of tax increases on their relative ability to attract industry and upper income residents, the federal government does not have these concerns; taxpayers cannot escape federal taxes by moving, unless they emigrate. Another advantage of the federal tax structure is that it is more progressive than that of states and localities. While most federal revenues are raised through levies on corporate and personal incomes, states rely primarily on regressive sales taxes and localities on the property tax, which is probably less progressive than the federal income tax. Finally, the federal revenue system is more elastic; in a growing economy, federal tax revenues will automatically increase much more rapidly than those of states or localities.

Of course the advantages of the federal revenue system may not be applicable to a major expansion of the federal role in school finance. Several studies have indicated that over the next five years existing federal programs, if expanded to keep pace with inflation and other built-in growth factors, will require more revenues than the federal tax system is likely to generate.[2] New initiatives are therefore likely to require new or increased federal taxes. If this is true of an increase in the federal role in school finance, the advantages of the federal tax system over those of the states and localities will depend on which new tax source the federal government develops or which existing taxes are raised.

The case for increasing the federal responsibility for financing elementary and secondary education rests first on the fact that the benefits and costs of education spill over state boundaries, and second on the superior fiscal

---

1. For a discussion of the geographical distribution of benefits of public programs, see the discussion in George F. Break, *Intergovernmental Fiscal Relations in the United States* (Brookings Institution, 1967), Chap. 3.

2. Charles L. Schultze and others, *Setting National Priorities: The 1973 Budget* (Brookings Institution, 1972), Chap. 13; and David J. Ott and others, *Nixon, McGovern and the Federal Budget* (Washington: American Enterprise Institute for Public Policy Research, 1972), Chap. 3.

ability of the federal government. Neither rationale, however, tells us what share of education expenditures should be borne by the federal taxpayer or offers a means of selecting among the wide range of possible objectives that could be pursued through federal educational programs.

Possible Federal Objectives

In expanding its fiscal commitment to elementary and secondary education, the federal government might choose to pursue any of a number of objectives: (1) the goals of existing federal programs, (2) state or local tax relief, (3) a reduction in expenditure and resource disparities, (4) a reduction in tax inequities, and (5) assistance for nonpublic schools. In addition to the choice of its objectives the federal government must also select the appropriate means of achieving them. It might mandate changes through regulations and requirements, or provide incentives that would lead states and localities to act in the desired way.

Strengthening Existing Programs

Most of the programs currently financed by the federal government are aimed at specific national educational objectives which for one reason or another states and localities are unwilling or unable to meet. The largest federal program at present is Title I of the Elementary and Secondary Education Act (ESEA) of 1965 which is directed at improving through compensatory education the educational opportunities of children from disadvantaged homes (see Table 6-1). Although compensatory services, ranging from remedial specialists to medical treatment, are supposed to be provided for eligible children, there is so far not much evidence that the Title I program has significantly upgraded the academic performance of disadvantaged children. Many reasons have been offered for the disappointing results. Among these is the fact that in some areas—especially rural districts—school expenditures, including Title I funds, are so low that they are not sufficient for a good education. There is also evidence that Title I funds have in many instances been substituted for local funds. If the target group does not actually get any special care or compensatory treat-

Table 6-1. Appropriations to the U.S. Office of Education for Elementary and Secondary Education, by Type of Program, Fiscal Years 1971–73

Millions of dollars

Type of program	1971 Actual	1972 Actual	1973ᵃ Estimated
Aid to educationally deprived childrenᵇ	1,500	1,598	1,810
Aid to federally impacted areas	551	612	681
Education for the handicapped	105	110	162
Vocational education	446	489	584
Emergency school assistance and civil rights education	94	20	271
Education renewal	301	324	303
Research and development	68	87	108
Otherᶜ	303	319	364
Total	3,368	3,559	4,283

Sources: *Congressional Record*, daily ed., August 6, 1971, pp. S13444–48; October 13, 1972, pp. H10018–21; and October 14, 1972, p. S18241; tables prepared by the U.S. Department of Health, Education, and Welfare for H.R. 16654 (September 14, 1972; processed); *Making Appropriations for the Departments of Labor and Health, Education, and Welfare*, House Conference Report 92-1591, 92 Cong. 2 sess. (1972); *The Budget of the United States Government—Appendix, Fiscal Year 1973*, p. 481.

a. Amounts approved by Congress in H.R. 16654, 92 Cong. 2 sess. (1972), and H.R. 17034, 92 Cong. 2 sess. In H.R. 16654, the Labor-HEW appropriation bill, Congress appropriated $30.5 billion for the two departments and related agencies, but included a provision (sec. 409) that permitted the President to reduce the total to $29.3 billion, provided that no specific item was reduced by more than 13 percent. President Nixon vetoed H.R. 16654 after Congress adjourned. Therefore the Ninety-third Congress will have to reconsider the appropriation. However, H.R. 16654 is useful as an indicator of what the Ninety-third Congress is likely to appropriate. The general supplemental appropriations bill for fiscal year 1973 (H.R. 17034) appropriates $271 million for emergency school assistance and $92 million for the National Institute of Education, with the additional provision that $16 million be transferred from education renewal to the National Institute of Education. Column 3 reflects these adjustments.

b. Under Title I of the Elementary and Secondary Education Act of 1965.

c. Includes the following: strengthening state departments of education, supplementary services, library resources, and equipment and remodeling.

ment, it is not surprising that its performance lags.[3] In some cases, disadvantaged children are so highly concentrated in particular schools that recent Title I funding, even without slippage of funds, cannot be expected to make any significant difference.[4] In such cases, either massive compensa-

3. A special study of the Title I comparability guidelines (which were established to ensure that school districts use state and local money to provide nearly equal services to all schools before the addition of Title I funds) found that Title I schools were noncomparable; that is, that Title I funds were actually used to raise the spending levels in schools serving the poor to the levels in schools serving wealthier students. "Special Report on Review of the Implementation of Comparability Provisions, Public Law 91-230" (U.S. Department of Health, Education, and Welfare, unpublished document, no date), especially pp. 44–49 and Appendix B.

4. In recent years Title I appropriations have been about $1.5 billion, or less than $200 per disadvantaged child.

tory funds or some system of breaking up the concentrations of low income children would seem to offer the only hope of success.[5]

A study by the Department of Health, Education, and Welfare shows that as spending per pupil for compensatory education programs rises, the likelihood of significant improvements in cognitive skills increases markedly.[6] On this basis, and for the political purpose of presenting an alternative to busing, there have been several proposals to increase federal funding of compensatory education.[7] With an estimated 8 million disadvantaged children of school age, each of whom would receive compensatory services worth $450 (approximately half the national average school expenditure, the original goal of Title I), a fully funded program would cost about $3.6 billion. Existing Title I funds of more than $1.5 billion can be counted toward this total only to the degree to which current funds reach disadvantaged children instead of replacing regular school expenditures. Given past difficulties in targeting these funds, additional federal spending of about $3 billion would probably be required to pursue the federal goal of providing significant compensatory services to the disadvantaged.

Impacted areas aid, the second largest of the federal programs that support elementary and secondary education, provides assistance to school districts that serve significant numbers of children whose parents either work for the federal government or reside on property owned by the federal government. The program was conceived during the Korean war as a means of compensating school districts for the rises in enrollment caused by military installations. The rationale was that since many of the children lived on tax-exempt federal property the schools did not enjoy the usual tax base increase that accompanies an inflow of population. Since that time, the program has been gradually expanded to include children of civilian government workers, most of whom live in taxable buildings or work in nontaxable buildings located in school districts other than those in which their children attend school. Children living in public housing have also been

5. A final reason sometimes offered for the lack of success of Title I programs is that "money does not make any difference" in education, not to speak of compensatory education. For a discussion of this issue, see Harvey A. Averch and others, *How Effective is Schooling? A Critical Review and Synthesis of Research Findings*, Prepared for the President's Commission on School Finance (Santa Monica: RAND Corporation, 1972).

6. U.S. Department of Health, Education, and Welfare, "The Effectiveness of Compensatory Education: Summary and Review of the Evidence" (HEW, 1972; processed).

7. Two examples are the Equal Educational Opportunities Act proposed by President Nixon in March 1972, and House Resolution 905, introduced by Congressman Carl D. Perkins, which would add $2.5 billion to the Title I appropriation.

added to the impacted areas aid program, despite the fact that public housing is usually owned by local authorities that make payments to local governments in lieu of taxes, and despite the absence of evidence that public housing leads to an increase in school population. In its current form, much of the program makes little sense. Recent administrations have repeatedly attempted to cut it back, but Congress has thwarted this effort.

The federal government also has long-standing categorical programs that benefit vocational education, programs for handicapped children, and school libraries. In 1971, the Nixon administration attempted to consolidate many of these categorical programs and convert them into a single grant to states. The idea behind this proposal was that the states could better determine the allocation of funds among these categories of programs. So far, special revenue sharing for education, the name given to this consolidation of programs, has not been adopted by Congress and its success may depend on increasing the funds for these programs as they are consolidated.

More recently, federal interest in supporting educational research has grown. The Education Amendments of 1972 authorized the creation of a National Institute of Education (NIE), which would take over and expand existing federal education research support.[8] NIE's budget in its first year will probably be around $100 million, but a preliminary plan projected a support level five times as high in five years.[9] With increasing acceptance of the notion of experimentation in education—the controlled testing of alternative curricula, staffing arrangements, and new education technologies—these projections may well prove conservative.[10]

Another new initiative contained in the Education Amendments of 1972 was the Emergency School Aid Act, which authorized $2 billion in fiscal years 1973 and 1974 to meet the special problems confronting school districts that are being forced to desegregate, to encourage voluntary elimination of minority group isolation, and to help overcome the educational disadvantages imposed by segregated schooling.[11] Although some of the

8. Title III, sec. 405 (b) (1), of Public Law 92-318, 92 Cong., approved June 23, 1972.

9. Roger E. Levien, *National Institute of Education: Preliminary Plan for the Proposed Institute*, A Report Prepared for the U.S. Department of Health, Education, and Welfare (RAND Corporation, 1971), p. 153.

10. In a limited demonstration program of the U.S. Office of Education called "Experimental Schools," the average annual cost of a project was $1.3 million. At this rate, supporting experiments in 5 percent of all school districts would cost $1.1 billion. (For a description of the program, see U.S. Office of Education, *Experimental Schools Program: 1971 Experimental School Projects; Three Educational Plans*, DHEW (OE) 72-42 [1972].)

11. P.L. 92-318, Title VII.

funds that will be expended under the act are clearly for transitional purposes, such other goals as overcoming the disadvantages of racial isolation in most major cities will create demands for funding beyond the two-year life of the legislation. Emergency school assistance may well become another permanent federal program.

Most of the existing federal aid to education programs have rationales that imply federal, rather than state or local, financing. The Title I program is of this nature, both because the failure to educate poor children affects the whole society and because poor children are concentrated in states that can least afford compensatory services. Similarly, the federal commitment to assist desegregation is the expression of a national concern, one that is frequently in conflict with local majority opinion. Research into new educational techniques must be a federal responsibility: the investment is large, the payoff is uncertain, and successful research will be broadly disseminated and benefit many school districts. In the older categorical and special purpose programs, federal funding usually reflects the feeling that states and localities if left to their own devices would not spend as much on such programs as vocational education and training the handicapped as the national interest requires.

A possible federal role in education finance over the next several years is simply the continuation and more adequate funding of aid programs that are already in being. This has been the actual course of the period from 1969 to 1972. Although the Nixon administration has tried to cut back or at least to hold down the support levels for most of the older programs, this effort has met with little success; the well entrenched congressional advocates of the programs have overridden one of three presidential vetoes of educational appropriation bills during this period, and have compromised on budgets that exceeded presidential requests in the other years. Federal planning for future educational support, if it is to be realistic, must thus reckon with some growth in congressionally favored programs. Even a modest expansion in existing programs might increase the federal commitment to $8 billion by the mid-1970s, more than doubling the education appropriations of fiscal year 1972.[12] Such an expansion of existing programs has significant implications for the other potential federal actions that will be discussed in this chapter.

First, expansion of existing programs may in part replace state and local funds that would have been used for education. To that extent, this type of

12. The $8 billion estimate is composed of $3–$3.5 billion for Title I, $0.5–$1 billion for research, $1 billion for desegregation aid, and $2.5 billion for all other programs.

federal strategy indirectly provides tax relief for state-local taxpayers. The various existing federal programs have different impacts on state-local tax burdens. Federal research support would not replace state-local funds at all, because these governments devote few of their own resources to such research. On the other hand, impacted areas aid is almost entirely a substitute for local funds; but it affects only selected school districts.

Second, the expansion of existing federal programs will have an effect on expenditure disparities among school districts. Of particular importance in this respect is the Title I program. Since Title I funds are distributed to districts within a state more or less in proportion to the enrollment of low income children, increased federal funding of the program might affect the manner in which state governments attempt to equalize expenditures. As Chapter 4 pointed out, some state aid reform plans would count a disadvantaged pupil as more than one student, thereby giving extra state aid to districts with such enrollees. If Title I were funded at a higher level than is now the case, states might feel less pressure to compensate districts for the higher costs of educating low income children. This could make equalization reform programs simpler, cheaper, and politically more acceptable for the states.

Tax Relief

A second major objective that might be pursued by the federal government is state and local tax relief. Both presidential candidates in 1972 made relief of the burdens of local residential property taxation a major objective of their aid to education plans, and both promised new federal assistance to bring about such relief.

If general state-local tax relief is desired, almost any additional federal grant-in-aid to state and local governments can produce it. A good example is the State and Local Fiscal Assistance Act of 1972 (general revenue sharing), which provides for the distribution of $5.3 billion in the first full year, one-third of which will go to state governments and the rest to local general purpose governments, not school districts. Such funds might relieve the local property taxes on homeowners and renters if states used their revenue sharing grants for enlarged state aid to education, and if school districts responded by reducing their own revenues by like sums.[13] Although the

13. For example, before the ink had dried on the revenue sharing act, the governor of New Jersey proposed allocating more than 70 percent of the state grant to localities for school aid. See Ronald Sullivan, "Cahill Proposed Using $40-Million in Revenue-Sharing Funds for School Aid," *New York Times*, October 15, 1972, p. 62.

federal funds paid to local governments cannot, under the legislation, be spent for schools, local general purpose governments could use their federal funds to finance existing levels of noneducational services. This would permit them to lower the general property tax, and school districts could increase their school taxes and expenditures without causing any overall increase in property tax rates. The point is that almost any rise in federal aid to state and local governments, even when it excludes school districts from its beneficence, permits a reduction in the state-local tax burdens. Just how much of a general grant-in-aid program is used for tax relief and how much for increased expenditures will depend on the reactions of state and local governments, as will the choice of the specific taxes that are reduced.

Most of the support for tax relief as a major federal objective is based on a desire to reduce property taxes, especially those on residential property. There are several ways in which the federal government could provide incentives for reducing the reliance on residential property taxes for schools or to relieve the onerous aspects of the tax.

One possibility is to require that states eliminate residential property taxes as a source of revenue for schools, and to provide a federal grant sufficient to "replace" the lost revenue. As Chapter 3 mentioned, the Nixon administration suggested such an approach in the material it transmitted to the Advisory Commission on Intergovernmental Relations (ACIR) for review in early 1972. Although the difficulties with this approach have already been discussed, it might be useful to review them briefly. First, such a plan would be expensive, requiring at least $12 billion a year. Second, since states vary widely in the use made of residential property taxes to support education (see Table 3-12), it is not feasible to distribute $12 billion in such a way that each state will have enough to replace its residential school tax. Under any conceivable distribution formula states like New Jersey would get too little federal money to replace their education property taxes, and would have to supplement the federal funds with new state-raised revenue. However, the magnitude of the proposed education aid is so great that all states would be likely to agree to eliminate residential school taxes. Third, *eliminating* the residential property tax for education means, in effect, that the level of education spending in each school district will be determined by the state. If local districts cannot impose property taxes on residences, they cannot finance any education expenditures at all at the local level because of the lack of alternative local tax sources. Thus, in practice, a federal program of property tax replacement is a federal program for full state assumption of the costs of education. Capacity equalization programs such as those discussed in Chapter 4 would not be possible.

A less drastic approach, one that would reduce but not eliminate the current reliance on property taxes, was suggested by the President's Commission on School Finance, which proposed a $5.5 billion, five year program of incentive grants designed to induce states to take over a greater share of responsibility for financing education.[14] If states respond to such a federal incentive, a lesser reliance on local property taxes to support education would be assured, since local educational revenues are overwhelmingly raised from property taxes (see Table 2-2). This solution, however, leaves open the possibility that states would replace the lost local revenue with a statewide property tax.

Two problems arise under a federal incentive program for raising the state share. First, there is the question of the effectiveness of a program like that advocated by the President's Commission: will a temporary federal contribution of $1.1 billion a year be sufficient to induce states to take on a significant share of the education costs now borne by localities? Since increasing the state share may entail costly "leveling up" of school expenditures, states may be reluctant to take the step. Second, a system of federal payments to reward states that increased the state share in education finance would suffer from an obvious, probably fatal, political flaw. States that "reformed" themselves before the introduction of the program, such as Hawaii, would get no rewards, while the most backward states would be able to institute the reform at the federal taxpayers' expense. Even for a transitional program, such characteristics are not likely to be popular.

A third technique by which the federal government might induce states to reduce their reliance on property taxes for education is relatively simple and straightforward, and involves no cost to the federal treasury. At present, owners of property can deduct property taxes from their individual tax returns, or count property taxes as a cost in computing rental income for federal income tax purposes. In effect, the federal government is now sharing the cost of property taxes with individual property owners, thereby encouraging the use of the tax. If the federal government wished to discourage the use of the property tax for education, it could simply change the income tax laws to reduce or eliminate the deductibility of the portion of property

14. President's Commission on School Finance, *Schools, People, & Money: The Need for Educational Reform*, Final Report (1972), App. H. Similar proposals have been introduced in Congress. Some would pay states for every percentage point reduction in locally raised funds; others would reimburse states that increased the state contribution. See, for example, H.R. 6521, 92 Cong. 1 sess. (1971).

taxes used for educational purposes. This simple change, one would expect, would pressure states into replacing school property taxes with sales or income taxes, both of which would continue to be deductible on federal tax returns. States that do not now use property taxes for education would be unaffected, and residents of states that shifted tax sources would not, in the end, lose any federal tax benefits. This proposal, of course, would require a shift to state-level financing and the attendant "leveling up," and might thus, like the other proposals here reviewed, create a demand for federal financial assistance for equalization of expenditure disparities. But since no federal budget dollars would be necessary to induce states to shift from local property tax finance, there would be more federal funds available for the goal of equalization. Elimination of the deductibility of property taxes has not been suggested by any major political leader.

Another form of property tax relief is the "circuit breaker" approach, which is intended to provide relief for families that are especially burdened by property taxation. Circuit breakers usually give cash rebates or income tax credits to those whose property tax liabilities are high in relation to their incomes. As was mentioned in Chapter 3, fourteen states already have circuit breaker programs, although their benefits are for the most part restricted to the low income elderly. In October 1972, President Nixon indicated that the first step he would take to fulfilling his pledge to relieve the burden of school property taxes would be to propose a national program of tax relief for the aged.[15] One way of doing this would be to incorporate a circuit breaker program in the federal income tax structure. One estimate is that it would cost the federal government roughly $1.4 billion to rebate to the elderly all residential property taxes paid in excess of 4 percent of household income.[16] On the grounds of ability to pay, restricting a circuit breaker program to the elderly makes little sense—if anything, an elderly couple with an income of $2,500 is better off than a younger couple with children who have an equivalent income. An extension of the program to all age groups would cost about $6.1 billion. This amount would be cut in half by a limitation of the program to households with incomes below $7,000.

15. See "Transcript of the President's News Conference on Domestic and Foreign Matters," *New York Times*, October 6, 1972, p. 28.

16. These estimates are taken from "Property Tax Relief and Reform: The Intergovernmental Dimension," Preliminary Draft Report of the ACIR Staff (Advisory Commission on Intergovernmental Relations, August 31, 1972; processed), Pt. 2, p. 3-35, and are subject to revision. (The final report will be entitled *Financing Schools and Property Tax Relief—A State Responsibility* [forthcoming].) It is possible that the federal government may recoup some of this expenditure because it will reduce the amount of property taxes itemized on federal income tax forms and therefore slightly increase receipts from the income tax.

As an alternative to building a circuit breaker directly into the federal tax structure, the federal government might provide states with incentive grants to establish state circuit breaker programs. For example, the federal government could agree to reimburse states for some fraction of the costs of any state program that conformed to federal guidelines.[17] In many ways this approach would make more sense than a unified national circuit breaker plan, since the dependence on property taxes varies so greatly across states that a single system would end up benefiting only those living in high property tax states. In most of the South, where property tax rates are very low, few persons would appear to have an "excessive" property tax burden by national standards. Individual state programs would take this variation into account. An "excessive" burden in a low property tax state like Mississippi might be defined as 1 percent of family income, while in a state like New Hampshire, which relies heavily on property taxes, the line might be drawn at 7 percent of family income.

Whether the federal government introduced circuit breakers directly into the federal tax system or wrote guidelines for state programs, a federal circuit breaker would have to resolve many difficult problems of eligibility (should the program be limited to the elderly? should it include all low income families or all families? should renters be included?), of administration (how can renters be guaranteed relief?), and of standards of relief (should all "excessive burdens" be relieved, or only a fraction, so as to preserve some check on the growth of taxes?).

There are also a number of serious objections that can be raised to property tax circuit breakers. In the first place, it is not clear why property taxes that take a large fraction of a person's income are any more onerous than other types of taxes; the poor and the elderly are also profoundly affected by sales taxes. It would therefore seem only logical that a national circuit breaker be designed in such a way as to relieve the excessive burden that arises from all forms of state and local taxes. At a minimum, a federal circuit breaker program would have to be coordinated with other federal efforts toward tax reform. Second, federally supported circuit breaker programs would by no means discourage states from using property taxes as a source of revenue for schools. To the contrary, they might provide an incentive for states to substitute property taxes for other taxes, since only the former would qualify for federal compensation.

Each of the tax relief programs reviewed here, if adopted, would greatly

17. Senator Edmund Muskie proposed a federal grant to states to relieve the property tax burden of the elderly. See "Muskie Proposes New Housing Security System," press release from office of Edmund S. Muskie, January 31, 1972.

affect both existing federal programs and potential new ones for equalization of education spending. Any program that shifts responsibilities from local property taxes to the state level should result in a rethinking of the federal impacted aid program. The rationale for these federal payments to school districts is that the school district cannot tax federal property and thus requires a compensatory payment. If education expenditures were made independent of local property taxes, the rationale would have no merit at all; the impacted areas aid program, to continue, would have to become a state-based program. In any event, budgetary savings should be possible from this existing program if some form of tax relief strategy is followed.

Any federal program that successfully induces states to abandon local property taxes entirely as a source of revenue for education places some constraints on equalization alternatives within states. If local property taxes cannot be used for add-ons at the school district level, proposals for equalization that involve local taxes—for example, capacity equalization—become infeasible. On the other hand, federal initiatives that are designed only to increase the state share of education spending will not necessarily eliminate expenditure disparities within states. In fact, federal rewards for greater state participation may not affect equalization at all. As a comparison of Tables 2-3 and 4-7 shows, some states with high state shares show substantial intrastate disparities.

Finally, it is important to remember that federal programs for tax relief will not lower total tax burdens, since increased federal aid will necessitate larger federal taxes. To be sure, many individual taxpayers and some states may find themselves better off after a shift from state and local revenue sources to federal ones, but there will be others who will be hurt. From the standpoint of state and local officials, probably the most important change would be that some of the onus for raising school taxes would be shifted to another level of government.

Reducing Inter- and Intrastate Inequities and Disparities

A third objective that might be pursued through increased federal support of elementary and secondary education is the reduction or elimination of the inequities and disparities that now characterize the nation's school finance systems. Although the emphasis in this book has been on the variations that exist among the school districts within states, similar disparities in educational quality and the ability to finance schools exist between states.

INTERSTATE DISPARITIES. As Table 6-2 indicates, the average expendi-

Table 6-2. Interstate Disparities in Educational Expenditure, Capacity, Tax Effort, and Need, 1970–71 School Year

Money amounts in dollars

State	Per-pupil expenditure	Capacity (per-capita personal income)	Effort (state and local school revenues as percent of personal income)	Need (public school enrollment as percent of total population)
Alabama	523	3,087	3.5	23.1
Alaska	1,401	4,875	7.1	25.6
Arizona	843	3,913	5.1	23.7
Arkansas	578	3,078	3.5	23.7
California	808	4,640	4.2	23.3
Colorado	819	4,153	5.0	24.1
Connecticut	1,116	4,995	5.5	21.5
Delaware	1,029	4,673	5.5	23.8
District of Columbia	1,134	5,870	3.5	19.7
Florida	819	3,930	4.1	20.3
Georgia	680	3,599	3.6	23.6
Hawaii	979	4,738	5.1	22.8
Idaho	678	3,409	4.8	24.9
Illinois	978	4,775	5.0	21.0
Indiana	797	4,027	5.3	23.3
Iowa	922	3,877	5.7	23.1
Kansas	804	4,192	4.6	22.7
Kentucky	625	3,306	3.8	21.8
Louisiana	797	3,252	5.1	22.9
Maine	767	3,375	5.2	24.4
Maryland	976	4,522	5.0	22.8
Massachusetts	882	4,562	4.3	20.3
Michigan	1,031	4,430	5.3	24.2
Minnesota	878	4,032	5.9	23.7
Mississippi	603	2,788	4.1	24.0
Missouri	759	3,940	4.0	22.7
Montana	858	3,629	5.4	24.7
Nebraska	676	4,030	3.6	21.9
Nevada	808	4,822	4.2	25.2
New Hampshire	781	3,796	4.3	20.8
New Jersey	1,163	4,811	4.8	20.3
New Mexico	735	3,298	5.3	27.7
New York	1,381	5,000	5.2	19.0
North Carolina	657	3,424	4.3	23.2
North Dakota	711	3,538	4.8	23.5
Ohio	793	4,175	4.1	22.5
Oklahoma	607	3,515	4.1	23.9
Oregon	934	3,959	5.4	22.2
Pennsylvania	969	4,147	4.8	19.9
Rhode Island	960	4,126	4.0	19.6
South Carolina	654	3,142	4.5	24.2
South Dakota	718	3,441	4.9	24.8
Tennessee	623	3,300	3.9	22.6
Texas	674	3,726	4.8	23.7
Utah	657	3,442	5.5	27.7
Vermont	1,100	3,638	6.9	24.6
Virginia	784	3,899	4.6	22.9
Washington	828	4,132	5.2	23.7
West Virginia	676	3,275	4.2	22.8
Wisconsin	973	3,912	5.4	22.2
Wyoming	900	3,929	5.6	25.6
U.S. average	868	4,156	4.7	22.3

ture per pupil in Alabama, the lowest spending state, is less than half that of New York. While some of the expenditure differences among states may be due to variation in the costs of educational inputs and to the differences in preferences for education, at least some of it is related to the states' varying fiscal capacities. As can be seen in the second column of Table 6-2, the relative tax base or ability of states to raise revenues for education varies considerably. Per capita personal income among states ranges from $2,788 in Mississippi to $5,000 in New York. The effort various states make in behalf of public education also differs greatly. As was the case within states, poorer areas often tax themselves harder yet spend less than do the richer states, although there are some notable exceptions. Finally, states differ, although not greatly, in their "need" for public education as crudely measured by the fraction of the population enrolled in public schools. Only the federal government has the ability to remove the tax inequities and equalize educational opportunity among states.

Federal policies might be directed either at the tax inequities or at the expenditure disparities. That is, the federal government could act so as to equalize the fiscal ability of each state and hope that the result would be a more equal interstate distribution of educational expenditures, or it could act to ensure that all children receive a minimum basic level of schooling. The first approach might take the form of a federal capacity-equalization grant similar to those discussed in Chapter 4, by which the federal government would ensure that each state exerting the same effort was capable of achieving the same educational quality or the same level of real educational resources. This technique equalizes the fiscal capacity of all states at a common guarantee level. The effect of such a grant would be to reduce the price of raising educational funds for states whose fiscal capacities were below the guarantee level, and to raise the price for those above the level. As in the intrastate case, unless the capacity guaranteed to all states was that of the richest, money would have to be taken away from some areas.[18]

Setting the guaranteed capacity at this high level, however, would entail

18. In other words, a federal capacity-equalization program would have to allow each state to spend as if it were as rich as New York, the state with the highest income per pupil. Income per pupil is the most commonly used measure of a state's ability to afford education, since it combines general revenue raising capacity (measured by income per capita) and need (measured by pupils per capita).

Footnote for Table 6-2:
Sources: Per-pupil expenditure and school enrollment from National Education Association, Research Division, *Estimates of School Statistics, 1971–72* (NEA, 1971), Table 11, p. 36, and Table 2, p. 27; total and per-capita personal income from U.S. Department of Commerce, Bureau of Economic Analysis, *Survey of Current Business*, Vol. 52 (August 1972), Tables 1, 2, p. 25; population data from U.S. Bureau of the Census, *Current Population Reports*, Series P-25, No. 468, "Provisional Estimates of the Population of States: July 1, 1971 and 1970" (1971).

substantial federal budget outlays. If the percentage increase in each state's expenditures for education (not including existing federal programs) was equal to one-half the percentage reduction in the price of education, and if the state took the rest of the federal grant as tax relief, the federal government would have spent about $12.6 billion in 1970–71 on such a complete capacity-equalization program.

As Table 6-3 indicates, such an extensive program could significantly reduce per-pupil expenditure disparities. Although the table shows what might happen under a federal capacity-equalization program it embodies several unrealistic assumptions. First is the assumption that existing federal programs would be completely unaffected by the new grant program; in all likelihood, they would be cut back. Second, it was assumed that states would ignore existing federal programs in deciding how much to spend under the new program; one would expect that the level of funding for these programs would influence state behavior. Third, the federal taxes required to pay for the new program have been assumed not to affect state spending. In fact, a program of this magnitude would require new taxes that would reduce disposable income and would probably in turn lead to a reduction of state outlays. Finally, the assumption that every state follows the same expenditure rule, increasing spending (other than for existing federal programs) by one-half the percentage change in price, is an oversimplification. Some states might want to spend more, while others might prefer greater tax relief.

Even a program that equalized capacity at the level of the richest state, so as to avoid negative grants, would probably be unrealistic from a political standpoint because it would mean that the wealthiest states would receive very little in comparison with the poorer ones (Table 6-3). While the federal government would pay $284 per student, or 45 percent of the educational bill, in Alabama, it would provide Connecticut with only $151 per student, or 13 percent of its educational spending, and New York would get no additional federal aid. Certain equalization formulas seek only partially to offset differences in fiscal capacity; such an approach would be more tolerable politically, but unfortunately, the price of greater political acceptability may be to worsen existing spending disparities. An example of a partial equalization scheme is given in the last three columns of Table 6-3: although the high spending states receive a small federal matching percentage, their expenditures actually rise more than those of most low spending states. [19]

19. The partial equalization formula is similar to one given by Russell B. Vlaanderen and Erick L. Lindman, *Intergovernmental Relations and the Governance of Education*, A

A common method of limiting costs in a full capacity-equalizing program is to put a limit on the amount of funds any state may receive. If no state were allowed to receive more than $300 per student under the full capacity-equalization program, federal budget outlays would be reduced by about $1.3 billion under the assumptions of Table 6-3. On the other hand, if political necessity required that every state be given a minimum grant of $100 per pupil, $355 million of the saving would be eliminated.

A program of capacity-equalization grants designed to lessen interstate disparities in fiscal ability to raise revenue for schools would affect the other federal objectives discussed in this chapter. On the one hand, states could use the federal funds to "level up" expenditures in low spending districts, thus reducing intrastate disparities. A comparison of the federal grants distributed under the full capacity-equalization formula of Table 6-3 with the leveling up costs reported in Table 4-7 discloses that forty-five states could achieve leveling at the ninetieth student percentile under such a federal program. On the other hand, if states reacted to the federal program as Table 6-3 assumes, much of an interstate equalizing grant program would be used for tax relief. Although federal grants of $12.6 billion would be distributed, education expenditures would rise by only $5.2 billion; the remainder would be used for tax relief at the state or local level.

Of course, the same federal dollar cannot be used for both intrastate equalization and tax relief. Even if a capacity-equalizing grant program were undertaken, it would be important for the federal government to decide whether to impose additional requirements that would induce states to either equalize expenditures or reduce taxes. In other words, a federal interstate capacity-equalization program does not preclude pursuit of other federal goals. It is important to note that an interstate capacity-equalization scheme may not result in much interstate expenditure equalization. Under the state spending assumptions of Table 6-3, the full capacity-equalizing program would reduce significantly disparities in interstate spending, but the partial capacity-equalizing program would not.[20]

The alternative to the capacity-equalization approach is to place a floor under educational spending in all the states. This would be a recognition

---

Report to the President's Commission on School Finance (The Commission, 1972), App. C, p. 1.

20. A measure of dispersion, the coefficient of variation, computed for the estimates, put existing dispersion at 0.216, dispersion after full capacity-equalization at 0.189, and dispersion after partial capacity equalization at 0.209. If the price elasticity of education differs systematically among states in such a way that states with low per-pupil expenditure levels or poor states respond less to a lower price than other states, a capacity-equalization program may even increase interstate expenditure disparities.

Table 6-3. Current Educational Expenditures per Pupil, and Estimated Distribution of Expenditures under Federal Full Capacity-Equalization and Partial Capacity-Equalization Formulas, by State, 1970–71 School Year

Money amounts in dollars

State	Current per-pupil expenditure	Full capacity-equalization formula			Partial capacity-equalization formula		
		Federal share (percent)	Per-pupil grant	New per-pupil expenditure	Federal share (percent)	Per-pupil grant	New per-pupil expenditure
Alabama	523	53	284	635	38	192	604
Alaska	1,401	34	459	1,597	31	413	1,580
Arizona	843	43	402	1,009	34	306	974
Arkansas	578	53	316	703	38	213	667
California	808	32	285	931	30	265	923
Colorado	819	40	362	970	34	300	947
Connecticut	1,116	13	151	1,187	25	307	1,252
Delaware	1,029	30	329	1,172	29	317	1,167
Florida	819	33	281	939	30	252	928
Georgia	680	45	334	816	35	249	786
Hawaii	979	26	266	1,097	28	289	1,106
Idaho	678	52	392	833	38	270	792
Illinois	978	14	139	1,043	25	262	1,094
Indiana	797	36	321	933	31	271	914
Iowa	922	40	428	1,100	33	343	1,069
Kansas	804	33	288	928	30	258	916
Kentucky	625	46	295	745	35	214	716
Louisiana	797	48	407	961	36	290	920
Maine	767	49	431	940	36	300	894
Maryland	976	27	282	1,100	28	293	1,105
Massachusetts	882	15	134	945	25	235	986
Michigan	1,031	35	408	1,205	31	355	1,185
Minnesota	878	40	403	1,046	33	323	1,016
Mississippi	603	59	331	730	41	214	692
Missouri	759	32	260	871	30	242	864
Montana	858	48	470	1,047	36	335	1,000
Nebraska	676	36	271	791	31	228	774
Nevada	808	30	260	921	29	250	917
New Hampshire	781	34	296	907	31	266	896
New Jersey	1,163	10	116	1,218	25	311	1,301
New Mexico	735	56	434	905	39	282	853
New York	1,381	0	0	1,381	23	304	1,517
North Carolina	657	47	324	788	35	229	755
North Dakota	711	53	429	881	38	289	833
Ohio	793	32	276	912	30	256	904
Oklahoma	607	46	307	732	35	223	702
Oregon	934	36	373	1,092	31	315	1,070
Pennsylvania	969	24	246	1,079	28	292	1,097
Rhode Island	960	22	218	1,058	27	273	1,080
South Carolina	654	53	361	797	38	243	756
South Dakota	718	52	421	885	38	290	830
Tennessee	623	49	325	753	36	226	719
Texas	674	43	320	806	34	244	778
Utah	657	57	441	829	40	289	777
Vermont	1,100	45	566	1,331	34	409	1,275
Virginia	784	40	337	924	33	270	900
Washington	828	35	315	962	31	275	947
West Virginia	676	49	359	820	36	250	782
Wisconsin	973	34	374	1,133	31	336	1,119
Wyoming	900	48	482	1,094	36	344	1,046
U.S. average	868[a]	30	274	982	30	273	984
U.S. total (millions of dollars)	...	...	12,617	...	...	12,553	...
Coefficient of variation	0.216	...	...	0.189	...	...	0.209

Sources: Current per-pupil expenditure from National Education Association, *Estimates of School Statistics, 1971–72*, Table 11, p. 36; per-pupil personal income from NEA, *Rankings of the States, 1972*, Table 60, p. 36. The federal share of expenditure (net of existing federal aid) was computed as follows:

of the responsibility of the federal government to guarantee that every child obtained the education necessary to function productively in society. For example, the federal government could provide every state with a grant equivalent to the average per pupil expenditure in the nation. States or localities, if they desired a better education for their children, could add to this amount. Since such a program would be enormously expensive, most of the basic federal grant proposals contemplate a much lower level of support—somewhere between 10 and 35 percent of the average expenditure level in the nation—or impose a minimum effort criterion on the states.[21] Whether such flat per-pupil grants would markedly reduce expenditure disparities is open to question. Much would depend on whether the proclivity to use the federal grant as a substitute for state and local resources is greater in high spending states or in low spending states. Some assurance that expenditure disparities would be reduced could be obtained if federal regulations required that states spending less than the national average maintained their existing educational tax efforts, or imposed maximum expenditure levels on high spending states.

A federal interstate equalization program might be designed to emphasize equalization of expenditures or of capacity. Capacity equalization does not guarantee a reduction of spending differences among the states, and "realistic" programs may actually widen them. If a federal program were to ensure a narrowing of interstate spending differences, restrictions on minimum and maximum state expenditures would have to be imposed, at some cost in state autonomy. Finally, limits must be imposed on the alternative uses—tax relief or intrastate equalization—of a federal grant under an interstate equalization program.

INTRASTATE DISPARITIES. Equalizing the fiscal capacity or average expenditure levels among states would not ensure that these objectives were achieved among the school districts within a state. For this reason, many have advocated that any increase in the federal commitment to elementary and secondary education be used to bring about a reduction in expenditure disparities or tax inequities within each state. One argument in favor of this objective is that "leveling up" or equalization at a high, politically tolerable

21. See, for example, H.R. 12367 and H.R. 10405, both introduced in the first session of the Ninety-second Congress (1971).

Footnotes for Table 6-2 (continued):
for the full capacity-equalization scheme, a federal matching ratio of 1 − (per-pupil personal income of state/per-pupil personal income of New York state) was used; for the partial equalizing scheme, a matching ratio of (0.43)/(per-pupil personal income of state/average per-pupil personal income of all 50 states) was used; the federal share, then, was calculated, for the respective programs, as (federal matching ratio)/ (1 + federal matching ratio).
 a. Average includes District of Columbia.

level would require significant amounts of new revenues that states are incapable of raising (see Table 4-7). While this may be true in a few cases, a preliminary analysis by the staff of the ACIR suggests that all but three states could generate considerably more money than is required to equalize at the ninetieth percentile student level if they exerted the same overall tax effort as New York. If all states were to impose the same tax effort as the state with the highest effort in their region, all but thirteen states could raise the money needed for equalization at the ninetieth percentile level.[22] While most states may have the overall fiscal capacity that is required, the will may be absent. Although court decisions could change the situation in many states, an added incentive in the form of federal aid would help speed introduction of intrastate equalization programs.

There are several ways in which the federal government might attempt to regulate the movement toward reform of intrastate disparities. One is to require that states submit plans demonstrating that they are moving toward a more equal system of education, and to give the Department of Health, Education, and Welfare the power to review and approve the plans.[23] While this approach has the advantage of encouraging diverse approaches to educational equality, it puts a very heavy burden on federal officials. If officials take a "hard stand" on states' equalization plans, and attempt to withhold funds from noncomplying jurisdictions, they will be subject to tremendous political pressure, as has been the case in numerous attempts to enforce civil rights legislation.[24] In many fields in which the federal government has tried to regulate behavior, the regulators have ended up serving the interests of the groups they were supposed to regulate.[25] In many existing programs, the federal bureaucracy has worked hand in hand with state boards of education, rubber stamping any plan that has been submitted.[26]

A second approach to the reduction of intrastate inequities would be to

22. "Educational Equality and Intergovernmental Relations," Preliminary Report of the ACIR Staff (Advisory Commission on Intergovernmental Relations, August 15, 1972; processed), Pt. 1, pp. 43, 44. These conclusions are subject to revision. The final report will be entitled *Financing Schools and Property Tax Relief—A State Responsibility* (forthcoming).

23. An example of this approach is the Educational Quality Act of 1972, introduced by Senator Henry M. Jackson (S. 3165, 92 Cong. 2 sess.).

24. For examples of how political pressure is exerted, see Leon E. Pannetta and Peter Gall, *Bring Us Together: The Nixon Team and the Civil Rights Retreat* (Lippincott, 1971).

25. See Roger G. Noll, *Reforming Regulation: An Evaluation of the Ash Council Proposals* (Brookings Institution, 1971).

26. See Jerome T. Murphy, "Title I of ESEA: The Politics of Implementing Federal Education Reform," *Harvard Educational Review*, Vol. 41 (February 1971), pp. 35–63.

require that a state attain a specific performance standard. Two kinds of standards of intrastate equalization can be envisioned. One is for the federal government to prescribe the method of intrastate reform; it might insist, for example, that all states adopt district capacity equalizing plans, or assume a minimum share of financing education. The latter approach was taken by the President's Commission on School Finance, which recommended that each state assume 90 percent of the financing of public education.[27] The other approach is to formulate minimum criteria for the results of state finance plans; for example, a state might be required to ensure that each district maintain an expenditure level above an amount based on the average of the previous year's spending in the state.[28]

Each of these approaches might be criticized on various grounds. There is, of course, the objection that true federalism requires that states be given the responsibility for keeping their own houses in order (with the courts occasionally supplying maid service), and that any federal rules are an unnecessary encroachment on state prerogatives. Whatever the merits of this argument, if states are to receive large new federal grants, their bargaining position is not very strong.[29]

The debate over whether there should be any federal influence on intrastate equalization is likely to revolve around how to balance federal constraints against a desire for diversity in state solutions. Whether the federal government tries to set minimum conditions for the process of reform or for its outcomes, there will inevitably be a conflict between the attempt to give the states freedom and the attempt to impose minimum conditions that will be effective agents of change. The balancing act is especially difficult because no one really knows how states would respond to various federal requirements.

Any federal attempt to spur on intrastate equalization will have to be coordinated with the other national objectives of school finance reform. An example of the interplay of goals occurs in the problem of improving schooling in large cities. Although most observers rank large city school problems at the top of the list of areas of need, city school systems often

27. *Schools, People, & Money*, p. 36.
28. A bill introduced in 1972 by Senator Walter F. Mondale (S. 3779, 92 Cong. 2 sess.) establishes as a condition for federal aid that each district spend 90 percent or more of what was spent the previous year by the ninetieth percentile district.
29. A similar case against federal encroachment was made when the comparability guidelines were introduced in the Title I program. Compliance with the standards for allocation of their own funds by school districts was made a condition of receipt of federal funds.

spend well above their own state's average expenditure per pupil.[30] If a federal incentive program for intrastate expenditure equalization were also to attempt to help cities, most states would have to bring their expenditures up to a very high level: leveling at the eightieth or ninetieth student percentile might be needed if the resources of the school districts in major northern urban centers were to be increased. As Chapter 4 noted, however, expenditure equalization at such high levels entails a large increase in state or federal spending, most of which would not benefit cities or other areas where education is inadequate. There would be less reason to raise expenditures to such high levels if the educational needs of cities were met in ways other than by the blunt instrument of intrastate equalization. For example, if the Title I program were expanded, the urban centers would receive a major share of the funds.[31] Similarly, if a new urban education aid program, such as that suggested by several groups, were enacted by Congress, the cities would not need a large intrastate equalization program.[32] Increased spending in the inner cities could take place without the added costs of equalizing expenditure at a high level in every state. A federal program for intrastate equalization will be efficient only if it does not try to solve all the fiscal problems of education; to be sensible, it must be undertaken in conjunction with other programs.

Another major issue in federal programs to provide regulations or incentives for intrastate equalization of school spending levels is whether the program should create biases toward higher aggregate spending levels in the states. In general, a federal program focused on disparity outcomes (one requiring, for example, that no district's per-pupil expenditure shall be less than 80 percent of that of the highest spending district) is neutral

30. See U.S. Office of Education, *Finances of Large-City School Systems: A Comparative Analysis* (1971), Table 7, pp. 50–51.

31. For example, New Jersey's six large cities (those with populations over 100,000), which enroll 13.3 percent of the state's public school children, receive 45.1 percent of the state's Title I funds. (*Robinson* v. *Cahill*, Docket L-18704-69, Superior Court of New Jersey, Hudson County [1972], p. 26 and App. A, and U.S. Bureau of the Census, *Statistical Abstract of the United States, 1971* [1971], pp. 21–23.)

32. Two such proposals for aid to the cities have been made; one by the President's Commission on School Finance, which recommended initiation of a $1 billion urban educational assistance program (*Schools, People, & Money*, pp. 44, 46), and the other by the HEW Urban Education Task Force in *Urban School Crisis: The Problems and Solutions Proposed by the HEW Urban Education Task Force*, Final Report of the Task Force on Urban Education of the Department of Health, Education, and Welfare [1970] [available from National School Public Relations Association, Washington, D.C.]). The latter's plan—to increase urban educational resources for cities with over 100,000 population by one-third—would cost $7.5 billion by 1975.

with respect to the aggregate level of spending in a state. While in most cases such a rule would lead to higher total spending, a state might choose to equalize disparities at a low spending level. On the other hand, a program that bases equalization requirements on the spending of a recent year (for example: "In 1973, no district may spend less than the expenditure of the eightieth percentile district in 1972") would effectively close off the option for a state to hold down its total spending level. Naturally, the decision whether to bias the intrastate equalization requirements toward higher spending levels depends on the importance attached to state and local tax relief as an objective of federal policy. Some degree of tax relief is more likely to come about if the federal intrastate equalization requirements allow states to reduce disparities at a low level of aggregate spending.

Changing the Structure of the Educational System

Although each of the proposed changes in the way public schools are financed would significantly affect the nonpublic school sector, the nature of the effect is not always clear. If federal programs can make city schools into more effective enterprises, there is little question that many families who have in desperation turned to private schools will return to public education. On the other hand, if states take over education finance, and leave little leeway for wealthy school districts to supplement expenditures, many parents who now are able to find high quality education in public schools may be forced to seek it in the private sector. Public school financial reforms will also bring many shifts in the after-tax income of families, and these may indirectly affect the ability of parents to send their children to nonpublic schools.

Direct federal aid programs for nonpublic schools might also significantly change the structure of the nation's educational system. Two general approaches to providing such federal aid have been put forward in recent years. The first of these is to include the nonpublic sector in any new federal effort to aid elementary and secondary education. The President's Panel on Nonpublic Education advocated a plan whereby a fraction of the expenditure equalization incentive grants proposed by the President's Commission be set aside by each state to reimburse parents for tuition paid to nonpublic schools.[33] In states with constitutional prohibitions against such aid, the

33. President's Panel on Nonpublic Education, *Nonpublic Education and the Public Good*, Final Report to the President's Commission on School Finance (1972), p. 42.

federal government could withhold a fraction of the incentive grant and administer the tuition reimbursement from Washington. A number of the federal educational aid programs introduced by members of Congress in recent years are similar in spirit to the panel's suggestion, in that they would provide money for the nonpublic school sector if such aid did not violate the state's constitution.[34] In general these programs attempt to avoid constitutional problems in much the same way as Title I of the ESEA and other existing federal programs: the funds designated to benefit nonpublic education are to be kept in the control of public agencies and expended only on "secular, neutral, or nonideological services, materials, and equipment."[35] If the funds for a new federal aid program are allocated to the states primarily on the basis of public school enrollments, inclusion of nonpublic school students in the program would mean that the moneys for assisting the nonpublic schools would be diverted from the public sector within the state in which the nonpublic schools are located. That is, once Rhode Island receives its allotment of federal funds, the money it allocates to nonpublic education is paid out of its federal share; in this way the plan avoids requiring Oklahomans to pay an extra sum to Rhode Islanders because the latter state has a large nonpublic enrollment. If, however, a state's allocation is based on the number of school-aged children, the taxpayers of all states share in paying the subsidy to the nonpublic schools, while only the taxpayers of the state in which the schools are located reap the benefits.

The second general approach that has received considerable attention is to provide aid through federal income tax credits to families of nonpublic school children. This approach has been endorsed by the Nixon administration, by the leadership of the Democratic party, and by a great number of congressmen.[36] The specific proposal that has received the most congressional support would provide a federal income tax credit for 50 percent of tuition paid (up to $400 tuition) to nonprofit private institutions.[37] The benefit of such a tax credit would be highly concentrated in a few areas (see Tables 5-1 and 5-2), while the benefits would be "paid for" by the general federal taxpayer. As was pointed out in Chapter 5, the Rhode

34. See, for example, H.R. 7796, 92 Cong. 1 sess. (1971).
35. See H.R. 12367, 92 Cong., 1 sess. (1971), sec. 4 (b)(4)(A)(i).
36. More than 140 bills to aid nonpublic schools were introduced during the Ninety-second Congress. A list of these bills is contained in *Material Relating to Proposals Before the Committee on Ways and Means on the Subject of Aid to Primary and Secondary Education in the Form of Tax Credits and/or Deductions*, 92 Cong. 2 sess. (1972), p. III.
37. H.R. 17072, 92 Cong. 2 sess. (1972), sec. 1.

Table 6-4. Estimated Effect of a Tuition Income Tax Credit of 50 Percent up to $200 under H.R. 17072, by Income Class, 1972–73 School Year

Adjusted gross income class (dollars)	Number of nonpublic school students (thousands)	Average tuition paid (dollars)	Amount of tax credit		Percentage distribution of total tax credit
			Per pupil (dollars)	Total (millions of dollars)	
Under 3,000	94.2	30	0	0	0.0
3,000–5,000	232.9	44	4	1.0	0.3
5,000–7,500	687.5	80	31	21.4	6.1
7,500–10,000	1,092.3	140	68	74.2	21.2
10,000–15,000	1,544.9	195	93	144.1	41.2
15,000–20,000	708.1	549	127	89.8	25.7
20,000–25,000	230.4	911	80	18.5	5.3
25,000 and over	268.2	1,038	4	1.0	0.3
All classes	4,858.5	288	72	350.0	100.0

Sources: Authors' estimates based on unpublished tabulation prepared by the Joint Committee on Internal Revenue Taxation as part of its Staff Study on H.R. 13495, February 10, 1972. It was assumed that tuitions were $400 or less per pupil for families with incomes under $15,000. For families with incomes between $15,000 and $30,000, authors' own estimates of distribution of tuitions paid and average incomes within income classes were used; all families were assumed to have the average number of children for their income class. For families with incomes over $30,000, only those with four or more students in nonpublic schools would be eligible for a tax credit. The total amount of such grants was assumed to be negligible. Figures are rounded and may not add to totals.

Island taxpayer, who had previously enjoyed substantial tax relief in not having to pay for nonpublic schools, would now have part of the costs of those schools borne by taxpayers in other states who received no such benefits. In addition, the benefits would be concentrated in a few income classes. Although the size of the credit would be reduced for those with income above $18,000 per year, most of the estimated $350 million in benefits would initially accrue to families with above average incomes (see Table 6-4).

The initial impact of the tax credit program is no measure of its long-term consequences. First, tuition and enrollment in existing nonpublic schools are likely to rise. If tuition rose to the $400 level aided under the tax credit program, federal tax losses would be almost doubled.[38] Second, a federal tax credit might initiate a vast restructuring of the system of education in the United States. Once the principle of federal subsidy for tuiton and fees was established, local school districts might attempt to supplement their federal support by charging tuition in formerly public institutions. Although tuition and fee charges are against the tradition of American public education and would require changes in state laws, it is

38. See press release, "Statement by the Honorable George P. Shultz, Secretary of the Treasury, before the House Ways and Means Committee," August 14, 1972.

hard to imagine the public sector idly watching the federal government give $200 to nonpublic school students when their students have never received comparable federal support. In the long run, then, a federal tax credit for nonpublic schools may represent the first step in developing a universal voucher system for all elementary and secondary education, with federal, state, and local sharing of the cost of the voucher.

The merits of a federal tax credit program must thus be judged in part by the likely benefits to be derived from the transformation of a predominantly publicly operated to a publicly subsidized, but privately run, industry. There is very little experience with such a system in the field of education in this country.

Future Federal Policy

The Ninety-third Congress will have to settle many of the questions about the federal role in school finance. Most of the current education legislation will expire during the 1973–75 period. The reports of the President's Commission on School Finance and of the Advisory Commission on Intergovernmental Relations will be available to policymakers who have delayed seeking new initiatives until the advice of these bodies was accessible. Also, the Supreme Court's ruling on the inequities of the existing school finance systems will be known. What are the basic choices that must be made? What are the constraints on the choices?

A number of major goals for the federal government have been discussed: expanding existing federal educational programs, providing tax relief, reducing interstate and intrastate disparities in expenditure or fiscal capacity, and changing the structure of the education industry to better accommodate the private sector. While the federal government need not choose one goal to the exclusion of all the rest, the clear conflicts among the objectives force certain choices.

The conflicts are easiest to understand in the context of a grant program to the states. To oversimplify, an interstate expenditure equalizing program would give poor states like Mississippi much larger grants per pupil than wealthier states like New Jersey. On the other hand, a grant formula that accomplishes this goal will put federal money in the wrong place to accomplish property tax relief: Mississippi depends little on such taxes, New Jersey a great deal. One way out of this conflict is to offer an equalizing grant program with a condition that states reduce property taxes for education. If the grant program were large enough to offer states with heavy property taxes a choice they could not refuse, reliance on the property tax might indeed drop precipitously. Requiring substantial reductions in the property tax would probably make it impossible for many states to "level up" and equalize educational expenditure disparities among districts, because leveling up would put substantial burdens on the state-level taxpayer, burdens that a state legislature could impose only if a state property tax could be used to replace a large part of lost local property tax support. Thus, if the federal government attempted to impose intrastate equalization requirements on top of property tax relief requirements, the federal contribution necessary to make states accept both requirements would be very high indeed. Naturally, the sum could be made smaller by the direction of federal funds to states with high property taxes and high needs for intrastate equalization; but that would mean abandoning the goal of interstate equalization of expenditures.

Any program of federal aid of finite dimension must settle upon priorities in the interstate and intrastate equalization areas and in property tax relief. The weakening of at least one of these objectives is a necessary price of insistence on any other goal. These constraints would be less compelling, however, in a very large federal grant program that provided enough federal funding to pay most of the costs of equalization and property tax replacement.[39]

Naturally, a program of this magnitude would have to compete with the existing federal programs in education, not all of which would be made redundant. Of especial importance in this regard are the Title I and federal educational research programs. Although the massive grant program would help some city school systems, an expansion of Title I would be necessary to provide adequate compensatory services. The need for educational research would not be affected by a program of school support grants to states or localities.

A program of federal support for nonpublic education along the lines of the tax credit program discussed in this chapter must also be evaluated in terms of its competition for scarce public funds. Since the tax credit ap-

---

39. An exact dollar figure cannot be placed on such a program, but some idea of the order of magnitude is given by these 1970–71 data: residential property taxes used for education, $12 billion; intrastate equalization to the ninetieth percentile student, $7 billion; interstate equalization in which states below the national average are raised to that level after intrastate equalizing has taken place, $3 billion. The sum of these costs is the total state and federal revenue requirement; the federal incentive required would be some major fraction thereof.

proach might lead to a large loss of federal revenue, it would inevitably take away funds from existing federal education programs or from public school finance reform initiatives.

The benefits derived from greater federal financing of education must be balanced against existing and prospective future claims on the federal budget in other areas. As we have noted, increased federal revenues over the next few years will probably be consumed by the expansion of existing programs. Thus, it is not likely that a massive federal grant program for education will be possible unless a major new tax increase is enacted or existing federal programs are substantially slashed. Under conditions of budget stringency, the key policy issue is whether the federal government completes its old initiatives, *or* supports partial equalization and tax relief, *or* aids in the creation of a voucher system.

Bibliography

I. Commission Reports

Benson, Charles S. (director). *Final Report to the Senate Select Committee on School District Finance.* Submitted by the Consultant Staff. Vol. 1. Sacramento: The Committee, 1972.

President's Commission on School Finance. *Schools, People, & Money: The Need for Educational Reform.* Final Report. Washington: U.S. Government Printing Office, 1972.

President's Panel on Nonpublic Education. *Nonpublic Education and the Public Good.* Final Report to the President's Commission on School Finance. Washington: U.S. Government Printing Office, 1972.

Report of the New York State Commission on the Quality, Cost and Financing of Elementary and Secondary Education. Vol. 1. The Commission, 1972.

School Finance Reform in Michigan—1971. State of Michigan, Executive Office, Bureau of Programs and Budget, 1972.

II. General Works

Advisory Commission on Intergovernmental Relations. *State-Local Revenue Systems and Educational Finance.* A Report to the President's Commission on School Finance. Washington: ACIR, 1971.

———. *Who Should Pay for Public Schools?* Washington: U.S. Government Printing Office, 1971.

Bendixsen, Marian F. *In Search of Equality: School Finance Revisited.* Washington: National Committee for Support of the Public Schools, 1972.

Coons, John E., William H. Clune III, and Stephen D. Sugarman. *Private Wealth and Public Education.* Cambridge: The Belknap Press of Harvard University Press, 1970.

Current History. Issues on "American School Finance: A History," "American School Costs," and "Financing America's Schools Tomorrow," Vol. 62 (June 1972) and Vol. 63 (July and August 1972), respectively.

175

Guthrie, James W., and others. *Schools and Inequality.* Cambridge: M.I.T. Press, 1971.

Jencks, Christopher, and others. *Inequality: A Reassessment of the Effect of Family and Schooling in America.* New York: Basic Books, 1972.

Johns, Roe L., and others (eds.). Volumes produced for the National Educational Finance Project: *Economic Factors Affecting the Financing of Education* (Vol. 2); *Planning to Finance Education* (Vol. 3); *Status and Impact of Educational Finance Programs* (Vol. 4); *Alternative Programs for Financing Education* (Vol. 5). Gainesville, Florida: National Educational Finance Project, all published in 1971 except Vol. 2, 1970.

Levin, Betsy, and others. *Paying for Public Schools: Issues of School Finance in California.* Washington: The Urban Institute, 1972.

————. *Public School Finance: Present Disparities and Fiscal alternatives.* A Report Prepared by the Urban Institute for the President's Commission on School Finance. 2 vols. Washington: The Commission, 1972.

National Educational Finance Project. *Future Directions for School Financing: A Response to Demands for Fiscal Equity in American Education.* Gainesville, Florida: National Educational Finance Project, 1971.

Sacks, Seymour. *City Schools/Suburban Schools: A History of Fiscal Conflict.* Syracuse: Syracuse University Press, 1972.

Wise, Arthur E. *Rich Schools, Poor Schools: The Promise of Equal Educational Opportunity.* Chicago: University of Chicago Press, 1968.

III. Does Money Matter?

Averch, Harvey A., and others. *How Effective is Schooling? A Critical Review and Synthesis of Research Findings.* Prepared for the President's Commission on School Finance. Santa Monica: RAND Corporation, 1972.

Bowles, Samuel, and Henry M. Levin. "The Determinants of Scholastic Achievement—An Appraisal of Some Recent Evidence," *Journal of Human Resources,* Vol. 3 (Winter 1968). Brookings Reprint 145.

Mosteller, Frederick, and Daniel P. Moynihan (eds.). *On Equality of Educational Opportunity.* New York: Random House, 1972.

U.S. Office of Education. *Do Teachers Make a Difference? A Report on Recent Research on Pupil Achievement.* Washington: U.S. Government Printing Office, 1970.

U.S. Department of Health, Education, and Welfare. "The Effectiveness of Compensatory Education: Summary and Review of the Evidence." Processed. Washington: HEW, 1972.

IV. Nonpublic Schools

Cohen, Wilbur J. (project director). *The Financial Implications of Changing Patterns of Nonpublic School Operations in Chicago, Detroit, Milwaukee and*

Philadelphia. A Report Submitted to the President's Commission on School Finance by the School of Education, University of Michigan. Washington: The Commission, 1972.

Erickson, Donald A., and others. "Crisis in Illinois Nonpublic Schools." Final Research Report to the Elementary and Secondary Nonpublic Schools Study Commission, State of Illinois. Processed. The Commission, 1971.

Fahey, Frank J. (director). *Economic Problems of Nonpublic Schools.* Submitted to the President's Commission on School Finance by the Office for Educational Research, University of Notre Dame. Washington: The Commission, 1972.

Gary, Louis R., and associates. "The Collapse of Nonpublic Education: Rumor or Reality?" The Report on Nonpublic Education in the State of New York for the New York State Commission on the Quality, Cost and Financing of Elementary and Secondary Education. 2 vols. Processed. New York City: The Commission, 1971.

Gurash, John T. (chairman). *The Report of the Archdiocesan Advisory Committee on the Financial Crisis of Catholic Schools in Philadelphia and Surrounding Counties.* Philadelphia: The Committee, 1972.

New York Department of City Planning. "Three Out of Ten: The Nonpublic Schools of New York City." Processed. New York: Department of City Planning, City of New York, March 1972.

Public Aid to Nonpublic Education. A Staff Report Submitted to the President's Commission on School Finance. Washington: The Commission, 1972.

Whelan, Charles M., and Paul A. Freund. *Legal and Constitutional Problems of Public Support for Nonpublic Schools.* Submitted to the President's Commission on School Finance. Washington: The Commission, 1972.

V. Selected Data Sources

National Catholic Educational Association. *A Statistical Report on Catholic Elementary and Secondary Schools for the Years 1967–68 to 1969–70.* Washington: National Catholic Educational Association, 1970.

————, Research Department. *A Report on U.S. Catholic Schools, 1970–71.* Washington: National Catholic Educational Association, 1971.

National Education Association, Committee on Educational Finance. *Financial Status of the Public Schools, 1971.* Washington: National Education Association, 1971.

————, Research Division. *Estimates of School Statistics, 1971–72.* Washington: National Education Association, 1971.

————, ————. *Rankings of the States, 1972.* Washington: National Education Association, 1972.

————, ————. *Salary Schedules for Teachers, 1970–71.* Washington: National Education Association, 1970.

Review of Existing State School Finance Programs, Vol. 2: *Documentation of Disparities in the Financing of Public Elementary and Secondary School Systems—By State*. A Commission Staff Report Submitted to the President's Commission on School Finance. Washington: The Commission, 1972.

School Management. "Cost of Education Index, 1970–71," by Orlando F. Furno and Paul K. Cunco, Vol. 15 (January 1971), and "The Cost of Education Index, 1971–1972," no author, Vol. 16 (January 1972).

Stollar, Dewey H., and Gerald Boardman. *Personal Income by School Districts in the United States*. Gainesville, Florida: National Educational Finance Project, 1971.

U.S. Bureau of the Census. *Current Population Reports*, Series P-20, No. 222, "School Enrollment: October 1970." Washington: U.S. Government Printing Office, 1971.

———. *Census of Governments, 1967*, Vol. 4, No. 1, *Finances of School Districts*. Washington: U.S. Government Printing Office, 1969.

———. *Census of Population, 1970, General Social and Economic Characteristics*. Final Report PC (1)-C (volumes for each state and U.S. Summary). Washington: U.S. Government Printing Office, 1972.

U.S. Office of Education. *Digest of Educational Statistics, 1970 Edition*. Washington: U.S. Government Printing Office, 1970.

———. *Projections of Educational Statistics to 1979–80*. 1970 Edition. Washington: U.S. Government Printing Office, 1971.

———. *Statistics of Local Public School Systems, 1968–69: Finances*. Washington: U.S. Government Printing Office, 1971.

———. *Statistics of Local Public School Systems, Fall 1969: Pupils and Staff*. Washington: U.S. Government Printing Office, 1971.

VI. Federal Programs

Schultze, Charles L., and others. *Setting National Priorities: The 1973 Budget*, especially Chapters 8, 9, 10, and 14. Washington: Brookings Institution, 1972.

U.S. Congress. House. General Subcommittee on Education of the House Committee on Education and Labor. *Needs of Elementary and Secondary Education for the Seventies*. A Compendium of Policy Papers. 91 Cong. 1 sess. Washington: U.S. Government Printing Office, 1970.

———. Senate. Select Committee on Equal Educational Opportunity. *Equal Educational Opportunity*. Hearings. 91 Cong. 2 sess. Washington: U.S. Government Printing Office, 1970. Parts 1A, 1B, 2, 7; *Equal Educational Opportunity—1971*. Hearings. 92 Cong. 1 sess. 1971. Parts 16A, 16B, 16C, 16D-1, 16D-2, 16D-3. *Ibid.*, 1972. Parts 20, 21.

VII. Legal Issues

Bittker, Boris I. "Churches, Taxes and the Constitution," *Yale Law Journal*, Vol. 78 (July 1969).

Coons, John E., William H. Clune III, and Stephen D. Sugarman. "A First Appraisal of Serrano," *Yale Review of Law and Social Action*, Vol. 2 (Winter 1971).

Dimond, Paul R. "Serrano: A Victory of Sorts for Ethics, Not Necessarily for Education," *Yale Review of Law and Social Action*, Vol. 2 (Winter 1971).

Goldstein, Stephen R. "Inter-District Inequalities in School Financing: A Critical Analysis of Serrano v. Priest and Its Progeny," *University of Pennsylvania Law Review*, Vol. 120 (January 1972).

Karst, Kenneth L. "Serrano v. Priest," *California Law Review*, Vol. 60 (May 1972).

Kurland, Philip B. "Equal Educational Opportunity: The Limits of Constitutional Jurisprudence Undefined," *University of Chicago Law Review*, Vol. 35 (Summer 1968).

Michelman, Frank I. "Foreword: On Protecting the Poor Through the Fourteenth Amendment," *Harvard Law Review*, Vol. 83 (November 1969).

Index

Aaron, Henry J., 27*n*
Advisory Commission on Intergovernmental Relations (ACIR): on leveling up, 166; on local control, 55, 56; on property tax, 24, 155; on state finance, 91; VAT study, 46–47
AFL-CIO: on nonpublic school aid, 113; teachers' unions, 102
Age: and circuit breaker program, 40, 157–58; and property tax, 26, 28, 30, 40, 70–71
Alabama: federal equalization effect, 162; per-pupil expenditure, 161; VAT effect, 46–47
American Civil Liberties Union (ACLU), 113
Americans United v. *Oakey*, 131*n*
Anderson, Wendell, 91
Andrew, Ralph, 67*n*, 122*n*
Arizona: school district inequality, 2, 59
Averch, Harvey A., 37*n*, 151*n*

Baird, Robert N., 20*n*
Bartell, Ernest J., 110*n*, 111, 137*n*, 138*n*, 144*n*
Beeman, William J., 27*n*
Benson, Charles S., 37*n*, 40*n*, 61*n*, 64*n*, 84*n*, 88*n*, 91*n*
Berke, Joel S., 80*n*
Birth rate: effect on Catholic schools, 109, 111
Bittker, Boris I., 142*n*
Black, David E., 27*n*
Board of Education v. *Allen*, 130*n*
Bond issues. *See* School bond issues
Borrowing. *See* Finance, public school
Boston: Catholic schools, 118; tax base disparity, 27, 42–43
Botter, Theodore I., 80
Brazer, Harvey E., 71*n*, 74*n*

Break, George F., 148*n*
Brickell, Henry M., 13*n*, 123*n*
Brown, Kenneth M., 105*n*, 108*n*, 112*n*, 114*n*
Building codes: discriminatory, 34
Burns, James A., 67*n*
Burruss v. *Wilkerson*, 58*n*, 74*n*
Busing: alternatives to, 151; equalization proposals, 83; opposition to, 23

Cahill, William T., 44*n*, 51*n*, 55, 91, 92*n*, 154*n*
Caldwell v. *Kansas*, 59*n*
California: equalization proposal, 92; full state funding proposal, 91; Greene bill, 92; local finance, 23; nonpublic schools, 142; school district inequality, 2, 58, 72–74; state property tax proposal, 45; VAT alternative, 47; Watson amendment, 92–93
California Senate Select Committee on School District Finance, 91, 92
Callahan, John J., 80*n*
Carliner, Geoffrey, 28*n*
Carnevale, Tony, 67*n*, 122*n*
Catholic schools: church subsidies, 14–15, 103, 111, 122, 137–38, 145; in city, 107–08, 118–19; concentration of, 97; consolidation plan, 137, 138; contributed services, 13–14, 110–11; declining preference for, 106; demographic factors, 107–08; enrollment, 2, 14, 99–111, 145; and federal aid programs, 16; future of, 109–12; and income level, 106–08; per-pupil costs, 13, 101–03; property tax attitude, 70; school lunch program, 138; teachers, 101–03, 110; tuition, 14, 103–06, 137–38. *See also* Finance, nonpublic school; Nonpublic schools